Iran and the International System

Much attention in the West has focused on Iran as a problem country—a potential nuclear threat, seen by George W. Bush as part of the "axis of evil" and by Barack Obama as a top priority for serious diplomatic engagement at the very highest levels. This book challenges the representations of Iran as a hostile regional power led by ideologues, and goes further by discussing how international relations are viewed from inside Iran itself, outlining the factors that underpin Iranian thinking on international relations and considering what role Iran, as a large and significant country in the Middle East, ought to play in a fairly constructed international system.

The book is written by leading scholars and policymakers from inside, as well as from outside, Iran and includes academics with unparalleled access and insights into the world-views of the Iranian leadership. Subjects covered include the rationale of Iran's Islamic constitution, including its electoral system, and the impact this has on international relations; Iran's view of the ideal international system, including the place therein of ethics, justice, and security; Iran's international interests, including energy needs; and relations with the West, including the clash between Iranian and Western views of the world order.

Anoushiravan Ehteshami is Dean of Internationalisation, Professor of International Relations, and was founding Head of the School of Government and International Affairs at Durham University, UK. His most recent books published by Routledge include *Geopolitics and Globalization in the Middle East: Old Games, New Rules* and *The Middle East's Relations with Asia and Russia*.

Reza Molavi received his Ph.D. from Durham University and recently acted as the Executive Director of the Centre for Iranian Studies, Durham University, UK.

Durham Modern Middle East and Islamic World Series
Edited by A. Ehteshami
University of Durham

Islands and International Politics in the Persian Gulf
The Abu Musa and Tunbs in strategic perspective
K. Ahmadi

Monetary Union in the Gulf
Prospects for a single currency in the Arabian Peninsula
E. Rutledge

Contested Sudan
The political economy of war and reconstruction
I. Elnur

Palestinian Politics and the Middle East Peace Process
Consensus and competition in the Palestinian negotiation team
G. Khatib

Islam in the Eyes of the West
Images and realities in an age of terror
Edited by T. Y. Ismael and A. Rippin

Islamist Extremism in Kuwait
From the Muslim Brotherhood to Al-Qaeda and other Islamist political groups
F. A. al-Mdaires

Iraq, Democracy and the Future of the Muslim World
Edited by A. Paya and J. Esposito

Islamic Entrepreneurship
Rasem N. Kayed and M. Kabir Hassan

Iran and the International System
Edited by A. Ehteshami and R. Molavi

The International Politics of the Red Sea
A. Ehteshami and E. C. Murphy

Iran and the International System

Edited by
**Anoushiravan Ehteshami
and Reza Molavi**

LONDON AND NEW YORK

This edition published 2012
by Routledge
2 Park Square, Milton Park, Abingdon, Oxon, OX14 4RN

Simultaneously published in the USA and Canada
by Routledge
711 Third Avenue, New York, NY 10017

Routledge is an imprint of the Taylor & Francis Group, an informa business

British Library Cataloguing in Publication Data
A catalogue record for this book is available from the British Library

Library of Congress Cataloging-in-Publication Data

Iran and the international system / edited by Anoushiravan Ehteshami and Reza Molavi.
p. cm. -- (Durham modern Middle East and Islamic world series; 20)
Includes bibliographical references and index.
(ebook) 1. Iran--Foreign relations--1997- I. Ehteshami, Anoushiravan. II. Molavi, Reza.
JZ1680.I73 2011
327.55--dc22
2011000312

ISBN: 978-0-415-55966-9 (hbk)
ISBN: 978-0-203-80913-6 (ebk)

Typeset in Times New Roman
by Integra Software Services Pvt. Ltd, Pondicherry, India

Printed and bound in Great Britain by the MPG Books Group

Contents

Figures and tables

Figures

Tables

Contributors

Arshin Adib-Moghaddam is a lecturer in comparative and international politics of the Middle East at the School of Oriental and African Studies, London. His research interests include Iranian foreign and domestic politics, United States foreign policy, and Islamic political and intellectual history.

Ali Akbar Alikhani is an academic based at the Institute for Social and Cultural Research in Tehran and is also currently an assistant professor at both Imam Sadiq and Tehran Universities. Winning respected researcher awards three times in Iran, his research interests over the course of several years have centred on political thought in the Islamic world.

Morteza Bahrani is Head of the Translation Department at the Institute for Social and Cultural Studies at the Ministry of Science, Research and Technology in Tehran and is also a researcher in the national project entitled, "Islamic Political Thought in Islam and Iran". His research interests are political philosophy in Medieval Islam and the political thought of Shi'ism and Iran.

Asghar Eftekhary is a lecturer at Imam Sadiq University in the department of Islamic Studies and Political Science and is a member of numerous research editorial boards. He has won two renowned researcher awards, and his research interests are centred on security studies and political thought.

Anoushiravan Ehteshami is a professor and Co-Director of the Economic and Social Research Council Centre for the Advanced Study of the Arab World in the School of Government and International Affairs at Durham University. He is also Dean of Internationalisation and Special Advisor to the Islamic Criminal Justice Project in the Centre for Criminal Law and Criminal Justice.

Dehghani Firooz-Abadi is chairman of the Committee of Political Sciences and Humanities Association, of the Ministry of Science, Research and Technology's High Planning Council in Tehran and also an associate professor at Allameh Tabatabaei University in Tehran. His field of research includes Iranian foreign policy, theories of international relations, and international cooperation.

Nadir Gohari is a doctoral candidate at Durham University in the School of Government and International Affairs. Previously, he earned his Master's degree in International Relations with a focus on the Middle East from the same institution.

Manouchehr Mohammadi is an advisor to the Minister of Foreign Affairs in Iran and has also held several political positions including Deputy Minister of Defence in Legal and Parliamentary Affairs in the Ministry of Defence. His research focuses on the Islamic Revolution and Iranian foreign policy.

Reza Molavi was a research fellow at the University of Durham's School of Government and International Affairs. He served as the Executive Director of the Centre for Iranian Studies until April 2010 at the University of Durham's School of Government and International Affairs. His research interests include Foreign Policy as well as Food, Water, and Energy Security in the Middle East.

Mohammad Javad Nateghpour is a senior visiting fellow in the School of Government and International Affairs at Durham University. He is also an associate professor of sociology at Tehran University.

Paul Rogers is the professor of Peace Studies at the University of Bradford. His main area of geographic focus is on the Middle East with special attention to the Persian Gulf. His research interests include political violence, terrorism, Middle East security, and arms control.

Mahboubeh Sadeghinia earned her Bachelor's degree in Political Science from Tehran University and her Ph.D. from Durham University. She has been involved in journalism and political analysis. She is currently a visiting research fellow in the School of Government and International Affairs at Durham University.

Hossein Salimi is a professor of International Relations and Political Science at Allameh Tabatabaei University. He is also a research fellow in the School of Government and International Affairs at Durham University.

Vahid Shalchi is a faculty member of the Cultural Studies Department at the Institute for Social and Cultural Studies in Tehran and is also deputy editor of two journals. His research focus is gender-based studies, lifestyles, youth cultures, and international as well as Islamic identities.

Luciano Zaccarra is a visiting research fellow at the Institute of Arab and Islamic Studies of the University of Exeter. He is also a research fellow in the department of Arab and Islamic Studies and the Director of Election Watch TEIM at Universidad Autónoma de Madrid.

Editors' acknowledgments

In addition to the many esteemed authors that have been so gracious as to contribute their work and unrivaled knowledge to form the many chapters within this book, we are greatly indebted to the Centre for Iranian Studies at Durham University and its interns for assisting with the demands of the project. In particular, we would like to extend our deepest gratitude to Nadir Gohari and Andrew Watts. Their devotion and tireless efforts that included reading, editing, organizing chapters, and contacting contributing authors have been invaluable to the development of this book and ensured that this endeavor will shed light on the sense of how the Iranian political elite view the existing international system and its many facets.

Introduction

Anoushiravan Ehteshami and Reza Molavi

This book was developed from a series of lectures given at the annual Farabi Conference at Durham University in June 2009 in an effort to provide a unique insight into Iran and its relationship with the international system. The chapters within this book contain works from academics and policymakers with unparalleled access to and understanding of the motivations of Iranian leadership, making this collection of particular significance to Western political analysts and those that seek to establish or strengthen relations with Iran. The international system has been experiencing considerable ongoing changes with shifts in power and influence, especially in the Middle East, where Iran has emerged as a regional power and worldwide energy provider. This position has inspired a newfound level of interest in Iran, which can provide grounds for a new era in international relations with this enigmatic state. It is important to note at this point that Iran is not the simplified and irrational country promoted by international media but rather a shrewd and deeply complex nation with a diverse population in search of its rightful place in the community of states.

In helping to understand Iran in this respect, the volume begins by addressing the moral and ideological fundaments that influence Iran's interaction with the international system. Fundaments in this sense refer to firm Islamic tenets and beliefs, which constitute the theoretical and ideological underpinnings of Islamic doctrine; this interpretation of course falls in line with Shi'ism. Chapter 2 elaborates on the political rationality of the Islamic Republic of Iran in contrast to contemporary fundamentalism. It is proposed that the political system of Iran as an Islamic state, especially in contrast to other fundamentalist organizations, regimes, and states, is in fact a rational entity. Policymaking in particular is used as an example to exemplify the political rationality of the state in comparison with other regimes in the region.

Subsequent chapters, following the brief overview and introduction to Iran's political system, offer an Iranian outlook towards the international system. The first perspective, provided in Chapter 3, shows that the Islamic Republic of Iran does not consider the existing international system to be ideal or reasonable. Iranian foreign policy consequentially is explained and demonstrated to help create an ideal international system by attempting to establish a just international order from an Iranian viewpoint. Chapter 4 discusses peace and security, investigating the aftermath of the disintegration of the Union of Soviet Socialist Republics (USSR) and the end of the Cold War, specifically addressing bipolar models and the loss of credibility of a system based on rivalries between two superpowers. Chapter 5 discusses the role major powers, especially the United States, played in shaping an international system catering to their respective national interests and Iran's response as a result. It is explained that Iran feels ignored in the international system and that the impact of the major powers upon it has been disregarded and overlooked, including the challenge of nonconformity with both East and West, instead adopting a "neither East, nor West" position. Chapter 6 further elaborates on Iran's relationship with the international system through the notion of transnational culture. Particular attention is given to the Iranian Diaspora and the role immigrants play in international relations, which is argued to create grounds for future understanding between nations, especially regarding Iran and other members of the international system. The relationship of Iran and the West is again revisited in Chapter 7 and is addressed by means of a post-structuralist approach. The goal would be to illuminate the opportunities for interaction between Iran and Western states, since dealings between the two are lacking. Chapter 8 then delves into the domestic and foreign policies of Iran. Elections are covered in this passage from previous years as well as the most recent ones, leading up to the question of legitimacy and credibility of the country abroad. It is argued that these characteristics must be regained in reassessing Iran's relationship with the rest of the world. Chapter 9 further discusses foreign policy in Iran but also ties in the social aspects to Iranian politics and the international system. Following up on foreign policy, Chapter 10 is concerned with the relationship between Iran and the United States. In particular, national interests are focused upon, including the notion of national sovereignty and the maximization of power. Emphasis placed on these elements, however, leads to factors that could also turn Iran into a globally influential power. Chapter 11 expands on Iran's role in the Middle East and potential global influence by focusing on energy, such as oil, and the increasing dependency on such commodities.

Elections are then discussed in the ensuing chapters, with Chapter 12 examining the international impact of the tenth elections. The geographical focus in this work would be the European Union and Mediterranean states. Finally, Chapter 13 presents different aspects to the tenth elections, providing a range of graphs and statistics to support the contrasting viewpoints.

The chapters in this book provide unique coverage and description of the topic, which is demonstrated in the following ways: the range of themes covered and addressed; the concepts of identity and politics distinctive particularly to Iran, such as the "neither East, nor West" legacy; the insight to the motivations of Iranian leadership; the providing of an Iranian perspective and outlook toward the international system; as well as creating the ground for future dialogue between Iran and other members of the international system in assisting individuals to reach a new understanding of the country and its citizens.

1 Iran's religious fundaments and principles in interaction with the international system

Ali Akbar Alikhani

Introduction

Every society has its own beliefs, attitudes, and tenets, on the basis of which the political system appropriate for that society is shaped. Today, there are about 50 Muslim countries in the world whose attitudes and beliefs come from Islam, though they differ in their compliance to Islamic principles and their interpretation of Islam in a political context. The Islamic Republic of Iran (IRI) is one of the countries that has based its political system as well as domestic and foreign policies on Islamic and Shia teachings. This chapter aims to explore Islamic principles and fundaments to which the Islamic Republic of Iran complies in its interaction with the international system and acts upon them.

"Fundament" here means non-revocable Islamic beliefs which constitute the theoretical and ideological infrastructures of all Muslims. These beliefs on which Muslims have consensus are fixed and unchangeable from the advent of Islam to eternity. "Principles" mean macro and basic strategies that can be applied at any time. These principles are constant within a certain period of time, but can change according to social conditions over the course of history. Of course, some principles can remain constant for long periods of time and new ones may be extracted from fundaments due to conditions of time and place. Principles that are rooted in fundaments are the link between "fundaments" and "policymaking." They should be defined in such a way as to both preserve unchangeable fundaments and give rise to policies that conform to conditions of time. "Interaction with the international system" means any form of relationship between a Muslim country and other countries, especially non-Muslim countries. Priority should be naturally given to political relations, which dominate other relations. "Religious" means principles and fundaments that exist or are capable of being taken from the Quran, the Prophet Mohammad's (S) Sunnah, and conduct of Imam Ali (AS), which delineate the Shia approach as laid out in this chapter. Therefore, principles and fundaments arise from the above three sources.

We will first discuss each of these fundaments before attending to the principles arising from them. Each fundament and principles has been analyzed by the author on the basis of original Islamic sources, especially the Quran and Sunnah. At the end of each discussion, principles and fundaments arising from Islam are explained.

We will also point to some articles of the Iranian Constitution which have their roots, directly or indirectly, in those fundaments and principles and which reflect the Islamic style of governance. Some fundaments are such that it has not been possible to include them in the Constitution, but they are among the indisputable points for the establishment of the Islamic Republic of Iran. The Preamble and Article 4 of the Constitution have clearly stipulated that the Iranian government is based on Islamic criteria. Article 2 of the Constitution has also noted that the Islamic Republic of Iran is based on God and Divine revelations and the sixth paragraph of the same article has pointed to the Quran and Sunnah as the main sources for the extraction of rules and principles.

Fundament 1: Respectful attitude to all people

Types of human dignity

Human dignity can be divided into two types, "inherent human dignity in this world" and "acquired human dignity in the Afterworld." Inherent human dignity in this world has been bestowed upon humans by God and is part of human nature. It will accompany them as long as they are alive and belongs to all human beings equally without having anything to do with religion, race, color, or gender. With regard to the inherent dignity in this world, besides God's stipulation in the Holy Quran that all human beings have been given dignity and superiority over other creatures,[1] other verses of the Quran have indicated in other ways that dignity and superiority by saying that God's spirit has been breathed into man,[2] man is God's surrogate on Earth,[3] and everything on Earth has been created for humans: these are all cases that denote the inherent dignity of human beings in this world.[4] The Quran has further stressed the negation of violence and bloodshed as evidence of the dignity of human beings.[5] The most important feature of this form of dignity is that it is constant and similar for all human beings because it belongs to mankind.

Acquired otherworldly human dignity is gained through a criterion called right-eousness and gives mankind superiority over other human beings in the other world. Although this kind of dignity is obtained in this world, its manifestation is seen in the Afterworld and the supremacy is manifested after death because nobody except for God can correctly measure or recognize it. This kind of dignity does not have a yardstick for assessment that can be understood in this world, and the Quran has stipulated that this form of dignity can be only given by God.[6]

Sin and disobedience to divine commands will not harm inherent human dignity in this world, and if God has drawn an analogy between infidels and animals,[7] this will be manifest only in the other world and denotes that they would be punished in the Afterlife. Ibn Arabi noted that the Prophet Mohammad (S) had stood up out of respect for the dead body of a Jew and had said that he (the Jew) was a carrier of the spirit of God.[8] He then concludes that the Prophet Mohammad (S) had, in fact, respected the holy spirit of the Jewish man and this proves that all human beings are alike in this regard.[9] Ibn Arabi also noted that the situation of people whose abode is Hell is like that of people who have lost a loved one or their home in this world and are suffering the consequences. Therefore, the innate dignity of humans is alike both for the pious and criminals. Ibn Arabi quoted from a Qushairi treatise that "he who considers himself more dignified than Pharaoh has failed to understand."[10] "Penitence," as an important principle of Islam, allows sinful human beings to have hope in the mercy of God. This shows that the essence of their humanity is intact and they can regain their lofty status when they want to.

Requirements of human dignity

The author maintains that human dignity is a right that cannot be taken from humans in this world under any condition. It is not that God has first created humans and then given them dignity; God has created them dignified from the very beginning, and depriving them of that dignity would change their true nature and existence.[11] Ayatollah Javadi Amoli believes that human dignity is not contractual, but a reality like the nobility of angels and the Quran, and all of them are symbols of dignity of God.[12] Therefore, committing any crime and sin or having any idea, thought and ... will neither deprive humans of their dignity, nor allow others to ignore that dignity. A man sentenced to death can be punished, but his dignity cannot be ignored because it is his innate right.

If human dignity was just a blessing and a virtue, it would be subject to conditions and could be taken away. If, however, it is considered a right, it cannot be taken away from humans under any condition and will have two important political and social consequences: first, everybody will be obliged to observe the dignity of other human beings and, second, when there is a correlation with the government and power. Therefore "human dignity is an inner and unalienable right for humans in society and in all fields of life."

Fundaments of human dignity in Islam

Intellect can be considered the main fundament for human dignity. Although many things have differentiated humans from other creatures, the most important distinction is human intellect. When interpreting the Quranic verse on "veneration"[13] some interpreters have noted that God has venerated humans by bestowing intellect upon them.[14]

The second fundament for human dignity is mankind's spiritual dimension and the spirit of God that has been breathed into him.[15] Muslim scholars maintain that humans consist of "material and spiritual" or "mundane and heavenly" or "animal and human" dimensions. His mundane dimension is related to his carnal soul while his spiritual dimension is related to God. It is his spiritual dimension that has made him distinct from other creatures.[16] The fundament of human dignity is his spiritual dimension. What imparts more significance to this dimension is the ability of the human spirit to evolve and soar.

The third fundament for human dignity is the power of understanding. Language—both meaning a means to speak and a system of concepts to make one understood—is an extraordinary power of which other creatures are deprived.

In other words, humanity hinges on understanding through concepts, propositions, languages, and cultures, which are exclusive to human beings.

The fourth fundament for human dignity is the essential unity of humanity and "external unity of humankind." This does not mean that all humans are alike, but that humanity is like a single body whose organs are human beings and that single body should have an objective manifestation. Every "person" is the same as "others" and "others" are the same as "I." This has been admitted by the Quranic verse which says that killing a single human being is tantamount to killing all people.[17] Mohammad Taqi Ja'fari has explained the verse through a mathematical formula stating that "one is equal to all" and "all is equal to one." He believes that this is a supernatural fact, not an ordinary legal principle.[18]

Principles

The following principles can be derived from the above facts:

Principle 1: Everybody is obliged to accept the requirements of his/her human dignity and avoid any measure that would undermine it.

Principle 2: Everybody is obliged to acknowledge the requirements of other people's human dignity and nobody is permitted to trespass against other people's human dignity.

Principle 3: Government is obliged to respect the dignity of all human beings with which it deals. In other words, first, it should avoid undermining their dignity and, second, no group should be allowed to harm that dignity, and third, all policies and plans, both at home and in international interactions, should aim to protect and promote human dignity.

Therefore, the fundaments and principles of human dignity have been taken into consideration in the Constitution of the Islamic Republic of Iran. Under its discussion of "mass communication media" in its preamble, it points to the dignity of all humans and in paragraph 6 of the second article, it has stressed the need to recognize and respect human dignity. Article 154 about foreign policy, mentions "human welfare throughout human society" as the ideal of the Islamic system. Article 39 bans insult to and the dishonoring of convicted persons, in whatever form and for any reason.

Fundament 2: Negation of violence

Conflict between violence and fundaments of political thought in Islam

For a number of reasons, the political thought of Islam and Shi'ism are basically at odds with violence and bloodshed. First, the most important goal of power and government in the political philosophy of Islam and Shi'ism is the guidance, evolution, and perfection of humans to ensure their happiness in this world and the Afterlife.[19] Guidance of humans is an epistemological discussion. People should know about and choose the correct path. They should seek perfection and sublimity and strive toward it. If somebody does not want to increase his/her knowledge or is not willing to move toward perfection, they should not be forced to. Therefore, the most important goal of Islam in politics can only be realized through people's will, and violence will be to no avail.

Second, the political thought of Shi'ism is based on ethics and values and seeks to establish moral, human, and divine values in the society.[20] Violence is immoral and a thought based on ethics and values cannot prescribe it.

Third, realization of justice[21] and right-centeredness[22] are the most prominent characteristics of Shia political thought and the most objective goal that it pursues in the political arena. These two important objectives can only materialize through people's will. People should want justice and strive toward it. If they do not want it for any reason, they cannot be forced to accept it. Moreover, violence is against the principle of justice and is considered an instance of corruption. When Imam Ali (AS) failed to put his reforms into force due to people's reluctance, he told them that he knew how he could bring them to the right path and that the only thing that could correct them was force and the sword but he would not resort to force and the sword because this would be corruption.[23] The Imam maintained that resorting to force, even to promote reforms, would be a kind of corruption and that people should yearn for reforms and justice.

Fourth, Shia political thought does not give priority to power and government; it considers them tools. Power is not the most important axis in the political thought of Islam, but right and justice are and the government is just a tool to help realize these goals.[24] Therefore, on this basis power and government are not valuable per se, and if the realization of right, justice, divine, moral, and human values is not possible through government, then government and power would be worthless and there would not exist any motives for attaining them.[25]

War and jihad in the Quran

The question may arise that if the Quran and Islam are against violence, why are there verses in the Quran that encourage people to go on with war and jihad? In response, we will first explain those verses. "Jihad" is used to describe any effort including "war." In the Quran, jihad has been used to mean both endeavoring toward good[26] and toward evil.[27] Jihad, however, is specifically used to mean "fighting in the way of God."

Quranic verses on jihad can be divided in three groups. The first group comprises verses which have limited jihad with conditions and restrictions, the outcome of which is that Muslims have not been allowed to wage war, have been banned from exerting cruelty during war, and are bound to observe ethics and humanitarian rights and principles, and have the right to use deterrent moves only to the extent of reciprocating—and not more than that. The second group consists of verses which encourage and recommend Muslims to fight and jihad in absolute terms, but according to the Quranic sciences, they are still bound by the aforesaid conditions—the first group.[28] The third group includes verses which intend to explain a situation related to war and jihad and subsequent rewards. In what follows these groups will be briefly explained.

(A) Restricted and conditional verses: Verse 61, Sura Anfal (Spoils of War) advises Muslims to prepare every weapon and all equipment to scare the enemies (of God and their own enemies).[29] The next verse commands them to accept enemy's offer of peace and ceasefire.[30] The first verse only exhorts Muslims to be militarily prepared in order to scare their enemies and merely promotes deterrence and a balance of power. Then immediately, it reminds Muslims of the necessity and priority of respecting peace. The next verse orders (calls on Prophet Mohammad (S)) to "rely on God if enemies tried to cheat on you because God will help you himself and by the faithful"[31] "that have been united by him."[32] "Therefore, encourage them to embark on war and jihad."[33] It is clear that the Quran has not encouraged or recommended Muslims to start war in those verses but the point is readiness for defense and in the next stage they are only encouraged to get prepared to face their enemies in case they attack or attempt to deceive them.

Another Quranic verse has allowed those on whom war has been imposed, or those who have been wronged, or have been unlawfully banished from their land, to start fighting in defense; those whose only sin was their faith and who had tyrants trying to deprive them of their rights.[34] Those verses denote fighting in defense of a natural right, which others violated in the first place and which God gives permission to Muslims to defend.

Mohammad Abdoh believes that jihad, especially warfare, despite what some may think, is not a pillar or goal of Islam and early Muslims always used jihad as a defense to protect their faith and their beliefs.[35] Muhammad Ammara maintains that war and jihad have not been of a religious nature in Islam, that is, Islam was not intended to be propagated through war and violence, and believes that those verses point to political and national issues because the heathens had banished Muslims from their land and tyrannized them and this was a good tenet by which Muslims were permitted to fight in order to defend themselves.[36]

The Quran clearly says that if non-Muslims did not fight Muslims and did not try to push them out of their land because of their religion, Muslims would not be blamed if they did justice to them and did good to them.[37] In view of the Quran's style,[38] the recent part of the verse in fact denotes the necessity of fair treatment of enemies and negates any kind of tyranny or illegitimate domination by Muslims.

Another Quranic verse says, "Fight in the cause of God those who start to fight you, but do not be unjust because God does not like tyrants."[39] Some principles can be extracted from that verse. First, war should only be waged for the cause of God and it is not prescribed for national, economic, political, ethnic, or other reasons. This condition basically denotes the opposition of Islam to war. Second, Muslims should only fight those who have fought with them and this means that the waging of war by Muslims is banned and not authorized. Third, if the enemy started to fight Muslims, they should respond in kind without going to the extremes and during war must not commit tyranny even toward their enemies. Some scientists maintain that the verse advises Muslims to observe moral and ethical principles and what is nowadays called "humanitarian law"; such as not punishing prisoners of war, deserters, injured soldiers, women and children, avoidance from contaminating food and water, and ....[40] Some also believe that the verse (do not commit tyranny) has advised Muslims not to start war.[41] Fourth, the fact that "God does not like tyrants," is a prohibition of any kind of tyranny and can both be a prohibition against starting war and any injustice in war. Then the Quran says, "kill them whenever you found them and drive them out of where they drove you out of (that is Mecca), because sedition is worse than murder."[42] Therefore, the reason behind the idea that you should kill them wherever you find them is that wherever they find you, they would kill you as they have started the war and therefore you should drive them out because they did the same to you. The interesting point is that Muslims have not been given carte blanche to banish their enemies, but they are to drive their enemies out of those places from where they themselves have been banished.

The reason behind said moves is clarified in the following verse and that is the enemies' sedition, which is worse than murder. Sedition means apprehending, imprisoning, torturing, and banishing Muslims, warmongering and killing Muslims; acts which pagans constantly did.[43] The next verse says "If your enemies desisted to fight, you should do so and give up fighting,[44] but if they insisted, you should continue fighting until there is no sedition."[45] That is, until arresting, torturing, and killing Muslims ends. But it reiterates immediately that as soon as enemies give up sedition, that is arresting, torturing, and killing you and put an end to it, Muslims should do the same,[46] otherwise they would be wrongdoers. Therefore, when enemies give up the persecution of Muslims, the war should come to an end unless some continue carrying out injustices. It is not correct to say that the word "sedition" in the verse is a general term and calls on Muslims to continue fighting until there is no sedition in the whole world[47] as previous verses have made the war dependent on enemies' aggression and insist that Muslims should not go to extremes, but should only respond in kind.[48] The said verses also command Muslims, first, to refrain from beginning the war; second, fight as long as it is needed; and third, observe the limits of justice and injustice. The Holy Quran orders Muslims to fight those who have fought them, but not go to extremes.[49] That is, extreme measures should be avoided in fighting an enemy who has started a war.

Some scholars maintain that the Quranic verse "anyone who does wrong to you, you should respond in kind," is a constant principle of the Quran which does not let Muslims start a war. Some claim that "fight with all of heathens"[50] has annulled the above command, but this is not true because all Quranic verses on war were revealed when Muslims were persecuted by their enemies, including said verse, which was revealed after aggression and the violation of covenants by heathens. Therefore, all wars waged by Prophet Mohammad (S) aimed to defend the truth,[51] and the general rule derived from verses which do not allow Muslims to begin a war can be applied at all times.

(B) Absolute verses: Absolute verses of the Quran about war and jihad are those that have unconditionally called on Muslims to embark on jihad. Two points are

noteworthy about these verses. First, according to the rule of "absolute and conditional verses," absolute verses are interpreted on the basis of conditional ones.[52]
Second, every one of those verses aims to elucidate a situation or encourage the
faithful to do certain acts which have already been prescribed under specific
conditions.

(C) Elucidating verses: The third group includes verses that elucidate various
aspects of jihad or the rewards that will be given to mujahids or martyrs. Those
verses have not commanded Muslims to embark on jihad, but shed light on various
aspects of it and indicate that jihad is subject to specified rules and conditions.

Violence in Sunnah and life of Prophet (S)

The tradition of Prophet Mohammad (S), especially throughout his rule in Medina,
was lenient, rational, and peaceful toward opponents and enemies. He treated
various groups of Jews in Medina on the basis of covenant, agreement, and
discourse, and even in times of crisis he avoided violence as a response to
problems.[53] When faced with infidels and pagans, Prophet Mohammad (S) took a
totally defensive stance, and his wars and military exploits were only defensive.[54]
In some cases when he overcame his enemies, his way with them was mercifulness,
tolerance, forgiveness, and lenience.[55]

The Shias believe that, due to various rational, narrative, political, and social
reasons, Imam Ali (AS) should have succeeded Prophet Mohammad (S) as the
leader and ruler of the Islamic society.[56] However, he relinquished his right and did
not use the leverage available to him. Imam Ali (AS) mentioned the prevention of
violence and bloodshed in society as the main reason behind his decision.[57] Imam
Ali (AS) avoided violence and bloodshed as they were basically incompatible with
his intellectual principles because his goal was to build a political system and
society in which justice would rule and the weak could claim their right from the
powerful without difficulty.[58] Such a society could not be built through violence
and bloodshed, but through peace and calm. Imam Ali (AS) told his son, Imam
Hassan (AS), not to invite anybody to fight[59] and also recommended the governor
of Egypt not to turn down an enemy's call to peace as God's satisfaction is in it
because peace will make soldiers comfortable, remove sadness, and make cities
secure. He also wrote to the governor in Fars to be just and avoid injustice and
tyranny, because tyranny would drive people out of homes and injustice would
unsheathe their swords.[60]

Imam Ali (AS) never initiated violence and war. In three wars of Jamal, Seffin,
and Nahravan, the war started only after negotiations with the opposite side failed.
Ultimately, the two armies lined up against each other. Imam Ali (AS) did his best
to prevent war and invited the opposite side to negotiations and peace talks before
the war started.[61] In most cases, he sent a copy of the Quran or told somebody to
hold the Quran over his head and called on the other side to quit war and accept
the arbitration of the Quran (which was accepted by the two sides). After those
measures failed, he would still be reluctant to start the war and waited for the enemy

to start it.[62] His sensitivity about avoiding bloodshed is evident in his letter to the governor of Egypt in which he calls bloodshed the biggest sin and points to many negative consequences of bloodshed in political, social, and ideological terms; he believed that bloodshed would weaken and destabilize power and the government.[63]

Striving to prevent violence

From the viewpoint of Islam, the most important duty of all people and organizations, including political players, is to prevent war by any means. Wars usually follow a period of escalation of tensions. The Almighty God orders Muslims to accept peace if their enemy is inclined toward it.[64] "If your enemy stopped fighting you and proposed peace, in that case, you are not permitted to go on fighting."[65] The first thing that Imam Ali (AS) did to prevent war was to argue with the enemy and convince them by using persuasive methods, on the one hand, and to recognize their rights and demands such as security and dispel their misunderstanding about insecurity,[66] on the other, so that they would not feel insecure and oppressed and embark on war. He also realized the political–social rights of Kharijites.[67]

The conduct of Imam Ali (AS), which is believed by the Shias to reflect the viewpoint of Islam, was based on avoiding starting war and violence. Even when negotiations failed to bear fruit, he told his army to sit down and not to begin the war.[68] This meant that if the other side did not start the war, there would be no war. Even when the two armies were deployed, he sent influential figures and envoys to mediate peace. He told them to stress both sides' interests and commonalities in their talks and pursued the negotiations not just from his own outlooks and interests. He not only sent one or more emissaries, but instead sent several different people[69] while he was also a party to belligerence. After the war began, Imam Ali (AS) continued to send emissaries in the hope of finding a solution to end the conflict.[70]

Principles

Thus far, we have proven that Islam is against all violence and rejects violence in interaction with others. The principles which can be derived considering the above facts and had been carried out by the Prophet of Islam (S) and Shia Imams are as follows:

Principle 1: Any form of physical violence is forbidden and unauthorized and defense is the only legitimate act.
Principle 2: Defense and response in kind should be only made in times of urgency and to repel a threat and no more than that.
Principle 3: Any form of violence or beginning a war is unlawful and prohibited.
Principle 4: Using weapons of mass destruction is unauthorized and forbidden.
Principle 5: It is prohibited to resort to unethical means such as blocking a water stream, spreading poisons or contaminating water and food, and …

Principle 6: Attacking women, children, seniors, religious missionaries, other civilians as well as religious sites and people's houses, and … is forbidden and if a war were to lead to these measures, that war should be prevented.

Principle 7: In the case of war and violence, every effort should be made to end these.

According to Islam's viewpoint about war and violence and in line with Principles 2 and 4 and what has been said in Preamble of the Iranian Constitution, which is considered a government based on Islam, the Islamic Republic of Iran cannot under any conditions initiate any war and can only defend itself. Therefore, Iran can never be considered a potential or actual threat to other countries or the international system because it is bound by ideological restrictions. Article 152 of the Iranian Constitution has noted that the country's foreign policy is based on peaceful reciprocal relations with other countries unless it is attacked by another country.

Fundament 3: Compliance with moral and humanitarian principles

Moral fundaments of Islam

Supplementing and completing moral virtues and values has been mentioned as one of the most important goals of Prophet Mohammad (S), something which he himself has admitted.[71] Any issue should be of the highest importance for which the Almighty God appoints a prophet, and any prophet directs all his efforts after appointment toward the goal he has been appointed for and does not overlook it under any condition for any interests, because if it were not for that objective, he would not have been appointed prophet. All performance and measures of the Prophet (S) to push the affairs of Muslims forward was carried out within in the framework of this exalted moral virtue.

Both in logical and rational terms and in view of Prophet Mohammad's (S) conduct, he always acted upon those moral values and divine criteria because he was not permitted to do otherwise. Prophet Mohammad (S) was appointed to a lofty goal toward which all means, including power and government, should be oriented. Any deviation from that original goal would defeat the main purpose of prophethood. God has admired Prophet Mohammad's (S) temper[72] and that good temper existed in him because The Prophet Mohammad (S) managed to manifest and be bound to all moral values and virtues that have their roots in divine teachings. Compliance with moral values will be more important when it is so under all conditions, including in weakness and power as well as in war and peace and will not be sacrificed for interests and prudence. The Prophet Mohammad (S) was always like that through thick and thin and under ordinary, critical, war and peacetime and at the peak of power and government. Therefore, God introduced him to all Muslims as a "good role model."[73] This is not only in personal aspects, but includes all social and personal, macro and micro dimensions of Muslims' lives including politics and governance.

There are two important points about the Prophet Mohammad (S) being a role model for Muslims. First, it is a totally objective and practical model, which cannot be realized through lip service and boasting. Second, as the subject grows in importance, so does the need to take Prophet Mohammad (S) as a role model. As a result, in politics and government, Muslims should follow suit with the Prophet Mohammad (S) "in practice" and "in reality." On the other hand, the Prophet Mohammad (S) has been appointed to complete moral virtues and God has admired his compliance with those virtues and has introduced him as a role model for Muslims. Therefore, politics and government in Islamic thought cannot be rationally and reasonably based on anything but ethics and their goal will be nothing but to promote divine values and moral virtues.

Necessity of observing ethics by Muslims in politics

Many things have been said about relativity of ethics[74] and moral values which will not be discussed here. In this chapter, we presume moral values to be absolute to prove that it is obligatory to comply with moral rules of Islam. A reason for that obligation, especially in the area of politics, is that compliance with moral values is one of Islam's goals. Government and power are tools and you can sacrifice tools for goals, but not vice versa. God has mentioned the purification of people as a goal of the Prophet Mohammad (S). Purification means to educate people in the right direction so as to habituate them to moral values and good deeds in order to achieve their perfection both in this world and the Hereafter.[75]

Another goal for Prophet Mohammad (S) and divine religions and even a goal of human perfection is mankind's happiness in this world and the other world.[76] As long as people observe moral values in personal and social domains, they will be happy in this world and the Afterlife. Therefore, moral values in Islam constitute a stage in achieving that qualitative goal.[77] Its quality would depend on the capacities and abilities of people, that is to say how and to what extent every person manifests these potentials inside themselves. It is not true that achieving anything less than the total goal would be in vain, but rather, every degree of it would be desirable. You cannot ignore or defy the main goal because it would undermine the whole effort. If, for example, we accepted that moral values—for the completion of which Prophet Mohammad (S) was appointed[78]—constitute part of Islam's goals, we would be questioning the very essence of Islam if we disregarded those values. No Muslim or Islamic government would be permitted to promote vice and undermine virtue; neither are they allowed to be deceitful. If the conditions and atmosphere are not healthy, you may refrain from concluding an agreement or contract or entering into political affairs, but when you do so you have no right to breach it or commit unjust bloodshed. Not acting in a direction against your goals is a human and rational principle and doing the opposite would be denounced rationally and inherently; ethics and promotion of moral values were among the goals behind the descent of Islam and appointment of Prophet Mohammad (S). In no time, that goal could be disregarded. Since Prophet Mohammad (S) was the last prophet of God after whom there has been no other prophet, his goals are still in force. Even if another prophet had come, he would not give up those goals because all divine prophets have been appointed to complete moral virtues[79] and no Muslim person or scholar has ever reached the conclusion that Prophet Mohammad's (S) goals have been wrong or should be changed due to special conditions. Some may reach the conclusion that although the goals are correct, Islam's moral policy cannot be implemented in present times. Such Muslims may even engage in political activities, but they have no right to move against Prophet Mohammad's (S) goals and use immoral means, thus undermining the moral system that has been established by Prophet Mohammad (S) and the Infallible Imams. They should look for and find ways to enforce moral politics and design a system which will conform to Prophet Mohammad's (S) ethics.

Compliance with ethics in wartime

According to Islamic teachings, all moral and humanitarian principles should be observed in wartime. Early Islamic texts have stipulated that no party to a war has the right to deprive the other party of water, food, medicine, and the like or poison them and make them unusable, even if the enemy is pagan.[80] The most important evidence in this regard is the Quranic verse that only allows Muslims to defend themselves in proportion to the aggression that has been pitched against them and does not allow them to take extreme measures or commit oppression and tyranny.[81] Prophet Mohammad's (S) conduct in war was to prevent his men from abuse of confidence or from killing women and children.[82] There are many instances in which Prophet Mohammad (S) has forbidden the killing of women and children.[83] Also, Prophet Mohammad (S) prohibited treacherous behavior in war and told his warriors to fight, but not to betray or breach their promises.[84] It is to be noted that authorized war tactics are quite different from treachery and deceit, which should not be used against the enemy in war.[85] In the battle of Seffin, Muawiyah's soldiers blocked access to water by Imam Ali's (AS) army, but when the situation changed in favor of the latter, they were prohibited by Imam Ali (AS) from doing the same. This happened several times and, at the end, they protested to Imam Ali (AS) who told them that such acts were immoral and, as such, unacceptable.[86] Also, when the Imam was stabbed by Ibn Muljam, he told his followers to provide his attacker with food and water so he may not be kept hungry.[87]

It is crystal clear in Islamic teachings and the political thought of Imam Ali (AS) that those wounded in war should not be mistreated, prisoners of war should not be killed, and enemy troops who have escaped should not be harassed, and all these principles were meant to reduce violence under the bitter conditions that have been created. In any war, Imam Ali (AS) told a caller to tell everybody that beside said cases, no dead body should be disfigured and when they entered the enemy's abode, no curtains should be torn down, no house should be broken into, and no property should be taken away.[88] In the battle of Jamal, some leaders of Imam Ali's (AS) enemies like Marwan and Walid were captured and brought to the Imam, but he let them go.[89] He prohibited mutilation of enemy dead bodies because even a dead body should be respected in Islam and buried under specific conditions and as per special rituals. Therefore, enemy bodies should be never defiled.[90]

In those wars, Imam Ali (AS) gave strict orders to soldiers not to molest women even if they insulted them or their commander and their noble ones.[91] When facing similar cases, Imam Ali (AS) himself did not permit any kind of aggression upon women. After the War of Jamal, Saffiyeh, the mother of Talheh, frequently insulted Imam Ali (AS), but he did not pay attention to her and prevented any harsh reaction by his men.[92] Many interpreters of the Quran have denounced the killing of women and children and believe the limits mentioned in the Quranic verse, which says not to transgress limits,[93] denotes avoiding killing women and children.[94] Although some jurisprudents believe that killing women and children who take part in war against Muslims is authorized, most Shia jurisprudents have absolutely forbidden killing women and children, even if they have taken part in war.[95] Also, killing the aged is forbidden provided that they have not taken part in war against Muslims.[96]

On the basis of Islamic law and three principles of: restrictions on use of weapons, compliance with moral principles in wartime, and good treatment of prisoners of war in international conflicts, Ayatollah Mohaqqeq Damad has noted that some social groups including: 1. Women and children; 2. The aged; 3. Business people and farmers; 4. Civilian passersby; and 5. The clergy and missionaries of various religions and sects, enjoy absolute immunity and support. Therefore, the following acts have been absolutely banned by Islam regardless of the religious tendencies of the people who fight Muslims:[97]

1. Genocide of enemies;
2. Depriving them of the right to surrender (that is, killing captives);
3. Acts of revenge;
4. Disrespect for the wounded;
5. Depriving the enemy of water or food;
6. Demolishing buildings and installations;
7. Destroying trees and environment.

Principles

The following principles can be deduced from what has been said about compliance with moral and humanitarian principles:

Principle 1: Moral and human frameworks constitute the basis of politics and governance in Islam.

Principle 2: International and political interactions should be based on moral principles and within their framework.

Principle 3: Under any condition, moral principles should be complied with. Wartime or other emergency conditions do not justify disregard for moral principles.

Obviously, the Islamic Republic of Iran, as a religious government, should be based on ethics and all policies should be made within the framework of moral principles.

Paragraph 1 of Article 3 of the Iranian Constitution has stressed the need to "create a suitable environment for growth of moral virtues on the basis of faith and piety." Also, paragraph 16 of the same article has noted that the Iranian foreign policy should be based on Islamic principles and its moral values. According to Article 39, insulting even the convicts is prohibited and punishable. Based on Article 14, the government of the Islamic Republic of Iran should interact with all non-Muslims according to principles of ethics and recognize their human rights.

Fundament 4: Precedence of dialogue as the main way of solving problems

In the Quran, God refers to numerous examples of divine prophets arguing with their opponents[98] and has ordered Prophet Mohammad (S) to pursue the policy of discourse with enemies and pagans.[99] Prophet Mohammad (S) started his mission by arguing with his opponents.[100] When he was deprived of required grounds for debate in Mecca through violent measures, he left that city[101] and went to another one where followers of different religions lived. There, in Medina, different tribes following various religions, including Jews and Christians, lived. There, dialogue was the basis of his mission and led to a social contract which recognized the political and social rights of all people and religions and guaranteed their security.[102] Shortly after the arrival in Medina of Prophet Mohammad (S), some people violated their pact and took violent action. Some of them were of the Bani Qainuqa tribe and Prophet Mohammad (S) tried to convince them to give up their measures and settle their problem through dialogue.[103] Before the battle of Badr, Prophet Mohammad (S) sent Omar ibn Khatab to negotiate with the opposite army to cease war, but they did not accept his logic, and one of their leaders, Abu Jahl, said that they would not swap cash for credit.[104]

Imam Ali (AS) also valued dialogue with opponents and enemies as a strategic policy to resolve problems. Before the battle of Jamal, he did his best both personally and through sending numerous envoys to negotiate with Talha, Zobair, and other leaders of the opposite side to convince them to give up hostilities.[105] His correspondence with Muawiyah still exists and negotiations with him continued up to the battle of Seffin.[106] He also negotiated with the Kharijites, who were his worst foes, to resolve misunderstandings.[107] When negotiations did not take place or failed, he acted moderately and waited for further opportunities. Before the battle of Nahrawan, Imam Ali (AS) sent out emissaries and then he started negotiations himself to persuade the opposite army to give up war.[108] Imam Ali (AS) divided the enemy into several groups in terms of their attitudes and backgrounds and talked to each group in a different way in proportion to their attitudes and commonalities.[109]

Principles

The following principles can be derived from Islam's attention to dialogue as an important basis for resolving problems:

Principle 1: Dialogue is the only logical way to solve political and international problems.

Principle 2: Dialogue should be based on commonalties and issues of agreement and proceed along the same lines.

Principle 3: If dialogue stops or reaches an impasse, the next way is still another dialogue according to the conditions of time and place.

Perhaps thinking, reasoning, and speech are the main distinctions between humans and other creatures. Islam has put special emphasis on dialogue and reasoning and although it has not been included in the Constitution, the Islamic Republic of Iran attaches great significance to it. If the Islamic Republic chose another way apart from dialogue to solve its international problems and did not choose it as an undisputable principle, it would be acting against Islamic principles.

Fundament 5: Compliance with covenants

Political and social importance of covenants

Although commitment to covenants is a moral necessity, it has been independently discussed due to its importance in political and international matters. It is very difficult for rulers and owners of power to act upon a covenant which imposes limitations on them and sometimes people/rulers may violate such covenants, if they conclude a covenant and then realize it is against their interests and power or that they will sustain losses due to the covenant. They will resort to various kinds of justification and deception, especially if the covenant has been signed with an enemy.

The Quran has put absolute emphasis on respecting covenants[110] and considers breaching covenants and contracts a great sin.[111] Imam Ali (AS) argued that if a ruler signs a covenant with his enemies he should observe it and no treacherous behavior and deception in the covenant would be permitted in these cases. It is because God has considered covenants as safe fortresses within which people will feel secure, confident, and calm. One can commit neither treachery nor encompass deception in a covenant. Imam Ali (AS) told his governor in Egypt that before signing a contract, he should scrutinize all its aspects because if, after singing it, he found it against his interests he had to tolerate its hardship and there would be no way to go back and breach that contact or take resort to deception to breach it, thus bringing the wrath of God on himself.[112]

All the above-mentioned outlooks and Imam Ali's (AS) recommendations to his governor were related to covenants with enemies and even enemies at war; that is, he had anticipated the worst conceivable situation and did not allow for breach of covenants so that there would be no place for justification of breaching the covenant or introducing deception, bringing in ambiguous sentences. Imam Ali (AS) sought to introduce a common point which would connect all human beings regardless of their native cultures and religion. He was trying to establish a point on which all human beings have a consensus and ensure the survival of human beings.

He maintained that the common point was respecting covenants, something that has been considered by God a strong sanctuary to make human societies feel secure. He did his best to defend that sanctuary and not let its stable sanctuary and bases be damaged and its respect ignored. He even sacrificed his power and government to preserve this sanctuary for mankind so that people have at least one thing they may trust, and within which they feel secure and calm.[113]

Compliance with content of covenants with anybody and at anytime

In the battle of Seffin, Imam Ali (AS) was forced into accepting a truce just as he was gaining victory over the enemy under the pressure and threat of a group of narrow-minded people in his own army.[114] When determining an arbitrator, the men he appointed were not accepted and another person who was not competent for that job was imposed on him. Finally, he signed a peace covenant with Muawiyah according to which two arbiters were to be appointed to determine the fate of Muslims and righteousness of one side; both sides promised to accept their judgments, which were supposed to be made on the basis of the Quran. Muawiyah used tricks so that the result of arbitration was against the interests of the Muslim society. Finally, those who had forced Imam Ali (AS) into accepting arbitration realized their mistake and came to the Imam urging him to breach the covenant because of the huge losses the arbitration inflicted on the Muslims and to restart the battle against Muawiyah. He told them that he had predicted the disadvantages of the covenant and had cautioned them, but they had not accepted. He added that he would not breach the covenant he had signed,[115] because God stipulated that:

> And fulfil the covenant of Allah when you have made a covenant, and do not break the oaths after making them fast, and you have indeed made Allah a surety for you; surely Allah knows what you do.[116]

The protesting group, which was later known as Kharijites, believed that agreeing to an arbitration covenant was the wrong thing to do and that war against Muawiyah was essential. Since they failed to convince Imam Ali (AS) to break that covenant, they concluded that they should fight both Imam Ali (AS) and Muawiyah. Imam did his best to be just to them and finally had to put them down,[117] though he believed that they were a group which was wrong in its interpretation of truth while Muawiyah was a corrupt element who knew exactly what he was doing and had waged war against the Imam with full knowledge and was acting according to immoral techniques. However, the Imam refrained from war against such a person just because of the covenant.

Principles

Compliance with covenants, as an Islamic and human fundament, leads to the following principles:

Principle 1: Respect for and commitment to covenants and their content is an absolute and undeniable necessity.

Principle 2: No deception, ambiguity and indistinctness are allowed with regard to covenants.

Principle 3: Suffering losses for any reason as a result of a covenant, is not a permit to breach the covenant, and those losses should be tolerated.

Today, Compliance with covenants is a rational issue and an inevitable necessity in political and social affairs. The Islamic Republic of Iran is no exception. Islam put so much stress on covenants in a primitive society about 1400 years ago and this shows how important they are in a modern society. Since this is an obvious fact, it has not been explicitly mentioned in the Iranian Constitution.

Fundament 6: Respect for all thoughts and religions

Trans-religious and trans-ethnical attitude

In his letter to Malik Ashtar, Imam Ali (AS) included many sentences that cover all human beings from any nationality, race, league, or religion. He put stress on such phrases as "the whole people," "the public," "servants of God," and "those who are like you in creation." In this connection the word "people" has been mentioned nine times, "peasant," meaning "citizen," in 19 cases, "the public" three times, "any human being" twice, "servants of God" once, and "your … in creation" once.[118] He opined that a ruler should have a humanistic and trans-religious attitude toward people. In this sentence, the Imam divided citizens of an Islamic society into two groups: first, those who are Muslims and religious brethren of rulers; and second, those who are not Muslims but who were created in the same way as rulers.[119] Imam Ali (AS) believed that being a human being is a basis of having human and citizenship rights. The Imam mentions a criterion which cannot be ignored under any conditions and is a part of the nature and essence of human beings and accompanies them up to their very deaths. Imam Ali (AS) has consistently considered humans, regardless of their nationality, ethnicity, or religion, to be on an equal standing[120] and all instances he has mentioned pertain to the social and political rights of human beings.

The important point is that when the Imam talks about non-Muslims, it is when the subject of his discussion goes beyond rights and commitments, because they are a form of obligation that should be observed according to law. The Imam, however, talks about kindness and a humanistic approach because merely being a human being, regardless of nationality and religion, is enough reason to love human beings and respect them.[121]

Respect for other religions and minorities

When Imam Ali (AS) saw a Christian mendicant, he ordered him to be paid through the Muslim treasury.[122] Although he was a Muslim and was the second most important Muslim figure next to Prophet Mohammad (S) who suffered the most for the cause of Islam and made utmost effort for its promotion, as the ruler of the society and in the peak of power he had a humane attitude toward all citizens and did not discriminate between a Christian—a minority—and Muslims. One of his rulers told the Imam that a Muslim and a Christian had committed a crime and asked him how they should be treated from a legal point of view. The Imam told him to punish the Muslim according to Islamic law and deliver the Christian to their leaders to punish him according to their laws.[123] This proves his respect for human personality and that he officially recognized the laws and beliefs of other people; although the Imam believed they were not righteous and their beliefs were not right and also they formed a minority living in the Islamic society where Islamic laws prevailed. The Imam could have easily punished the Christian according to the Islamic law, as the Muslim offender was punished, but commitment to ethical principles and respect for dignity of human beings required the Imam to respect everybody and safeguard their rights although their beliefs were contrary to his own or even if they were not acceptable to him.

When Imam Ali (AS) was told that enemies had attacked a city and robbed a Jewish or Christian woman of her anklet, he became so angry that he told his followers if a man died out of sorrow for that incident and for aggression upon a non-Muslim woman (living in an Islamic society), he should not be blamed.[124] The issue here was the enemy's aggression upon a human being and that the sanctity of a human being was violated. It did not matter to the Imam whether the citizen was a Muslim or not.

Principles

The following principles can be deduced on the basis of respect for all thoughts and religions:

Principle 1: All religions, thoughts, and attitudes should be respected in political and international interactions.
Principle 2: It is necessary to guarantee security and the political and social rights of all people.

Article 4 of the Iranian Constitution obligates the government and people according to a Quranic verse[125] to respect all non-Muslims, treat them with good manners, and do them justice in their interactions, except for those who conspire or launch acts of violence against the Islamic government.

Fundament 7: Attention to realities and power equations

It is logical to assume that in every situation, attention should be paid to existing conditions and realities, and decisions and actions should be affected accordingly. However, many faithful look for documented examples from the Quran and Sunnah. There are many verses in the Quran which advise Muslims to pay attention to realities. One of them, for instance, orders Muslims not to insult gods of pagans and enemies because they will, in turn, insult their God.[126] This verse clearly and transparently takes into consideration a reality without paying attention to idealistic or emotional issues or unrelated issues. Naturally, from the viewpoint of the Quran, the god of the opposing side is false and unacceptable but here the discussion is not on the legitimacy of the worshiped but that Muslims should regulate their conduct and performance on the basis of an outer reality, though this reality is not pleasant or true. Here, attention should be paid to two points. First, if a reality is not true, this does not mean that it should be ignored. Second, Muslims should not forget their principles, but the goal is to interact with others while preserving their ideological principles.

When Prophet Mohammad (S) was appointed, he invited people to Islam in secret and did not make public his mission for three years because conditions in Mecca did not let him do so. In other words, the Prophet (S) regulated his behavior in relation to the social realities the pagans had created, part of the Prophet's audience were the very same pagans, and no move was possible without taking into consideration the existing realities. Immigration of Muslims to Abyssinia[127] and Prophet Mohammad's (S) immigration to Medina were subject to social realities caused by enemies' conduct. The same was true with wars of the Prophet (S) when he had to defend himself against pagans.[128] Withdrawal of Imam Ali (AS) from power and government after the demise of Prophet Mohammad (S) was also subject to social realities as was his coming to power. The correctness or incorrectness of those realities or conditions of players are not an issue here, but the main issue is that we are faced with a reality and should decide and act in proportion to it, whether it is sweet or bitter, false or true. Imam Ali (AS) followed his own political and social principles during five years of his rule, but his decisions and actions to achieve these policies were based on social and political realities. He had to engage in three battles against his will. He was succeeded by his older son, Imam Hassan (AS), who ruled for about eight months before giving in to social realities and signing a peace accord with Muawiyah. The reason for accepting peace was the military superiority of Muawiyah.[129] Therefore, realities are determinants in the arena of policies and governance and not ideals and aspirations.

Principles

The following principles result from paying attention to realities and power equations:

Principle 1: Attention to realities and power equation is the main factor when interacting with international system.
Principle 2: There is no room for idealism and sloganeering in practical political and international interactions.

This is indicative of a necessity in politics and governance. This has nothing to do with constitution and, therefore, has not been directly mentioned in the

Constitution. The style and general spirit of the Iranian Constitution show that this issue has been a concern for Iranian politicians. We aim to prove that teachings of Islam and Sunnah of religious leaders are based more on realities of time than on pure sentiments and slogans.

Before drawing any conclusion to this chapter, it is imperative to answer one question: Has the Islamic Republic of Iran been able to act and behave precisely on the basis of these principles and foundations? In response I would like to raise another question: Are the Western and developed countries practicing what is said and written in anticipation of democracy? Any country and political system accepts principles and bases as ideal goals and lays its foundation on the basis of those goals. But the extent to which a country succeeds in attaining its goals depends on the existing political and social realities and conditions. However, the international system is obligated to help any country achieve its own defined sublime and human goals. We, as researchers and writers of the scientific community, are obliged to help governments to take steps in the direction of human and ethical goals and reach an ideal stage from the status quo.

Concerning the Islamic Republic of Iran, there are several points that must be taken into account. First, some 30 years have passed since the birth of the Islamic Republic government and this period of time is not long for the theoretical and ideological infrastructures of a government to take shape. More time is needed for gradual explanation and proper application in an Islamic government today of the ethical and religious principles and fundaments of Islam.

Secondly, the Islamic Republic of Iran has faced numerous political and social crises during its lifetime, including armed struggle by opposition groups in the early years after the revolution as well as assassination of people and IRI leaders and thinkers, which has turned the country into a security state.

This was followed by an unwanted war imposed on the IRI for eight years, which inflicted heavy material and human losses. On the one side of the conflict was the Islamic Republic of Iran alone and on the other side were almost all material, military, media, and diplomatic assistance of the Arab world and Western countries in support of Iraq.

As far as our discussion is concerned, the difficult situation and socio-political crises after the revolution which took some ten years had two consequences: First, the most important scientific and intellectual theoreticians of the revolution and the IRI were killed and this caused a very significant intellectual vacuum. Secondly, the heavy blows inflicted by the opposition, as well as domestic and foreign enemies made the IRI officials act with more caution and, based on their repeated experiences, not trust anyone too much.

In general, these two events slowed down the shaping of the religious and ethical fundaments and principles of the IRI and their realization through state rules and regulations.

Thirdly, putting aside the first decade, over the past 20 years, the Islamic Republic of Iran has faced numerous obstructions and animosities from most of the world's powerful and influential states in the international arena, particularly in the West.

In addition to widespread sanctions, the Western mass media have always tried to portray a negative and false image of the Islamic Republic of Iran. All these conflicts as well as ceaseless and strong pressures left the IRI with little chance to precisely theorize and materialize the fundaments and ethical-human principles of Islam within the components of its domestic and foreign policies.

Conclusion: introduction to "intersection theory" in international relations

Islam takes a human and universal approach to all issues. As for religious rites, religious rules, and some legal regulations, there are differences between Muslims and non-Muslims that are natural and even desirable, but when it comes to human dignity and justice, commitment to moral principles, and, especially, humanitarian law, there is no difference between the two groups. Although most historical evidence and attributions produced here are related to the internal affairs of Muslims, and they have roots in the fundaments and main teachings of Islam, these laws and rights are also true for and apply to non-Muslims and foreigners.[130]

Therefore, in view of the facts delineated in this chapter, we may be able to proceed toward presenting a general theory in international relations on the basis of Islamic teachings. This theory might help Islamists to interact with other countries and international systems away from extremism, tension, or pessimism, and while maintaining their own religious principles and fundaments. This interaction and cooperation will happen within an "intersection framework."

This means that every human being or country has common viewpoints, interests, and teachings with other human beings or countries. Even if there is no other common point, they are the same as humans[131] and have similar parents.[132] They have been divided into different nationalities and ethnicities and groups due to the conditions of life as well as social, historical, and geographical necessities and have different attitudes, interests, and demands. In some cases, the attitudes, demands, and interests of people, groups, and nations are similar due to the same necessities while in other cases, they differ. If we consider commonalties between groups and people as circles, the intersecting parts of those circles are "points of intersection." The closer people and groups are in terms of ideology, attitudes, culture, or material interests, the broader their area of concurrence will be. Such commonalties are not accidental but are rooted in attitudes, beliefs, demand, and interests. Therefore, factors creating those points of concurrence and common area are important for both sides. A collection of such factors creates frameworks which can give birth to agreements, contracts, and actions; we call these common factors "intersection frameworks" and they should be taken as the basis for movement, decisions, and actions in the international arena. People, groups, and countries enjoy commonalties in one or several different areas which help them shape intersection frameworks. In the absence of any commonalty or common interests, their humanity is their common ground and this can serve as a minimum contract basis for them.

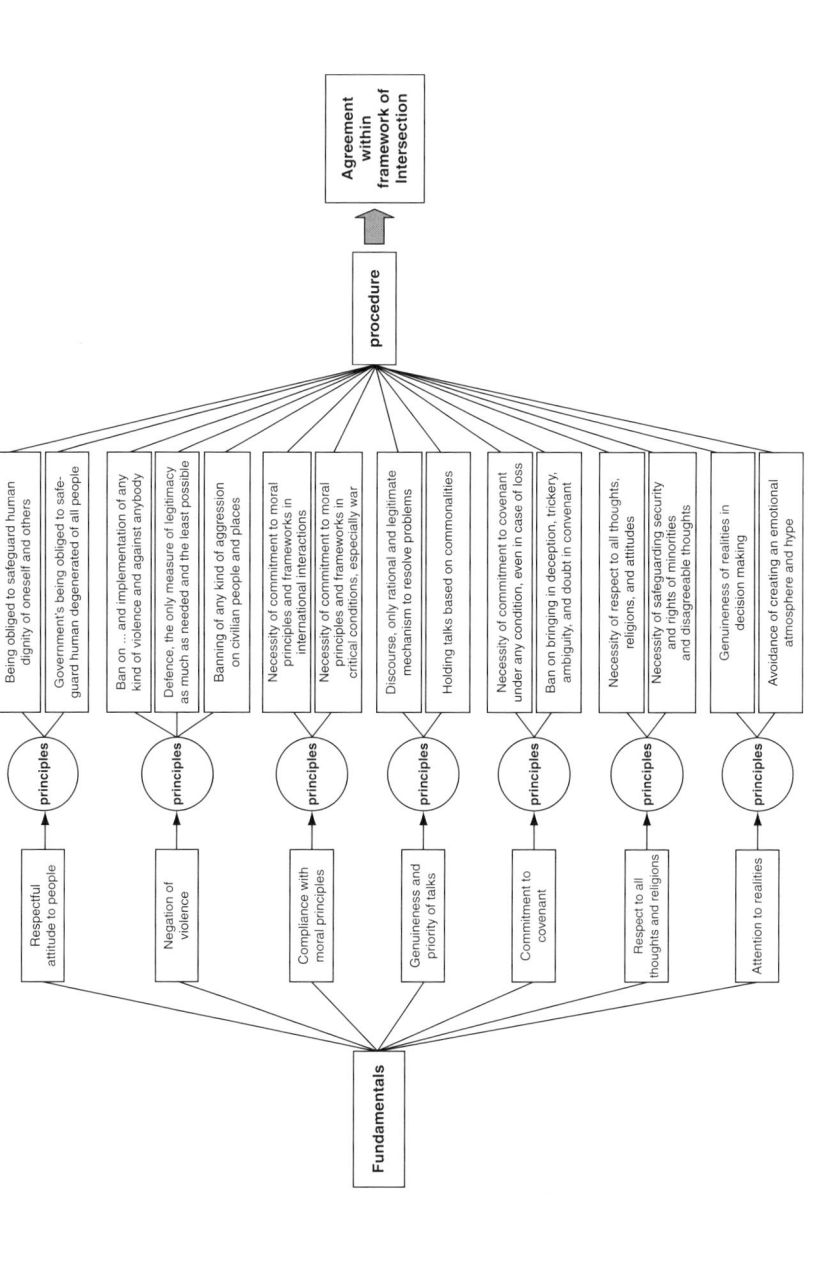

Figure 1.1 Intersection theory in international relations.

Rules and methods should be taken into consideration to move and act in the intersection frameworks, most of which have risen from the fundaments and principles discussed in this chapter. These rules and methods are as follows:

1. Centrality of human dignity: That is, the essential dignity of humans should always be taken into account in negotiations and interaction.
2. Détente: This means that raising issues and leading talks toward tension and carrying out any probable acts escalating tension and violence should be avoided.
3. Ethics: All negotiations and interactions should be conducted within the framework of moral rules and a commitment to them.
4. Focus on commonalties for agreement: Issues of differences should be passed over in favor of convergence, and agreement and issues and points agreed by both sides should be the focus.
5. Attention to realities and power equation: Aspirations, ideals, causes, dos and don'ts should not be taken as a basis for decision-making, and decisions should be based on realities. A Muslim country should first assess its own power and that of other players before making a decision.
6. Dignity of Muslims in foreign lands and security of non-Muslims in Islamic lands: Performance of Islamic governments should be such that any Muslim in any part of the world would be dignified and respected at a high level. Also, Islam never allows humiliation of Muslims by non-Muslims. On the other hand, a non-Muslim entering an Islamic country should enjoy the highest degree of comfort and security.

Notes

1　"And surely we have honoured the children of Adam, and we carry them in the land and the sea, and we have given them of the good things, and we have made them to excel by an appropriate excellence over most of those whom we have created," Asra (17): 70.
2　"... and breathed into him of my spirit," Hijr (15): 29.
3　"And when your lord said to the angels, I am going to place in the earth a caliph," Baqara (2): 30.
4　"... created for you all that is in the Earth," Baqara (2): 29.
5　"... whoever slays a soul, unless it be for manslaughter or for mischief in the land, it is as though he slew all men," Maeda (5): 32.
6　"... therefore do not attribute purity to your souls; he knows him best who guards (against evil)," Najm (53): 32.
7　"O you men! surely we have created you of a male and a female, and made you tribes and families that you may know each other; surely the most honourable of you with Allah is the one among you most careful (of his duty); surely Allah is knowing, aware," Hujarat (49): 13; Prophet Mohammad (S) said, there is no superiority for Arab over non-Arab, nor for whites over blacks; Ahmad ibn Abi Yaghoub, *Tarikh Yaghoubi*, translator Ibrahim Ayati, Tehran, Book Translation and Publication Corporation, 1968, vol. 1, p. 504
8　Muhammad (47): 12; A'raf (7): 179.
9　Muhiaddin ibn Arabi,, *Alfotouhat al-Makkiyah*, Beirut, Dar Sader, BITA, vol. 1, pp. 527–528
10　Abdulkarim bin Hawzan Al-Qushairi, *Al-Risalat al-Qishriyah*, research Abdulhalim Mahmoud and Mahmoud bin Sharif, Qom, Bidar Press, 1995, p. 70

11 Rahim Nobahar, Religion and Human Dignity, in: *Theoretical Fundaments of Human Rights*, Qom, Mufid University, 2005, p. 620

12 Abdollah Javadi Amoli, *Philosophy of Human Rights*, Qom, Asra Press, 1996, pp. 161–162

13 "… and surely we have honoured the children of Adam," Asra (17): 70

14 Seyed Mohammad Hossein Tabatabaei, *Al-Mizan fi Tafsir al-Quran*, Beirut, Al-A'lami Lilmatbuat Institute, 1393 AH, vol. 13, p. 156; Ahmad al-Ansari Al-Qartabi, *Al-Jami' Lil Ahkam al-Quran*, Beirut, Dar ul-Ehya al-Toras al-Arabi, 1966, vol. 10, p. 294

15 "… and breathed into him of my spirit," Hijr (15): 29

16 Abu Nasr Mohammad Farabi,, *Fosoul Montaze'ah*, translated by Hassan Malekshahi, Tehran, Soroush, 2003, p. 17; Ikhwan al-Safa wa Khillan al-Wafa, *Rasaeil*, Beirut, al-Dar al-Islamiyah, 1412 AH, vol. 2, p. 383

17 "… whoever slays a soul, unless it be for manslaughter or for mischief in the land, it is as though he slew all men," Maeda (5): 32

18 Mohammad Taqi Jafari,, *A Study of Two Universal Human Rights Systems of Islam and the West*, Tehran, Office for Propagation of International Legal Services Press, 1991, p. 406

19 Shahidi, *Nahj-ul-Balagha*, Tehran, Islamic Revolution Publications and Education, 1992, Sermon 105, p. 98

20 See "Compliance to Moral and Humanitarian Principles" below.

21 Nisa (4): 58; Nahl (16): 90; Maeda (5): 8 & 42; Shoura (42): 15; also see: Abdolkarim ibn Muhammad Yahya Qazvini, *Survival or Collapse of Government in the Political Words of Imam Ali* (AS), collected by Rasoul Ja'farian, Qom, Library of Grand Ayatollah Mar'ashi Najafi, 1992, pp. 97, 98, 100, 112, and 125; Jamaleddin Mohammad, Khansari, *Comments on Ghurar ul-Hikam wa Durar ul-Kalim*, corrections and comments by Mir-Jalaleddin Hosseini Armavi, Tehran, University of Tehran Press, 1981, vol. 1, pp. 11, 104, 198, and 216; and vol. 2, pp. 30 and 90; and vol. 3, pp. 205, 374, and 420.

22 See Khansari, *Comments*, vol. 3, p. 239; vol. 5, pp. 153, 168, and 338; Shahidi, *Nahj-ul-Balagha*, Sermon 87, pp. 69–70; Sermon 216; p. 248, Sermon 72, p. 250, and Brief Writings No. 125; pp. 54–55.

23 Al-Sheikh al-Mufid, Muhammad bin Muhammad bin Nu'man, *Al-Jamal*, Beirut, Dar-ul-Mufid, 1192, pp. 272–273; Shahidi, *Nahj-ul-Balagha*, Sermon 69, p. 53.

24 Shahidi, *Nahj-ul-Balagha*, Sermon 3, p. 11; Sermon 23, p. 34; Sermon 131, p. 129; Sermon 205, p. 239; Sermon 173, p. 179; also: Al-Sheikh al-Mufid, Muhammad bin Muhammad bin Nu'man, *Al-Irshad*, Beirut, Dar-ul-Mufid, 1193, vol. 1, p. 247.

25 Al-Sheikh al-Mufid, Muhammad bin Muhammad bin Nu'man, *Al-Irshad*, vol. 1, p. 247; Shahidi, *Nahj-ul-Balagha*, sermon 33, p. 34; and sermon 224, p. 259.

26 "… and strive hard in (the way of) Allah, (such) a striving a is due to him," Hajj (22): 78.

27 "… and if they contend with you that you should associate with me what you have no knowledge of," Luqman (31): 15.

28 Jalaleddin Abdulrahman Siouti, *al-Itqan fi Ulum al-Quran*, Seyed Mehdi Haeri Qazvini, Tehran, Amir Kabir Press, 1984, vol. 2, p. 103.

29 Al-Anfal (8): 60. وَ أعدوّالهم ماستطعتم من قوّةٍ و من رباط الخيل ترهبون به عدواالله و عدوّكُم...

30 Al-Anfal (8): 61. وَ ان جنحُوا للسّلم فاجنح لها و توكل على الله و انّهُ هو السميع العليم

31 Al-Anfal (8): 62. وَ ان يريدوا أنَّ يخدعوك فإنَّ حسبك اللهُ هو الذى أيّدكَ بنصرةٍ و بالمؤمنين

32 Al-Anfal (8): 63–64. و ألّفَ بين قلوبهم لو انفقتَ ما فى‌الارض جميعاً ما ألّفتَ بين قلوبهم و لكنَّ الله ألّف بينهم إنّهُ عزيزُ حكيمٌ يا أيُّهاالنبيُّ حسبُكَ الله و من اتّبعك منالمؤمنين

33 Al-Anfal (8): 65. يا ايُّها النبيُّ حَرِّض المؤمنين على القتال

34 Al-Haj: 39–40. الذين أُخرجوا من ديار هم بغير حق إلا أن يقولوا ربُّنا الله و ، ذن للذين يقاتلون بأنّهم ظُلموا و إنَّ الله على نصرهم لقدير (39) لولا دفع الله النّاس بعضهم ببعض لهدمت صوامع و بيع و صلوات و مساجد يذكر فيهااسم الله كثيرا و لينصرن الله من ينصره إنَّ الله لقوى عزيز(40)

35 Abdoh, Muhammad, *al-A'mal al-Kamelah*, research: Muhammad Ammara, Beirut, 1972, vol. 2, p. 733.

36 Muhammad Ammara,, *Islam and War and Jihad*, Ahmad Fallahi, Tehran, Nashr Press, 2004, p. 32.

37 al-; لا ينهاكم الله عن الذين لم يقاتلوكم فى الدين و لم يخرجوكم من دياركم ان تبرّوهم و تقسطو إليهم أنّ الله يحب المقسطين; Mumtahina (60): 8.

38 When Quran talks about corruption, it adds that God does not like corrupt people. It means that the faithful should stay away from corruption. Or it says that God likes the faithful to invite people have become faithful. In other words, when Quran says that God likes or does not like something, it means that the faithful should or should not do that.

39 ; و قاتلو فى سبيل الله الذين يقاتلونكم و لا تعتدوا ان الله لا يحبُ المعتدين; Cow (2): 190.

40 Muhammad Rashid Reza, *al-Minar Commentary*, Beirut, Dar-ul-Ma'rifah, BITA, vol. 2, p. 20 and vol. 9, p. 666.

41 Abolfazl ibn Hassan ibn Al-Tabarasi,, *Majma-ul-Bayan*, Tehran, Maktabat Ayatollah Mar'ashi al-Najafi, 1403 AH, vol. 1, p. 284.

42 ; واقتلوهم حيثُ ثقفتموهم و أخرجوهم من حيثُ أخرَجوكم و الفتنة أشدُ من القتل; The Cow (2): 191.

43 Rashid Reza, *al-Minar Commentary*, vol. 2, p. 209; Tabatabaei, *Al-Mizan fi Tafsir al-Quran*, vol. 2, p. 61; Akbar Hashemi Rafsanjani, *Guiding Commentary*, Qom, Islamic Propagation Office at Qom Seminary, 1992, vol. 1, p. 476.

44 ; فإن انتهوا فإنَّ الله غفور رحيم; The Cow (2): 192.

45 ; و قاتلوهم حتّى لاتكوا فتنة و يكون الدين لله; The Cow (2): 193.

46 ; فإن انتهوا فلا عدوان الا على الظالمين; The Cow (2): 193.

47 Najafabadi, Nematollah Salehi, *Jihad in Islam*, Tehran, Nei Press, 2003, p. 17.

48 الشهر و الحرام بالشّهر الحرام قتال فيه و الحُرَمات قصاصٌ ضمن اعتدى عليكم فاعتدوا عليه بمثل ما اعتدى عليكم و اتقواالله و اعلموا أنَّ الله مع المتقين; The Cow (2): 194; the verse is about the peace covenant of Hudaibiyah when the Prophet Mohammad (S) and a group of Muslims embarked on Haj pilgrimage and heathens of Mecca were planning to attack them; Abolfazl ibn al-Hassan ibn al-Tabari, op. cit., vol. 1, p. 287.

49 و قاتلو فى سبيل اللهالذين يقاتلونكم و لا تعتدوا إنَّالله لا يحبُ المعتدين, The Cow (2): 190.

50 و قاتلوا المشركين كافّة; al-Tawba (9): 36.

51 See Rashid Reza, *al-Minar Commentary*, vol. 2, p. 215.

52 Siouti, *al-Itqan fi Ulum al-Quran*, vol. 2, p. 103.

53 For more details on interactions between Prophet Mohammad (S) and Jews in Medina see: Ali Akbar Alikhani, "Interaction of Prophet's Government with Jews," in Ali Akbar Alikhani *et al.*, *Politics of Prophet Mohammad (S)*, Tehran, Cultural and Social Studies Research Institute, Ministry of Science, Research and Technology, 2007, pp. 269–293.

54 For more details on Prophet Mohammad's (S) wars see Ali Akbar Alikhani, "Analysis of Prophet Mohammad's (S) Wars with Pagans," in Ali Akbar Alikhani *et al.*, ibid., pp. 487–504.

55 See Tavakkol Habibzadeh, "War, Peace, and Humanitarian Law in the Life of Prophet Mohammad (S)," in Ali Akbar Alikhani *et al.*, ibid., pp. 419–450 and 457–480.

56 Ibn Asakir, *al-Imam Ali ibn Abi Talib (AS)*, research by al-Sheikh Mohammad Baqer al-Mahmoudi, Beirut, Dar ul-Ta'aruf lil Matbu'at, 1975, Section III, pp. 84–94.

57 Ibid., p. 92.

58 Shahidi, *Nahj-ul-Balagha.*, letter 53, p. 336.

59 Abbas Mahmoud, *Abqariyah al-Imam Ali (AS)*, Beirut, al-Maktabat al-Asriyah, 1967, p. 18.

60 Shahidi, *Nahj-ul-Balagha*, letter 53, p. 338.

61 Sebt ibn Al-Jozi, *Tazkirat-ul-Khawas*, Tehran, Maktaba Neinavi al-Hadisah, BITA, p. 69.

62 Abulhassan Ali ibn Hassan Al-Massoudi, *Moruj al-Zahab*, Abolqasem Payandeh, Tehran, Scientific and Cultural Press Company, 1991, vol. 1, pp. 718 and 763; Abi Yaghoub, *Tarikh al-Yaghobi*, Beirut, Dar Sader, BITA, vol. 2, pp. 94 and 184; Nasr ibn Muzahim Al-Minqari, *War of Seffin*, Parviz Atabaki, Tehran, Islamic Revolution

Publications and Education Press, 1991, pp. 75, 432, 530, 270, and 277; Al-Sheikh al-Mufid, Muhammad bin Muhammad bin Nu'man, *Al-Jamal*, p. 399; Mohammad ibn Jarir Al-Tabari, *Tarikh al-Tabari*, Beirut, Al-A'lami Lilmatbuat Institute, 1979, vol. 3, pp. 517–520; Abi Hanifeh Ahmad ibn Davoud Al-Dinvari, *al-Akhbar al-Tawal*, research: Abdul Muneim Amer, Cairo, Dar al-Ihya al-Kutub al-Arabiya, 1960, p. 147.

63 Shahidi, *Nahj-ul-Balagha*, letter 53, p. 339.

64 و إن جَنحوا للسِّلم فاجنح لها و توكّل على الله ;Al-Anfal (8): 61.

65 ...; فإن اعتزلوكم فلم يقاتلوكم و ألقو إليكم السَّلَمَ فما جَعَلَ الله لكم عليهم سبيلا ;Al-Nisa (4): 90.

66 Ahmad ibn Yahya bin Jaber Albalazari, *Ansab al-Ashraf*, Beirut, Dar-ul-Fikr, 1996, vol. 2, p. 387.

67 Abu Ubaid Qasem ibn Sallam, *al-Amwal*, Cairo, Dar-ul-Sharq, 1353, p. 321; Shahab-ud-Din Ahmad Naviri, *Nahayat al-Irb fi Fonounil Adab*, translated by Mahmoud Mahdavi Damghani, Tehran, Amir Kabir Press, 1985, vol. 5, p. 213; Abulfada al-Hafiz Ibn Kasir al-Dameshqi, *Al-Bidaya val Nahaya*, Beirut, Dar-ul-Kotob al-Elmiyyah, 1415 AH, vol. 7, pp. 295–300.

68 Al-Massoudi, *Moruj al-Zahab*, vol. 1, pp. 763 and 718; Ahmad ibn Abi Yaghoub, Beirut, op. cit., vol. 2, pp. 94 and 184; Al-Minqari, *War of Seffin*, pp. 75, 432, 530, 270, and 255; Al-Sheikh al-Mufid, Muhammad bin Muhammad bin Nu'man, *Al-Jamal*, op. cit., p. 399; Al-Tabari, *Tarikh al-Tabari*, vol. 3, pp. 517–520; Al-Dinvari, *al-Akhbar al-Tawal*, p. 147; Abu Jafar Muhammad ibn Abullah Eskafi Mo'tazeli, *Al-Me'yar wal Mowazenah*, Mahmoud Mahdavi Damghani, Nei Publications, 1995, p. 140; Mohammad Baqer Al-Majlesi, *Bihar-ul-Anwar*, research and comments: Sheikh Mohammad Baqer Al-Mahmoudi, Tehran, Ministry of Culture and Islamic Guidance, 1408 AH, vol. 32, p. 213.

69 Al-Jozi, *Tazkirat-ul-Khawas*, p. 69; Shahidi, *Nahj-ul-Balagha*, Sermon 122, p. 120.

70 Ali Akbar Hassani, *Analytical and Political History of Islam*, Tehran, Islamic Asceticism Promotion Office, 1994, p. 416; Rasoul Ja'farian, *History of Caliphs*, Qom, Al-Hadi Press, 1477 AH, p. 267.

71 Al-Majlesi, *Bihar-ul-Anwar*, vol. 16, pp. 210 and 287; vol. 18, p. 269; vol. 21, p. 98; vol. 22, pp. 56 and 356; vol. 24, p. 292; vol. 51, p. 249; vol. 69, pp. 370, 375, 386, 394, 397, and 405; vol. 70, pp. 371 and 374; vol. 71, pp. 373, 382, 391 and 420; vol. 74, p. 286; vol. 77, p. 158; vol. 78, p. 345; vol. 92.

72 "And most surely you conform (yourself) to sublime morality," Qalam (68): 4.

73 لَقد كانَ لكُم في رسول الله أسوَة حَسَنة ,Ahzab: 21.

74 See Mawla Mehdi Naraqi, *Islamic Ethics* (translation of Jami us-Sa'adaat), Seyed Jalaleddin Mojtabavi, Tehran, Hekmat Press, 1987, pp. 6–12; Mohammad Javad Moghniyeh, *Philosophy of Ethics in Islam*, Tehran, Badr Press Research Office, 1982, pp. 31–58.

75 Seyed Mohammad Hossein Tabatabaei, *Tafsir Al-Mizan*, Seyed Mohammad Baqer Mousavi Hamedani, Tehran, Tabatabaei Scientific and Theoretical Foundation, 1996, vol. 19, p. 535.

76 Sheikh Tousi, *Tahzib-ul-Ahkam*, Tehran, Dar-ul-Kutub al-Islamiyah, 1985, p. 80.

77 This will be discussed in more detail in Chapter 2.

78 See Chapter 2.

79 Al-Majlesi, *Bihar-ul-Anwar*, vol. 69, p. 397; vol. 70, p. 374; and vol. 78, p. 245; vol. 69, p. 394, and vol. 70, p. 371.

80 Al-Koleini, Abi Ja'far Muhammad ibn Yaghoub, *Forou'il Kafi*, Tehran, Darul Kutubil Islamiyah, 1983, vol. 5, p. 28.

81 "... whoever then acts aggressively against you, inflict injury on him according to the injury he has inflicted on you and be careful (of your duty) to Allah and know that Allah is with those who guard (against evil)," Baqara (2): 194; "... and fight in the way of Allah with those who fight with you, and do not exceed the limits, surely Allah does not love those who exceed the limits," Baqara (2): 190.

82 Ibn Hosham, *al-Sira al-Nabaviyah*, research by Mustafa Saqqa *et al.*, Beirut, Dar al-Ihya al-Turas al-Arabi, p. 992; Ahmad ibn Muhammad ibn Hanbal, *al-Musnad*, research: Ahmad Muhammad Shakir, Cairo, Maktabat ul-Turas al-Islami, 1414 AH, vol. 8, p. 41.

83 Abi Abdullah Muhammad ibn Yazid Qazvini Ibn Maja, *Traditions*, Beirut, Dar al-Ihya al-Turas al-Arabi, 1395 AH, vol. 2, p. 947 and vol. 2, p. 101; Sulaiman ibn al-Ashas al-Sajestani al-Azodi Abi Davoud, *Traditions*, Dar ul-Ehya al-Sunnat al-Nabavi, Bita, vol. 3, p. 52; Tousi, *Tahzib-ul-Ahkam*, 1985, vol. 6, p. 138.

84 Ibn Hosham, *al-Sira al-Nabaviyah*, p. 992.

85 See Seyed Mostafa Mohaqqeq Damad, *International Humanitarian Law*, Tehran, Center for Propagation of Islamic Sciences, 2004, pp. 94–97.

86 Al-Minqari, *War of Seffin*, pp. 219–222 and 253; Al-Jozi, *Tazkirat-ul-Khawas*, pp. 88–89.

87 Asir, *Alkamil Fittarikh*, vol. 2, pp. 197–198; al-Majlesi, *Bihar-ul-Anwar*, vol. 42, p. 288.

88 Naviri, Shahab-ud-Din Ahmad, pp. 178, 154–155, and 152; Al-Dinvari, Abi Hanifeh Ahmad ibn Davoud, op. cit., p. 151; Al-Tabari, *Tarikh al-Tabari*, vol. 3, p. 518; Shahidi, *Nahj-ul-Balagha,*, letter 14, p. 280; Al-Majlesi, *Bihar-ul-Anwar*, vol. 32, p. 213.

89 Al-Sheikh al-Mufid, Muhammad bin Muhammad bin Nu'man, *Al-Jamal*, op. cit., p. 339; Shahidi, *Nahj-ul-Balagha*, sermon 73, p. 55; Al-Aqqad, Abbas Mahmoud, op. cit., p. 200.

90 Shahidi, *Nahj-ul-Balagha*, letter 47, p. 321; letter 14, p. 280.

91 See previous footnotes and Shahidi, *Nahj-ul-Balagha*, letter 14, p. 280.

92 Al-Tabari, *Tarikh al-Tabari*, vol. 3, p. 544.

93 و لا تعتدوا إن الله يحب المعتدين, The Cow (2): 190.

94 Tabatabaei, *Tafsir Al-Mizan*, vol. 2, p. 61; Seyed Qutb, *Fi Zilal al-Quran*, Beirut, Dar-ul-Sharq, 1402 AH; Abolfazl ibn Hassan ibn Al-Tabarasi,, *Majma-ul-Bayan*, Tehran, Maktabat Ayatollah Mar'ashi al-Najafi, 1403 AH, vol. 1, p. 285.

95 Muhaqqiq Helli, *Sharayeh al-Islam*, Najaf, Matba'at al-Adab fil Najaf al-Ashraf, 1389, vol. 1, p. 312; Sheikh Mohammad Hassan Al-Najafi, *Jawahir al-Kalam fi Sharh Sharaye al-Islam*, vol. 21, Beirut, Dar ul-Ehya al-Toras al-Arabi, 1981, p. 70.

96 Abi Davoud, *Traditions*, p. 52; Hor Ameli, Sheikh Mohammad ibn Hassan, *Wasael ush-Shia*, research Abdolrahim Rabbani Shirazi, Tehran: Maktabat-ul-Islamiyah, 1403 AH, vol. 11, p. 43; Al-Najafi, *Jawahir al-Kalam fi Sharh Sharaye al-Islam*, p. 75.

97 Mohaqqeq Damad, *International Humanitarian Law*, pp. 55–57.

98 Noah's dialogue with opponents: A'raf (7): 59–64; Hud (11): 25–36; Shuara (26): 105–124; Abraham's dialogue with opponents: Ana'am (6): 83–84; Shuara (26): 69–104; Abraham's dialogue with Nemrud: The Cow (2): 258; Hud's dialogue with opponents: A'raf (7): 65–72; Moses' dialogue with Pharaoh: Taha (20): 49–76; Shuara (26): 18–56.

99 "Call to the way of your lord with wisdom and goodly exhortation, and have disputations with them in the best manner," Nahl (16): 125.

100 Munir Muhammad Ghazban, *Political Policy of Prophet Mohammad* (S), translated by Omar Qaderi, Ehsan, 2000, vol. 1, pp. 207–209, 135–138.

101 Rafiuddin Ishaq ibn Muhammad Hamedani, *Biography of Prophet Mohammad (S)*, corrected by Asghar Mahdavi, Tehran, Iran Culture Foundation, 1980, vol. 1, pp. 268–269, 459–476.

102 For the text of the covenant see Mohammad Hamidollah, *Political Letters and Covenants of Prophet Mohammad (S)*, Seyed Mohammad Hosseini, Tehran, Soroush Press, 1995, pp. 103–110. The original covenant can be found in different sources including, Ibn Hosham, *al-Sira al-Nabaviyah*, vol. 2, pp. 501–504; Ibn Kasir, *al-Sira al-Nabaviyah*, vol. 2, pp. 320–323; *al-Sira al-Jaliliya*, vol. 2, p. 96; *A'lam ul-Wara*, p. 45; *Uyun ul-Wasr*, vol. 1, pp. 260–262; Sallam, *al-Amwal*, pp. 202–206; Nar ud-Dur, vol. 1, pp. 222–223; Ahmad Miyanji, Makatibul Rasul, pp. 241–263.

103 Ibn Hosham, *al-Sira al-Nabaviyah*, vol. 1, pp. 50–51; Abolfazl ibn Hassan ibn Al-Tabarasi, *A'lam ul-Wura*, Beirut, Dar ul-Ma'rifa, 1979, pp. 89–90; Constant Virgil Gheorghiu, *The Life of Muhammad, Zabihollah Mansouri*, Tehran, Zarrin Press, 2005, p. 267.

104 Muhammad ibn Omar Waqedi, *Mughazi, Mahmoud Mahdavi Damghani*, Tehran, Tehran University Press, 1990, p. 45.
105 Muhammad bin Muhammad bin Nu'man Al-Sheikh al-Mufid, *The Battle of Jamal*, translated by Mahmoud Mahdavi Damghani, Tehran, Nei Press, 1988, pp. 200–204.
106 Al-Minqari, *War of Seffin*, pp. 125–130, 153, 156, and 207–209.
107 Al-Tabari, Mohammad ibn Jarir, *Tarikh Tabari*, translated by Abolqasem Payandeh, Tehran, Asatir Press, BITA, vol. 6, pp. 2606–2610.
108 Ibid.
109 Ibid., pp. 2610–2615.
110 Nahl (16): 91.
111 "Surely the vilest of animals in Allah's sight are those who disbelieve; then they would not believe. Those with whom you make an agreement, then they break their agreement every time and they do not guard (against punishment)," Anfal (8): 54–55.
112 Shahidi, *Nahj-ul-Balagha*, letter 53, pp. 338–339.
113 Ibid.
114 Al-Minqari, *War of Seffin*, pp. 661–668; Al-Tabari, Mohammad ibn Jarir, op. cit., vol. 4, p. 34; Al-Massoudi, *Moruj al-Zahab*, vol. 2, pp. 389–391; Naviri, Shahab-ud-Din Ahmad, *Nahayat al-Irb*, translated Mahmoud Mahdavi Damghani, Tehran, Amir Kabir Press, 1985, vol. 5, p. 197.
115 Al-Minqari, *War of Seffin*, p. 717.
116 "… and fulfill the covenant of Allah when you have made a covenant, and do not break the oaths after making them fast, and you have indeed made Allah a surety for you; surely Allah knows what you do," Nahl (16): 91.
117 Al-Minqari, *War of Seffin*, pp. 716–717; Al-Tabari, Mohammad ibn Jarir, op. cit., vol. 4, pp. 39 and 45–48; Al-Massoudi, *Moruj al-Zahab*, vol. 2, pp. 391 and 404–407; Naviri, Shahab-ud-Din Ahmad, op. cit., pp. 209–218.
118 Mohammad Taqi Ja'fari, *Fundaments of Political Principles of Islam*, Tehran, Nahj-ul-Balagha Foundation, 1990, p. 319.
119 Shahidi, *Nahj-ul-Balagha*, letter 53, p. 326.
120 Mohammad Taqi Ja'fari, op. cit.
121 Shahidi, *Nahj-ul-Balagha*, letter 53, p. 326.
122 Hor Ameli, Sheikh Mohammad ibn Hassan, op. cit., p. 49.
123 Ibid., vol. 18, p. 415; Abu Ishaq Ebrahim ibn Muhammad Saqafi Kufi Esfahani, *Al-Gharat*, Tehran, National Works Society, 1976, vol. 1, pp. 230–231.
124 Ibid., vol. 2, p. 476.
125 Al-Mumtahina (60): 8.
126 و لا تسبّوا الذين يدعون من دون‌الله فيسبُّوا اللهَ عَدواً بغير علم An'am (6): 108.
127 Rafiuddin Ishaq ibn Muhammad Hamedani, vol. 1, p. 312.
128 Ibid., pp. 413–463.
129 Al-Sheikh al-Mufid, Muhammad bin Muhammad bin Nu'man, *Al-Irshad*, translated by Seyed Rasoul Mahallati, op. cit., 2001, vol. 2, pp. 9–13.
130 Al-Koleini, *Forou'il Kafi*, vol. 5, p. 28.
131 ... فأنهم صنفان، اما اخٌ لك في‌الدين و اما نظير لك في‌الخلق, Shahidi, *Nahj-ul-Balagha*, letter 53, p. 326.
132 "O you men! surely we have created you of a male and a female, and made you tribes and families that you may know each other," Hujarat (49): 13.

Bibliography

Abelhadid, Ezzeddin ibn, *Commentary on Nahj-ul-Balagha*, research: Mohammad Abolfazl Ebrahim, Beirut, Dar ul-Ehya al-Toras al-Arabi, 1967.
Abi Davoud, Sulaiman ibn al-Ashas al-Sajestani al-Azodi, *Traditions*, Dar ul-Ehya al-Sunnat al-Nabavi, BITA.

Abi Yaghoub, Ahmad ibn, *Tarikh al-Yaghobi*, Beirut, Dar Sader, BITA.

Abi Yaghoub, Ahmad ibn, *Tarikh Yaghoubi*, translated by Ibrahim Ayati, Tehran, Book Translation and Publication Corporation, 1968.

Ahmab ibn Hanbal, al-Imam, *al-Musnad*, Beirut, al-Maktab ul-Islami, BITA.

Ibn Hanbal, Ahmad ibn Mohammad, *al-Musnad*, research: Ahmad Muhammad Shakir, Cairo, Maktabat ul-Turas al-Islami, 1414 AH.

Albalazari, Ahmad ibn Yahya bin Jaber, *Ansab al-Ashraf*, Beirut, Dar-ul-Fikr, 1996.

Al-Aqqad, Abbas Mahmoud, *Abqariyah al-Imam Ali (AS)*, Beirut, al-Maktabat al-Asriyah, 1967.

Arabi, Muhiaddin ibn, *Alfotouhat al-Makkiyah*, Beirut, Dar Sader, BITA.

Asir, Ezeddin Ali ibn, *Alkamil Fittarikh*, Beirut, Dar Sader, Beirut, 1965.

Beihaqi Neishabouri, Qutb-ud-Din Abulhassan, *Divan Imam (AS)* (collection of Imam's poems), correction: Abolqasem Emami, Tehran, Osveh press, 1996.

Al-Bokhari, Abi Abdullah Muhammad ibn Ismaeil ibn Ibrahim, *Sahih*, Beirut, Dar-ul-Fikr, 1420 AH.

Al-Dinvari, Abi Hanifeh Ahmad ibn Davoud, *al-Akhbar al-Tawal*, research: Abdul Muneim Amer, Cairo, Dar al-Ihya al-Kutub al-Arabiya, 1960.

Eskafi Mo'tazeli, Abu Jafar Muhammad ibn Abullah, *Al-Me'yar val Mowazenah*, Mahmoud Mahdavi Damghani, Nei Publications, 1995.

Farabi, Abu Nasr Mohammad, *Fosoul Montaze'ah*, translated by Hassan Malekshahi, Tehran, Soroush, 2003.

Hassani, Ali Akbar, *Analytical and Political History of Islam*, Tehran, Islamic Asceticism Promotion Office, 1994.

Hor Ameli, Sheikh Mohammad ibn Hassan, *Wasael ush-Shia*, research: Abdolrahim Rabbani Shirazi, Tehran, Maktabat-ul-Islamiyah, 1403 AH.

Ibn Hosham, *al-Sira al-Nabaviyah*, research by Mustafa Saqqa *et al.*; Beirut, Dar al-Ihya al-Turas al-Arabi.

Ibn Kasir al-Dameshqi, Abulfada al-Hafiz, *Al-Bidaya val Nahaya*, Beirut, Dar-ul-Kotob al-Elmiyyah, 1415 AH.

Ibn Maja, Abi Abdullah Muhammad ibn Yazid Qazvini, *Traditions*, Beirut, Dar al-Ihya al-Turas al-Arabi, 1395 AH.

Ikhwan al-Safa wa Khillan al-Wafa, *Rasaeil*, Beirut, al-Dar al-Islamiyah, 1412 AH.

Jafari, Mohammad Taqi, *A Study of Two Universal Human Rights Systems of Islam and the West*, Tehran, Office for Propagation of International Legal Services Press, 1991.

Ja'farian, Rasoul, *History of Caliphs*, Qom, Al-Hadi Press, 1477 AH.

Javadi Amoli, Abdollah, *Philosophy of Human Rights*, Qom, Asra Press, 1996.

Al-Jozi, Sebt ibn, *Tazkirat-ul-Khawas*, Tehran, Maktaba Neinavi al-Hadisah, BITA.

Al-Koleini, Abi Ja'far Muhammad ibn Yaghoub, *Forou'il Kafi*, Tehran, Darul Kutubil Islamiyah, 1983.

Al-Majlesi, Mohammad Baqer, *Bihar-ul-Anwar*, Beirut, Al-Wafa Institute, 1403 AH.

Al-Majlesi, Mohammad Baqer, *Bihar-ul-Anwar*, research and comments: Sheikh Mohammad Baqer al-Mahmoudi, Tehran, Ministry of Culture and Islamic Guidance, 1408 AH.

Al-Massoudi, Abulhassan Ali ibn Hassan, *Moruj al-Zahab*, Abolqasem Payandeh, Tehran: Scientific and Cultural Press Company, 1991.

Al-Minqari, Nasr ibn Muzahim, *War of Seffin*, Parviz Atabaki, Tehran, Scientific and Cultural Press Company, 1991.

Misbah Yazdi, Mohammad Taqi, *Legal Theory of Islam*, Qom, Imam Khomeini Educational and Research Institute, 2001.

Mohaqqeq Damad, Seyed Mostafa, *International Humanitarian Law*, Tehran, Center for Propagation of Islamic Sciences, 2004.

Muhaqqiq Helli, *Sharayeh al-Islam*, Najaf, Matba'at al-Adab fil Najaf al-Ashraf, 1389 AH.

Al-Najafi, Sheikh Mohammad Reza, *Jawahir al-Kalam*, vol. 21, Beirut, Dar ul-Ehya al-Toras al-Arabi, 1981.

Al-Najafi, Sheikh Mohammad Hassan, *Jawahir al-Kalam fi Sharh Sharaye al-Islam*, vol. 21, Beirut, Dar ul-Ehya al-Toras al-Arabi, 1981.

Naviri, Shahab-ud-Din Ahmad, *Nahayat al-Irb*, translated by Mahmoud Mahdavi Damghani, Tehran, Amir Kabir Press, 1985.

Nobahar, Rahim, Religion and Human Dignity, in *Theoretical Fundaments of Human Rights*, Qom, Mufid University, 2005.

Al-Qartabi, Ahmad al-Ansari, *Al-Jami' Lil Ahkam al-Quran*, Beirut, Dar ul-Ehya al-Toras al-Arabi, 1966.

Qomi, Sheikh Abbas, *Safinat ul-Bihar*, Beirut, Dar-ul-Mortez, BITA.

Al-Qoshairi, Abdulkarim bin Hawzan, *Al-Risalat al-Qishriyah*, research: Abdulhalim Mahmoud and Mahmoud bin Sharif, Qom, Bidar Press, 1995.

Quran.

Qutb, Seyed, *Fi Zilal al-Quran*, Beirut, Dar-ul-Sharq, 1402 AH.

Al-reishahri, Muhammad, *Mosuat al-Imam Ali ibn Abi Tablib*, Qom, Dar al-Hadis, 1421 AH.

Sallam, Abu Ubaid Qasem ibn, *al-Amwal*, Beirut, Dar-ul-Fikr, 1408 AH.

Shahidi, Seyed Jafar, *Nahj-ul-Balagha*, Tehran, Islamic Revolution Publications and Education, 1992.

Al-Sheibani, Muhammad ibn al-Hassan, *Kitab al-Seir al-Kabir*, Mohammad ibn Ahmad al-Sorkhi, Cairo, 1958.

Al-Sheikh al-Mufid, Muhammad bin Muhammad bin Nu'man, *Al-Irshad*, Beirut, Dar-ul-Mufid, 1192.

Al-Sheikh al-Mufid, Muhammad bin Muhammad bin Nu'man, *Al-Jamal*, Beirut, Dar-ul-Mufid, 1192.

Al-Sheikh al-Mufid, Muhammad bin Muhammad bin Nu'man, *The Battle of Jamal*, translated by Mahmoud Mahdavi Damghani, Tehran, Nei Press, 1988.

Al-Sheikh al-Mufid, Muhammad bin Muhammad bin Nu'man, *Al-Irshad*, translated by Seyed Rasoul Mahallati, Tehran, Office for Propagation of Islamic Culture, 2001.

Al-Tabari, Mohammad ibn Jarir, *Tarikh al-Tabari*, Beirut, Al-A'lami Lilmatbuat Institute, 1979.

Al-Tabari, Mohammad ibn Jarir, *Tarikh Tabari*, translated by Abolqasem Payandeh, Tehran, Asatir Press, BITA.

Al-Tabarasi, Abolfazl ibn Hassan ibn, *Majma-ul-Bayan*, Qom, Maktabat Ayatollah Mar'ashi al-Najafi, 1403 AH.

Al-Tabarasi, Abolfazl ibn Hassan ibn, *Majma-ul-Bayan*, Tehran, Maktabat al-Ilmiyah al-Islamiyah, BITA.

Tabatabaei, Seyed Mohammad Hossein, *Al-Mizan fi Tafsir al-Quran*, Beirut, Al-A'lami Lilmatbuat Institute, 1393 AH.

Tabatabaei, Seyed Mohammad Hossein, *Tafsir Al-Mizan*, Seyed Mohammad Baqer Mousavi Hamedani, Tehran, Tabatabaei Scientific and Theoretical Foundation, 1996.

Tousi, Sheikh, *Tahzib-ul-Ahkam*, Tehran, Dar-ul-Kutub al-Islamiyah, 1985.

2 Political rationality of the Islamic Republic of Iran in comparison with contemporary fundamentalism

Morteza Bahrani

Introduction

Conflict is a violent form of unjust human material. Most conflicts throughout history have resulted from a lack of an inclusive concept of justice among peoples. In the absence of such a concept, a nation will become hostile and in the most optimistic case interaction will give way to rivalry and even hostility. Although, in the past, geographical distance led to mental and theoretical distance, now that the world has become a smaller place due to revolutionary changes in industries and communications, the way is paved to give some thought to this issue.

Yet most theories related to interaction among governments have been based on traditional realism and rationality. They considered states as rational entities which would do everything possible to secure the interests of their nations (even resorting to war and deceit). Most recent approaches have attached more importance to peoples than states and have laid more stress on reason than rationality.

Considering the above points, great efforts have been made to that effect, especially through adopting a political philosophical approach, the prominent examples of which are the works of John Rawls and Thomas Pangle. We follow two goals in this chapter. The first goal is (A) to confirm Rawls' belief that decent countries can be a partner to peace and justice, and (B) that the Islamic Republic of Iran can be considered a decent nation. The second goal is (A) in order to take part in a theoretical plan on international peace and justice, the Islamic Republic of Iran should first formulate a domestic theory of justice, and (B) Iran can formulate such a theory on the basis of Islamic and Iranian theoretical teachings. Theoretical and practical efforts made in recent years and after the Islamic Revolution (1979) attest to this fact.

Theoretical framework

Immanuel Kant has begun his discussion in *Perpetual Peace* by asking whether politicians who simply think about conflict would heed the viewpoints of philosophers who are more concerned about the future outlook of humanity (Kant, 1983, p. 7). When talking about justice at international level, the question is whether practitioners of international relations and political sciences have anything to say apart from philosophical thoughts and what political philosophers have offered. Important theoretical efforts in international relations, especially in the past decade, have managed to turn conflict into less fraught relations among nations and to explain it, but they have failed to prevent injustice and there is a distinct lack of peace in international relations. Therefore, while admitting to the moral complexity of the world, understanding the moral fundamentals of international relations is a pre-requisite for the establishment of international justice and peace in a world which is characterized by such terms as nuclear age, post-modernism and post-Cold War.

Thomas Pangle and Peter Ahrensdorf have noted in their book *Justice among Nations* that, while voicing the concern that a review of international relations requires serious attention from masters of political philosophy, no theory of justice or injustice among nations can be put forward without a careful analysis of what constitutes justice within political domestic societies and among people. Therefore, an explanation of justice among citizens of any given society without due attention given to its international mission would be flawed. Explaining justice in a society goes hand in hand with explaining it in the foreign relations field of that nation (Pangle and Ahrensdorf, 1999, p. 12). From this viewpoint, in addition to the fact that common interests are fewer and tension is higher at the international level compared to the national and domestic level, and the issue of justice is more of a problem, the theory of domestic justice can be a basis for theorizing on international justice.

John Rawls, the author of *A Theory of Justice*, *Political Liberalism* and *The Law of Peoples*, uses the domestic theory of justice to achieve his theory of international justice. In fact, he generalized the theory of justice for an individual society to that for all peoples. The idea of *The Law of Peoples* (which is the focus of this chapter) has been derived from the dialectics of *A Theory of Justice* and *Political Liberalism*. Rawls stresses that he has presented foreign policy principles of a reasonably just (liberal) people by drawing on a liberal concept of justice. Therefore, his concerns are the foreign policy concepts of a liberal people. It is a form of assuring liberal peoples that ideals and foreign policy principles of a liberal people can also seem worthy of acceptance to a non-liberal yet decent nation. He maintains that the need for such assurances is an innate aspect of the liberal interpretation of justice because *The Law of Peoples* maintains that there is a non-liberal yet decent viewpoint (Rawls, 1999, pp. 4–9, 23).Therefore, the question of how to deal with non-liberal nations is a basic one in any liberal foreign policy. The benefit of this plan is that there is also room for non-liberal nations, which he calls 'decent nations', and, as he himself asserts, it may also include Islamic nations.

The important point when discussing Rawls' *The Law of Peoples* (and the reason behind this chapter) is that according to his theory, justice can be established in a society (either domestically or internationally) only when that concept has been promoted to an understanding of what it entails exactly to reach an overlapping consensus (at least before representatives of the concerned parties), so that the goodness of justice, as a meaning of justice, has been accepted by all peoples. The problem is that a liberal theory of justice cannot be put into action without giving some attention to the principles and policies of what constitutes a decent nation when it comes to formulating the foreign policy principles of a liberal people. Thus, compiling the principles and ideals of a liberal nation's foreign policy cannot be done without attention to the principles and policies of a decent people. If this prelude is accepted, then the second prelude is that the principles and policies of a non-liberal people, called 'decent' by Rawls, cannot be achieved in the absence of an international theory of justice. Finally, an international theory of justice (which is supposed to present principles of foreign policymaking) cannot be reached without first presenting a national and domestic theory of justice. Therefore, *The Law of Peoples* is like a pigeon with one wing that needs a second wing to fly and that second wing comprises peoples deemed decent by Rawls: peoples that are not only reliable and worthy of cooperation, but who also lay claim to a theory of justice at national and international levels.

Between rationality and reasonability

The difference

According to John Rawls, the difference between the rational and the reasonable could be outlined as follows: rational people pursue their ends intelligently and egoistically; reasonable people are willing to govern their conduct following a principle which they and others can accept in common and take into account the consequence of their actions on the well-being of others. A further basic difference between the reasonable and the rational is that the reasonable is public in a way the rational is not. This means that it is by the reasonable that we enter as equals the public world of others and stand ready to propose or to accept fair terms of cooperation with them. Insofar as we are reasonable, we are ready to work out the framework for the public social world. The reasonable is not altruistic, nor is it the concern for self. The reasonable can be applied to persons, institutions, doctrines or societies but the rational is applied to a single united agent (Rawls, 1993, pp. 49–53).

Thus, as the liberal peoples, in Rawls' theory, are the so-called 'reasonable', its realistic being requires that the decent peoples be rational and in transit to a reasonable situation, or what he called 'liberalizing the decent people'. This whole project is 'the law of peoples'.

The law of peoples

By this, Rawls means a particular political concept of right and justice that applies to the principles and norms of international law and practice. In fact it presupposes a 'society of peoples' that all follow the ideas and principles of the law of peoples in their mutual relationships. These peoples have their own internal governments, which may be constitutional, liberal democratic or non-liberal, but are deemed decent governments. This society of people is reasonably just in that its members in their relations follow the law of peoples. This idea of justice is based on the familiar idea of the social contract, and the procedure followed before the principles of right and justice are selected and agreed on is in some way the same in both the domestic and international case, and because they lack knowledge behind the veil of ignorance, their commitments are fair. The principles of the concept of justice presuppose reasonable pluralism and must satisfy the criterion of reciprocity (Rawls, 1999, pp. 3, 14).

For such an end, Rawls used the term 'peoples' and not 'states'.

Why peoples and not states?

As the title shows, the actors and parties who formulate the law of peoples are peoples and not states, like the domestic case in which the citizens are the actors within society. The merits of peoples over states are that the former lack traditional sovereignty, which endorses the powers, including the right to go to war in pursuit of state policies – Clausewitz's pursuit of politics by another means – with the ends of politics given by a state's rational prudential interests (Rawls, 1999, p. 25). The powers of sovereignty also grant a state a certain wrong autonomy in dealing with its own people. In this view, the peoples are free and equal.

So the law of peoples has two important factions: the liberal peoples and the decent peoples.

The decent peoples

In the performance and execution of 'the law of peoples', two types of society have a moral role. The first is composed of liberal peoples who have three basic features: a reasonably just, constitutional, democratic government that serves their fundamental interests; citizens unified by what Mill called 'common sympathies'; and, finally, a moral nature that requires a firm attachment to a political (moral) concept of right and justice. The second type of society is that of decent peoples. The basic structure of one kind of decent people has what Rawls called 'decent consultation hierarchy' and is worthy of membership in a society of peoples. These two types are 'well-ordered peoples'. Rawls asserts that there may exist decent non-liberal peoples who accept and follow the law of peoples. To this end he gave an imagined example of a non-liberal Muslim people, calling it Kazanistan. This people satisfy the criteria for decent hierarchical peoples: it is non-aggressive against other peoples, it honours and respects human rights and its basic structure contains a decent consultation hierarchy (Rawls, 1999, pp. 4, 5, 23).

The main component of the law of peoples is not a fantasy that cannot be reached.

Being realistic

Political philosophy is realistically utopian when it extends to what is normally thought to be the limits of the politically practicable and, in so doing, it reconciles us to our political and social conditions. What makes it possible is the diversity among well-ordered peoples, therefore, the law of people as acceptable and fair and effective in shaping the larger schemes of their cooperation. The society of well-ordered peoples is realistic in this way: it is workable and may be applied to ongoing cooperative political arrangements and relations between peoples. It does not require religious unity. Rather it concentrates on toleration. In this way the great evils would vanish and such peoples would not seek to convert others to their religion, or to conquer more territory or to wield political power over another people. Through negotiation and trade they can fulfil their needs and economic interests (Rawls, 1999, pp. 11, 17, 19).

The case of the Islamic Republic of Iran

Deserving membership

The criteria

When adapting the theoretical framework of Rawls, two points are noteworthy: firstly, the law of peoples can go beyond a liberal idea of justice and, secondly, according to set criteria, a country like Iran can be considered a decent nation. Decent nations enjoy the following characteristics. Firstly, they are not aggressors and achieve their legal goals through diplomacy, trade and other peaceful means. Secondly, three points need to be considered. (A) The legal system of this people guarantees human rights for all members of the community of nations (including the rights to life, security and liberation from slavery and forced labour, freedom of conscience and private property). In this sense, human rights cannot be rejected on the grounds that it is a Western idea. (B) The legal system of a decent nation imposes benevolent obligations and duties (apart from human rights) on all those who live within its territory. Those people are capable of learning and of moral perfection and know the difference between right and wrong according to their local culture. (C) Judges and other judicial officials should honestly believe that the law is based on a common idea of justice (Rawls, 1999, p. 32). All these criteria exist in the Iranian Constitution and the teachings of Islam. For example, Islam has forbidden all forms of violence (Alikhani, 2007).

Intersubjectivity

It is also true that mere awareness of cultural plurality in a modern world, without due attention to other cultures, will even cause problems for people of one culture to have faith in their own culture and to practice peace and justice. This will be a threat to that culture and increase the challenge of relativism or hegemony; then human beings would lose their trust in a single culture or tradition. On the other hand, the plurality of societies translates into plurality of philosophical, moral and religious teachings. Therefore, finding a single theoretical basis for justice is very difficult, if not impossible. Just in the same way that a single definition of rationality cannot be offered, nobody can come up with a single society whose every political action is based on rationality, because in that case the society will try to dominate other societies and eliminate plurality of cultures. Even if a liberal theory of justice were apt to assimilate other peoples, including decent ones, it could not determine obligations for others and give viewpoints on their behalf. According to the principles of justice, not resorting to inclusive doctrines is a requisite for the formulation of a justice theory. Therefore, political liberalism, as a philosophical theory, may itself impede the realization of a law of peoples. The Iranian government and people seek not only to observe such a law, but to also have a role in its formulation. This has been reflected in the Constitutional articles.

The constitution

The prologue of the Iranian Constitution has noted that 'in view of the nature of this great uprising, the Constitution guarantees negation of any form of theoretical and social despotism and economy monopoly and will endeavour to distance itself from dictatorship and to enable people to determine their own destiny'. Article 22 has noted that honour, life, property, rights, homes and jobs of people are immune to aggression. According to Article 34, a lawsuit is the inalienable right of every Iranian and every person can file lawsuits with a competent court. According to Article 23, inquisition is forbidden and nobody can be prosecuted for holding a belief. In Article 152, it has been noted that the foreign policy of the Islamic Republic of Iran is based on the negation of domineering policies, protecting independence and the territorial integrity of the country, defending the rights of all Muslims, with no commitment to hegemonic powers and maintaining cordial relations with all non-belligerent states. Based on Article 14, the government of the Islamic Republic of Iran is duty-bound to treat non-Muslims according to Islamic ethics, fairness and justice and observe their human rights. The Constitution has paid attention to the rights of minorities in its Articles 13 and 67. Imam Khomeini, the founder of the Islamic Republic, frequently announced that 'we want to be friends with all nations. We want to have good relations based on mutual respect' (Imam Khomeini, 1982, vol. 8, p. 252). 'We are not a nation to bully other nations when in power and there is no place for injustice and aggression in Islam' (ibid., vol. 16, p. 233). These principles and fundamentals produce an image of the Iranian Constitution in which a series of rights, which include equality before the law; security for life, property, employment and beliefs; and the right to just procedure, nationality and participation in political affairs, have been recognized for all Iranian nationals, regardless of their ethnicity, language and religion. All members of Iranian society may take advantage of those rights without discrimination.

Iran's membership in international treaties

Iran's membership in international treaties and instruments can be evidence of the decency of the nation in order to assure other liberal states that they should not fear aggression or violation of human rights on the part of Iran. Some treaties include: the United Nations Charter ratified in 1945; the International Covenant on Civil and Political Rights and the International Covenant on Economic, Social and Cultural Rights adopted in 1975; the Convention on the Prevention and Punishment of the

Crime of Genocide adopted in 1955; the International Convention on Elimination of All Forms of Racial Discrimination adopted in 1968; the Convention on the Rights of the Child adopted in 1993; Protocol 111 of the International Labour Organization adopted in 1967; the Non-Proliferation of Weapons of Mass Destruction (NPT) and Comprehensive Nuclear-Test-Ban Treaty (CTBT), as well as the Universal Declaration of Human Rights. Although the latter is not binding, its great influence on different aspects of human rights is undeniable and the Iranian government has voted for it.

Qualification for formulating a theory of justice

The aptitude

If a theory of justice is to be formulated, it should be done by scholars and theorists relying on the philosophical heritage of their society. Therefore, the formulation of a theory of justice calls for political thinking in the theoretical tradition of every nation. As put by the late Professor Mohsen Mehdi, the whole process of political thinking – or in his term, 'rationalism' – in Islam starts with the quality of the government and its political power. If there is rationality in the realm of the Islamic civilization, it should be sought in political and civil affairs. From this viewpoint, political philosophy in the Muslim world is a result of a rational approach to political issues. The crux of rational life of an Islamic society hinges on the answer to such questions as who should be the leader, how he should be elected or appointed, and what are the limits of his power (Mehdi, in *Daftari*, 2000). All these questions were the flip side of efforts that aimed at formulating the theory of justice. Majid Khadduri has considered seven aspects for the concept of justice in Islamic works and has enumerated them in his book *The Islamic Conception of Justice*: 1) political justice, 2) divine justice, 3) moral justice, 4) legal justice, 5) social justice, 6) justice among nations, and 7) philosophical justice (Khadduri, 1984).

Necessity

Formulation and developments in the domestic theory of justice will refine the international theory of justice. Therefore, while liberalism, overall, has one theory of domestic justice which has been taken as the basis for the international theory of justice, (according to Rawls) it is imperative for the Islamic Republic of Iran, as Muslims and decent peoples, and its theorists to reach a consensus over a single theory of domestic justice to achieve a general level of agreement before introducing it as a basis for an international theory of justice. Therefore, the fact that in a liberal theory of international justice the Islamic Republic of Iran can be trusted as a decent and honest player is a step forward to the realization of international peace and justice. The second step would be to offer an 'Islamic' concept of justice to supplement its liberal concept, in which the presence of a liberal ideology could be accepted as an honest player. Although it is presumed that religious teachings or other basic doctrines of an Islamic society are among those comprehensive doctrines that affect the government and social policies, and that society also respects political and social order in other societies. If such a society intended to promote its interests and to enhance its influence on other societies, it would act in ways which would not be incompatible with the independence of other societies, including their religious and civil freedoms. This feature of such societies, which arises from their comprehensive doctrines, will bolster the institutional fundamentals of peace-seeking behaviour and will differentiate that society from aggressive states. Therefore, as Rawls noted, the understanding of a hierarchical decent people of 'individuals' does not require acceptance of this liberal idea that individuals are citizens and enjoy equal basic rights. In that understanding, however, individuals are cooperative and responsible members of their special groups (Rawls, 1999, p. 47). Thus persons may recognize their obligations and moral tasks as members of those groups, understand them and act on their basis.

Conclusion

Despite such critiques and problems as 'distribution and redistribution of wealth in international relations' (Beitz, 2000), 'lack of due attention to the structure of globalization', 'doubts about the idea of one people/nation – one culture' (Buchanan, 2000), lack of agreement on basic principles of the law of people due to less importance being given to dialogue as a tool to determine overlapping principles among nations (Butler, 2001), considering decent nations as secondary members of the international system in favour of a minimal stability (Butler, 2001; Sadurski, 2003), indirect ethnocentric positions taken by Rawls and inattention to the plurality of cultures among nations (Tasioulas, 2002), and, finally, founding that theory on rich moral principles and inattention to communitarian requirements (Hosseini Beheshti, 2003), the idea of inter-peoples justice which has been presented by Rawls on the basis of justice for a single liberal society can be taken as a beginning for philosophical reflections to realize that goal – or in his phrase, 'realistic utopia". The most important acceptable feature of the plan is that, unlike the realistic approach taken by Clausewitz, war is no longer a continuation of politics in another language. Unlike the ideas of Kant, in this viewpoint, the production of weapons of mass destruction is not supposed to lead to perpetual peace (Sullivan, 1997, p. 52).

1. If multiple concerns make the liberal side potentially receptive to rival and diverse understandings of the nature of justice and society on the international scene, this is now a bilateral problem. The issue now is not that the Islamic Republic of Iran is a security and political concern for the West, but conversely, it is the liberal West that has emerged as a concern for Iran in its natural march towards humanitarian and justice-seeking ideals. Iran and Iranians, with *the intertwined sources of identity (Iranian nationalism, Islam and Westernization)* go their own way (Sariolghalam, 2008); if that way is not blocked by the preventive measures set up by Western countries, it will lead to peace and justice for the whole world. The fact that a people accept such heavy human

and non-human costs at the international level proves that it is restless to share its plan for international peace and justice. Understanding this point could be a first step towards any liberal move aimed at the establishment of global peace and security. Even if a foreign force thinks about the improvement and uplifting of the Iranian nation, it would have nothing to do with politics. It would be more of a political philosophical theory, which can be really influential in interacting with the religious ideas of the political system of Iran.

2.   If 'the law of peoples hopes to say how a world Society of liberal and decent peoples might be possible' (Rawls, 1999, p. 6), then all the parties should make a meaningful contribution in working it out. I mean that the extension of the domestic theory of justice to one of international justice is not bound and obligated to the concept of justice in a liberal domestic society, but that the theory of justice in the case of a decent domestic society is also needed. Rawls asserts that 'in developing the law of people, the first step is to work out the principles of justice for domestic society' (Rawls, 1999, p. 26). Accordingly, domestic theories of justice of both parties are needed to work out an international theory of justice. Therefore, it would have been better if Rawls had written his book on the Law of Peoples in cooperation with a thinker from one of the decent nations.

Bibliography

Alikhani, Ali Akbar, 'Political Analysis on Prophet Mohammad's (PBUH) Wars', *Political Sciences Research Magazine*, No. 7, summer 2007.

Beitz, Charles R., 'Rawls's Law of Peoples', *Ethics*, No. 110, July 2000.

Buchanan, Allen, 'Rawls's Law of Peoples: Rules for a Vanished Westphalian World', *Ethics*, No. 110, July 2000.

Butler, Brian E., 'There are Peoples and There are Peoples: A Critique of Rawls's The Law of Peoples', *Florida Philosophical Review*, Vol. 1, No. 2, 2001.

Constitution of the Islamic Republic of Iran. Available online at: http://www.iranonline.com/iran/iran-info/Government/constitution.html.

Daftari, Farhad (ed.), *Rational Traditions in Islam*, I. B. Tauris, 2000.

Hay, Colin, *A Critical Introduction to Political Analysis*, Palgrave, 2002.

Hosseini Beheshti and Seyed Alireza, 'Dialogue among Cultures and Political Theory', *International Journal of Humanity of the Islamic Republic of Iran*, Vol. 12, No. 3, 2003.

Hosseini Beheshti and Seyed Alireza, 'The Expanse of Rawls' The Law of Peoples', *Political Sciences Research Magazine*, No. 7, summer 2007.

Kant, Immanuel, *Perpetual Peace and Other Essays*, translated by Ted Humphrey, Hackett, 1983.

Khadduri, Majid, *The Islamic Conception of Justice*, The Johns Hopkins University Press, 1984.

Khomeini, Imam, *Sahifeh Nour (Book of Light)*, Islamic Revolution Cultural Documents Organization, Ministry of Culture and Islamic Guidance, 1982.

Morgenthau, Hans G., *Politics Among Nations*, McGraw-Hill, 1993.

Pangle, Thomas and Peter J. Ahrensdorf, *Justice among Nations: On the Moral Basis of Power and Peace*, The University Press of Kansas, 1999.

Rawls, John, *A Theory of Justice*, Harvard University Press, 1971.

Rawls, John, *Political Liberalism*, Columbia University Press, 1993.

Rawls, John, *The Law of Peoples*, Harvard University Press, 1999.

Rousseau, Jean-Jaques, *Social Contract*, Penguin Books, 1968.

Sadurski, Wojciech, 'The Last Thing He Wanted: Realism and Utopia in The Law of Peoples by John Rawls', EUI Working Paper Law, No. 2003/16.

Sullivan, Roger, *An Introduction to Kant's Ethics*, Cambridge University Press, 1997.

Tasioulas, John, 'From Utopia to Kasanistan: John Rawls and the Laws of Peoples', *Oxford Journal of Legal Studies*, Vol. 22, No. 2, 2002.

3   The Islamic Republic of Iran and the ideal international system

Dehghani Firooz-Abadi

Introduction

The Islamic Republic of Iran (IRI) as a revolutionary government hailing from the Islamic Revolution maintains a critical approach towards the current international system. In its view the present international order that dominates and the international system that goes with it is not suitable and should be revised. For this reason the IRI is considered a revisionist country and, contrary to the status quo countries, is trying to bring about revision and gradual changes in the existing international order and system. But the basic question is what type of international system is the country seeking to establish? In other words, what is the most suitable international system in the IRI's view? Does the IRI aim to overthrow the Westphalian order and the nation-state system that is based on it, or is it working to structurally reform it?

The present chapter aims to provide an answer to this question. A temporary response is that, although based on the Islamic theory of international relations, the Westphalian nation-state system is not a suitable one, and the IRI as a nation-state is trying to establish and create a just international order which is devoid of domination and structural violence. The discussion and testing of this hypothesis will be conducted in three stages. First, definitions and different types of international system will be elucidated. In the second stage, revisionist and justice-seeking principles and sources of the IRI will be reviewed. The third part will be devoted to the enquiry and analysis of mechanisms for the establishment of a just and suitable system that the IRI would find acceptable.

Different types of favourable international order

On the basis of the literature on international relations, different types of change in the international system are possible and conceivable. Kenneth Waltz differentiates between 'changes of the system' and 'changes in the system' (2000, p. 5). Only changes of the first type would make the anarchic nature of the international political system evolve. But changes at the unit level or even changes in the structure of the international system, despite their deep effects and outcomes, would not change the anarchic nature of the international system. Although structural changes would form different types of international systems, the nature of international politics is constant in all of them (ibid., p. 6). However, democratic peace theorists (Doyle, 1983, 1986), institutionalists (Keohane and Nye, 1989) and interdependence theorists (Keohane and Martin, 1995), as Waltz elaborates, believe that as a result of the expansion of democracy, mutual dependence and the effective role of international institutions, the anarchic nature of the international system and international politics all change. K.J. Holsti (1988, chapter 2) in the definition of different types of international systems, refers to the constituent units of each international system as one of the aspects that highlights their difference and distinction. Therefore, the Greek city-state system is different and distinct from the modern nation-state system.

So it should be argued which of these changes are essential and would guarantee the formation of a favourable international system in the eyes of the IRI in place of the present one. Is Iran seeking substantial changes in the anarchic nature of the international system and international politics, or is it trying to change the Westphalian nation-state system? The preferences of the IRI in a change of system and the establishment of a more suitable one could be regulated in a hierarchical order and gradually followed up on the basis of national potentials and capabilities. Such a hierarchical order of preferences is: structural reform of the international system; evolution in the anarchic nature of the international system; reform of the Westphalian order and nation-state system based upon it; and finally formation of an Islamic world society.

An Islamic world society

The IRI as an Islamic state that has its roots in a transnational revolution has goals and interests in the world order. Based on Nuechterlein's definition (1979, pp. 76–77), Iran's goals and interests are development and establishment of an international political–economic order and system (either regional or world) in which it feels itself secure and enabled to deal with its political, economic and cultural activities peacefully. What would be ideal and desirable in its eyes is the establishment of an Islamic world system, one that is formed through the efforts of human beings utilizing worldwide Islamic values, common human interests, ethical principles and justice. A just Islamic world society would be devoid of power relations, domination, suppression and violence, and would proclaim the freedom and equality of all human beings as citizens of an Islamic world government (Dehghani, [1386] 2007, pp. 142–143).

Perhaps it could be claimed that this is an Islamic example of world society that has been referred to by Hedley Bull (1977–1984) and other theorists of the English school. Formation of an Islamic world society necessitates the spread of Islamic values and norms throughout all societies, together with consolidation of the Islamic world within a united Ummah. As will be explained later – and many writers have written about it – the Islamic political and international order does not conform with the Westphalian order and nation-state system, so an Islamic world society within the framework of a state-centric Westphalian order is not possible (Bromley, 1994, pp. 90–94; Tibi, 2000, pp. 87–89; Vatikiotis, 1987, pp. 42–44; Zubaida, 1989). This is because, using Philpott's words, 'Islamic cosmopolitanism' does not consider the natural and legal division of human beings within the framework of geographical borders of any nation-state (Philpott, 2002, p. 86).

The formation of an Islamic world society as one of the main ideals and a foreign policy strategic goal of the IRI has been explicitly asserted in the country's Constitution and in statements made by its leaders. For example, in the introduction to the Constitution, with regard to the goal and application of this law, it has been stated:

> The Constitution, with regard to the Islamic nature of the Revolution of Iran which was a movement for the victory of all the oppressed over the oppressors, will prepare the ground for the continuation of this revolution both inside and outside the country. Especially in further expansion of international relations with other Islamic and popular movements, it will try to pave the way for the formation of a unified Ummah in the world (*This is your Ummah which is a united Ummah and I am your Creator, therefore worship me*) and the continuation of the struggle for the salvation of the needy and oppressed nations in the entire world will be enforced (author's italics).

The Founder of the Islamic Revolution, Imam Khomeini, also stated: 'Nothing should bring about aberration from the superb objective of the Revolution which is Islamic world government' (Khomeini, [1371] 1992, p. 108).

However, it should be noted that the formation of an Islamic world society as a world system proposed to replace the Westphalian order and nation-state system is a long-term goal in the foreign policy of Iran. Therefore, contrary to the claims of some writers, present-day Iran under the status quo is not aiming to disturb the nation-state system, and indeed has recognized its main infrastructural institution, namely the principle of national sovereignty, and acts within its framework – in fact the Constitution of the IRI explicitly prohibits interference in the internal affairs of other countries (Article 154).

An Islamic international society

Formation of an Islamic international society is the second preference and priority of the Islamic Republic of Iran. Islamic internationalism, as expressed by Philpott, does not necessitate or ensure negation of the Westphalian order and nation-state system. That is to say, division of nations into separate political units of a nation-state are accepted, but commitments and responsibilities of Islamic nation-states go beyond national interests and embody Islamic and human values (Philpott, 2002, p. 86). According to Bull's (1977, p. 13) definition of international society, an Islamic international society is based on Islamic 'common interests and common values' and Islamic rules will govern relations of countries that have membership in common institutes.

From theoretical and practical points of view, formation of an Islamic international society takes priority over an Islamic world society, for direct transition from an existing anarchic international system into an Islamic world society is not possible. Rather, after the formation of an Islamic world society, its government and citizens would gradually become aware of their interests, values and common fate, and this would prepare the ground for the establishment of an Islamic world society under a unified sovereignty and government. Such a process of transition would start in the Islamic world and, through the unity within the Ummah, would then spread throughout the entire world.

The Islamic international society stands for justice, common interests of nations which would bring about prosperity, peaceful coexistence, non-interference in internal affairs of others, mutual respect, peace and international security. The *Constitution* of the Islamic Republic of Iran has pointed to these principles and norms either explicitly or implicitly. 'The government of the Islamic Republic of Iran and Muslims are required to treat non-Muslims with good manners and Islamic equity and justice and observe their human rights' (Article 14). Also, in Article 154 it has been asserted: 'The Islamic Republic of Iran regards the happiness of Man in Human Society as its aspiration and recognizes independence, freedom and the right to just government as the right of all the people of the world.' The formation of an Islamic international society would ensure change in the anarchic nature of international politics.

Although the Constitution of the Islamic Republic of Iran embodies principles and definitions of Islamic internationalism, such goals and principles provide for ideal circumstances. This ideal order too, like the Islamic world society, is attainable under certain conditions in the long-term future. Therefore, the IRI, while acknowledging this ideal international situation under the status quo by accepting the nation-state order and system and respecting the right to sovereignty by other countries, will pursue the establishment of a just international system that is devoid of domination and domineering tendencies.

A just international system

As previously mentioned, what the Islamic Republic of Iran is pursuing as world-order goals and interests is the establishment of a just international order and system through structural, normative and institutional reforms rather than disturbing the present Westphalian order and nation-state system. These multi-dimensional reforms would be such that the present anarchic nature of the international system based on power politics and a power hierarchy would evolve, resulting in the formation of an international society based on the partnership of all nations and common human interests. Because Iran sees the existing international system as unnatural, illegitimate and unsuitable in all the three structural, normative and institutional dimensions, it therefore should be changed. All active political factions in the IRI, who represent minor different facets of Islamic discourse in foreign policies, have reached a consensus in this regard. Their difference of opinion is merely confined to the mechanisms and tools for reform of the existing international system (Dehghani, [1384] 2005).

So, the international system favoured by the Islamic Republic of Iran enjoys certain characteristics and components which make it different and distinct from the existing international system. The most important principles and components of this international system are: the equality of governments, a rule of law and international law, positive peace, the absence of domination by any one bloc and common human values.

Equality of states

One of the major principles of the present system is the principle of the equality of independent and sovereign states, as asserted in the first paragraph of Article 2 of the United Nations Charter: 'This organization is based on the equality of all member states.' But this principle has never been observed and respected within the international system and in relations among countries, to such an extent that it is the great powers that are enjoying great financial and physical power and influence. Therefore, contrary to the views of Van Dyke (1966), countries are not enjoying equal rights, for their rights are not equally respected by mighty governments. The international political scenario that is so reliant on power shows only too well that all countries (contrary to the opinion expressed by Kelsen, 1966) are not equal before the law. The big powers because of their superior might could refrain from obeying international rules and such regulations would not be applied to them, as would be the case with other countries.

The most important signifier and manifestation of the inequality of countries in the existing international system is the permanent membership of the five big powers in the Security Council of the United Nations and their power to veto – a specific right that has been granted to those five countries, according to the present power politics, because of their military power. Therefore, the IRI has opposed the right to veto of the big powers and is seeking the strengthening of the UN General Assembly and granting of more authority and eligibility for decision-making to UNGA. Leaders of the IRI have constantly expressed their criticism and protested against this exclusive right for the big powers as a symbol of injustice in the international system. For example, Iran's Foreign Ministry in a statement in 1982 said: 'For the big powers, the use of the right to veto in the Security Council of the United Nations Organization is not in accordance with human standards and the principle of human equality and is a weapon which is used by the superpowers against oppressed and tyrannized nations of the world' (*Ettelaat* daily, 16 January 1361).

Over two decades later, Iran's president in his address to the General Assembly of the United Nations Organization in 2006, criticized the Security Council by stating: 'The existing structure and work process at the Security Council is not responsive to the expectations of the present generation and the needs of contemporary mankind. This structure and work process is the heritage of World War II. As long as this institution fails to make efforts as the representative of the entire international community transparently, justly and democratically, it will be neither legitimate nor efficient ... As long as the structure and work process is not reformed, we should not expect injustice, tyranny and oppression to be rooted out in the world or not to spread ... Today, serious amendments in the structure and work process of the Security Council are more essential than ever' (Ahmadinejad, [1385] 2006).

Rule of law and independent international organizations

The second principle of a just international system favoured by the Islamic Republic of Iran is the implementation and practice of an international rule of law in all countries with the result that all nations – whether powerful or weak – are equal within international law. The proper mechanism for the realization of this goal is the existence of independent, legitimate, efficient and democratic international organizations and institutions, which reflect common human interests and, irrespective of a power hierarchy and exertion of influence by the big powers, implement and exercise international rules and regulations that are compiled and approved regardless of power relations and through the active participation of all countries.

Under this international system, countries would treat each other with mutual respect. Meanwhile, based on the principle of sovereignty, powerful governments would refrain from interference in the internal affairs of other countries and recognize the interests and sovereignty of weaker countries. Furthermore, international rules and regulations and the decisions of international independent and legitimate organizations would be applied to all countries without discrimination and under unified standards. In this case, there would be no trace of double or multi-dimensional standards in international relations and within the international community.

It is the view of the IRI that in the international system none of these principles and norms is implemented or practised completely. Thus the big powers, using double standards and in a discriminatory manner, are not committed to international rules, regulations and responsibilities, but instead through the use of force and power impel other countries to follow them. So international organizations and institutions are also a reflex of the division of international power and maintain the interests of the powerful nations to such an extent that they become instruments which, instead of confining the activities of the big powers, legitimize their power and behaviour.

Therefore, the IRI has constantly criticized and protested against the unjust and discriminatory nature of the existing international system. Although such criticisms have varied, the IRI has never been happy with the status quo. For example, in a harsh criticism of the international organizations, Imam Khomeini said: 'The world today is suffering from organizations subservient to the big powers, especially the US, that operate under hollow names such as the Security Council, Amnesty International and Human Rights and such empty concepts serve the big powers and are, in fact, implementing their verdicts and are assigned to condemn the oppressed and innocent people of the world in the interest of the world-devouring big powers' (Khomeini, [1374] 1995, p. 427).

Iran's Foreign Minister Manouchehr Mottaki says in this regard: 'The Islamic Republic of Iran has a critical approach towards international organizations; we believe that after sixty years the United Nations Organization should undergo a pathology test in order to maintain the interest of all countries. We support the multiplicity of permanent members of the Security Council of the United Nations and believe that the international situation has evolved and now different regions with differing levels of power should take part in decision making and participation in the Security Council of the United Nations Organization. Not only the United Nations Organization but all international economic organizations should represent the interests of the developing countries and medium-range powers of the world' (Mottaki, [1385] 2006).

Under these circumstances, President Ahmadinejad considers reform and change in the structure of the United Nations Organization, the Security Council and other international organizations on the basis of democratic principles and observance of equal rights for all the members as the only option to come out of the status quo: 'The United Nations Organization should take steps in truly defending the rights of nations and the domination of any one country or centre over this organization should be prevented. To realize this important task, we need basic changes in the structure of the United Nations Organization' (Ahmadinejad, [1384] 2005).

The IRI has also severely criticized the double standards in international relations and international organizations and has called for an end to this unjust procedure. It has constantly been critical of and protested against the double standards in areas such as human rights and resolutions passed by the Security Council. The climax of its criticism has centred around Iran's nuclear issue and the performance of the International Atomic Energy Agency (IAEA) and the Security Council. Iran believes that the IAEA and the UN Security Council have failed to exercise unified standards in the implementation of the NPT, to such an extent that while ignoring the military nuclear build-up in Israel, they violate Iran's explicit rights within the IAEA and NPT (Rohani, [1384] 2005, pp. 12–13).

A just peace

A just peace is one of the most important elements of the international order and system favoured by the IRI. Without the realization of justice, peace and security would not be maintained. It is for this reason that former President Mohammad Khatami has also stressed that 'the first prerequisite to attain true peace is the recognition of equal rights for all human beings. We need to create a word society wherein all human beings are equal and enjoy equal rights. These are principles that replace struggle and bloodshed. And world peace would become sustainable only under such circumstances' (Khatami, [1379] 2000). President Ahmadinejad also states: 'Justice and the preservation of human dignity are two major foundations for the preservation of peace and security, the right for all nations and states' (Ahmadinejad, [1385] 2006). Manoucher Mottaki too reminds us that 'the Islamic Republic of Iran defines a direct relationship between justice and security' (Mottaki, [1385] 2006).

What Iran regards as a just peace goes far beyond a negative and minimal peace, meaning an absence of war, and is tantamount to the definition of the positive peace expressed in Galtung and Schmid's theories. Positive peace goes beyond an absence of physical violence and, for it to be realized, conditions other than the annihilation of war should be present. Thus peace means social, political and economic justice and the integration of human society. Positive peace places war and violence in a more expanded context in social, economic and political processes and does not confine it to political trends, because political violence is only a manifestation of gaps and deeper social and economic inequalities (Galtung, 1964, p. 1; 1969, p. 190; Schmid, 1968).

Therefore, for peace to be established, in addition to controlling disputes and fighting, quarrels with the potential to lead to structural violence should be prevented, for this kind of violence is a type of social relations in which one side is capable of exerting its domination completely, while the other side is deprived of expressing itself and its potential. Deprivation, famine, suppression, starvation, inequality, racism and racial discrimination, imperialism, dependency and under-development are examples of structural violence that are institutionalized in political, social, economic and national and international cultural structures and institutions. In this definition of peace, contrary to a negative and minimal peace, social-economic justice has priority over the annihilation of war, because with the realization of a positive peace and in the absence of structural violence, there would remain no need for resorting to force, war and physical violence (ibid.). Thus the IRI feels that in order to gain access to a sustainable peace and security, relationships based on power, hegemony, domineering structures and structural violence should be erased.

Absence of domination

Another fundamental factor and principle of a just international system is the absence of any tendency to dominate, for this brings about violence that threatens and weakens international peace and security. As previously mentioned, Iran feels that the most blatant form and type of domination in international relations is the hegemony of a superior power in the international system, for the hegemonic power imposes its favourite order, which maintains its interests within that international system. The post-Cold War international system is an example of the hegemonic order in which the US tries to impose its superpower domination over other countries, including Iran.

Therefore, with this unipolar system in mind, Ayatollah Khamenei, leader of the Islamic Revolution, states that as a criterion for the IRI's foreign policy: 'We can by no means accept the behaviour associated with the system of domination … in no way will we undergo domination, and we consider the criterion for our diplomacy to be confrontation with the domination system that reigns at present in the world order and departure from the rule of the domineer over the dominated' (Khamenei, [1386] 2007).

President Mohammad Khatami too has said: 'Islamic Iran would not accept the thought and idea of hegemony, nor does it have any intention of being hegemonic … We are strongly opposed to a unilateral world in the sense that a certain power may try to impose its wishes and policies on the world simply because it enjoys material facilities' (Khatami, [1379a] 2000a, p. 2). Thus the Ahmadinejad administration has determined and defined one of its foreign policy priorities and goals as a 'confrontation with post-modern colonialism and a struggle with schemes of the world domination system' (Office of the President). Meanwhile, Manouchehr Mottaki sees one of the tasks of the government as a 'struggle with power monopoly at world level' under the leadership of the US (Mottaki, [1385] 2006). Elsewhere he reiterates: 'We believe that the international world system is suffering from a lack of justice and hegemony and the domination of one or several big powers is not effective in this international system' (Mottaki, [1986] 2007, p. 5).

Common human values

The fifth element and principle to be aimed at in a just international system is common human interests and values. Common human values are not necessarily in contradiction with national interests; it rather means that national interests should acknowledge and accommodate the collective interests of other nations and countries. Maintenance of this goal necessitates a change in the present international system with its dominating powers, so that collective security would replace the principle of unlimited and unrestrained self-help, for 'by changing the logic of international relations and keeping away from the logic of power' security and human prosperity could be attained. 'Countries should not behave according to a power-inclined resolve but according to a dialogue-inclined firmness which would finally bring about a resolution based on affection and morality' (Khatami, [1379b] 2000b, p. 2).

Discursive sources of Iranian revisionism

Iranian revisionism originates from three discursive sources: Islamic ideology, the concept of the importance of the Third World, and the search for and spread of justice. The coming together of these three discourses determines and enhances the revision of the international system that is visualized by the Islamic Republic of Iran.

Islamic ideology

The most important factor in Iranian revisionism is Islam and Islamic teachings. Islamic discourse is based on the political theory of Islam according to which the international system based on nation-states and geographical borders has no inherent value. The Islamic world order is based on the pillars of ideological borders. Such a demarcation has been defined and determined as the *Dar-ol-Islam* (the abode of Islam) and *Dar-ol-Kofr* (the abode of infidels) in the international arena. The *Dar-ol-Islam* is a territory where Muslims reside and rule and constitutes a united *ummah*, a territory and political authority or sovereignty (Adib-Moghaddam, 2005). The *Dar-ol-Kofr* embodies all territories outside the Islamic and Muslim sovereignty. Given its relationship with the *Dar-ol-Islam*, the *Dar-ol-Kofr* is also divided into the *Dar-ol-Harb* (the abode of war), the *Dar-ol-Hayad* (the abode of neutrality) and the *Dar-ol-Ahd* (the abode of covenant). The *Dar-ol-Harb* refers to regions and societies that are openly at war with the Muslims, the *Dar-ol-Hayad* is neutral, and the *Dar-ol-Ahd* is a land which has signed peace and truce treaties with Muslims and would not be hostile to them (Zyaee-Bigdeli, [1368] 1988).

Therefore, the existing state-centric international order and system, which is incompatible with Islamic ideas, is not favoured and should be changed to the

Islamic world system. But, as previously mentioned, such a transition from the status quo to what is considered a suitable Islamic order could take place gradually, peacefully, step by step and be reformist to such an extent that although the final target is the formation of an Islamic world society, the realization of such a goal is first attained through the amendment of and change in the present international system, leading to the desired formation of an Islamic international society. However, Islamic discourse requires the adoption of a revisionist foreign policy towards the present international system (Dehghani, [1384] 2005, pp. 71–72).

Third worldism

The second source of revisionism in the foreign policy of the IRI is what could be termed Third Worldism, which has an anti-colonialist, anti-imperialist and anti-hegemonic nature. This is an idea that opposes the present international political–economic order and is about amending and adjusting to reach a suitable situation and order for maintaining the interests of the Third World, or developing countries of the South. In other words, this discourse, by accepting the principles, rules, norms and fundamental institutions of the present international order, such as the political unit of the nation-state (national and territorial state), national sovereignty and non-interference in the internal affairs of countries, believes that the economic order especially should be changed in the interest of the Third World countries (Dehghani, [1386] 2007, pp. 132–133).

The most important goals of Third Worldism are: international justice; economic development; the practical equity of countries; independence and practical freedom; non-dependence on the great powers; reform, adjustment or change of rules, institutions, norms and international organizations; respect for national sovereignty and the territorial integrity of countries; positive international cooperation; non-participation in military acts and the provision of military bases to big powers; support for the United Nations Charter and international law; combating colonialism, imperialism and racism; general disarmament; non-interference in the internal affairs of countries, and fighting against underdevelopment and Third World internationalism (Holsti, 1988, chapter 4).

Therefore, Third Worldism is based on 'justice' and 'independence', the latter termed by Bull as the first wave of the revolt against the West. But independence of the Third World countries in the process of decolonialization did not mean they gained freedom of action in the international system. So, with justice in mind, the Third World tried to gain equal economic and political rights in the second wave of its revolt against the West. Today, in the third wave, the Third World is trying to achieve cultural independence and autonomy from the West (Bull, 1988, p. 223).

The historical background and positive and negative experiences of the Iranians throughout history, especially during the 19th and 20th centuries, has strengthened their enthusiasm for Third Worldism. The rich Iranian background of culture and civilization surely entitles the country to a more enhanced standing in the world – even promotion to the status of a superpower, which would encourage it to pursue the foreign policy aim of reforming and changing the international order and system. But, on the other hand, aggression and invasion of Iran by foreigners, from Alexander the Great to Mahmoud Afghan, have resulted in some form of national humiliation. Furthermore, interference by colonialist Russia and Great Britain in Iran turned the country into a semi-colonized state. Such bitter experiences enforce the seeking of justice and independence in foreign policy and push it to further efforts to bring about change in the West-dominated and unjust international order (Moshirzadeh, 2007, pp. 529–533).

The search for justice

Justice and justice-seeking is the third stimulus for revisionism in the foreign policy of the Islamic Republic of Iran. Seeking justice is rooted in the Iranian culture and civilization, and has been strengthened and stabilized by the Shia sect of Islam to become a part of Iranian identity throughout history, even of Iranian society prior to the arrival of Islam (Mojtahedzadeh, [1383] 2004).

In Islam, especially in the Shia sect, justice enjoys a high value and importance, being one of the principles of Shi'ism. According to Islamic teachings, both individual Muslims and the Muslim community are required to implement justice and try to establish it both within and without their community. Therefore, the Islamic government and ruler are not merely responsible for the prevalence of justice within the country, but should make efforts for its establishment within human society as a whole. Therefore, the IRI sees itself as commissioned to expand justice throughout the world and establish a just international order and system (Ramazani, 1990).

The historical experience of the Iranians strengthened the justice-seeking spirit in them too, especially the bitter experience of the imposition of pacts on Iran in the 19th and 20th centuries by the colonialist powers, and the failure of the oil nationalization movement. The most important and evident example and symbol of its quest for justice is its support for the struggle of the oppressed against the oppressors, perceived as between evil and good powers or, in other words, between falsehood and justice, in which it is committed to supporting the rightful and just front.

The administration of President Ahmadinejad has been forthright in upholding the above. The Foreign Minister Manouchehr Mottaki has asserted: 'The Islamic Republic of Iran with the help of supportive countries is interested in becoming a standard-bearer in moving towards the realization of international justice.' To this end, 'the foreign policy of the 9th administration is to enforce a discourse based on justice, acceptance of equal rights for countries in playing their role in the creation of a new and justice-seeking world order' (Mottaki, [1385] 2006).

Mechanisms for development of a just international system

The Islamic Republic of Iran offers proposals both at practical and theoretical levels for the establishment of a suitable international system. As for theoretical proposals, first the present international order and system should be deconstructed and then a just order and system should be elucidated and promulgated. At a practical level, too, change in the international system through the two strategies of unity within the Islamic world and formation of an anti-hegemony front or coalition would be followed up by revisionist and anti-domineering countries and players.

Deconstruction of the present international order

In the deconstruction process an attempt would be made to disrupt and displace the present binary oppositions and polarizations through revision, a redefinition and a rereading of the present international system, with the intention of bringing about a system that is natural, logical and legitimate.

The Islamic Republic of Iran has embarked on the deconstruction of the present international system. Through describing and elucidating the unjust nature of the status quo and the established order, it is trying to denaturalize and delegitimize it. Denaturalization means showing the reality that the present international system, like any other social phenomenon, has its time and place and under special conditions it has found the opportunity to exist and with the passage of time and as a result of its position of dominance, has been considered natural. The continuation and consistency of this supremacy has entailed some type of legitimacy. In the process of denaturalization the IRI has tried to disclose the contingent nature of the present international system and deprive it of the legitimacy it has obtained over the course of time (Dehghani, [1386] 2007, pp. 85–86).

The denaturalization and delegitimization of the present international system is essential for its deconstruction but it is not enough. Therefore, in the second step, the Islamic Republic of Iran intends to bring about change and establish a more favourable system. Such a goal is perceived as attainable through campaigning against the present system, unipolar and unjust relations and international centres of power, as well as criticizing international organizations and institutions and making efforts to reform them, for one of the manifestations of the unjust international system is improper and inefficient organizations and institutions that institutionalize injustice, discrimination and domination of the big powers and legitimize them (ibid., p. 87).

Unity of the Islamic world

One of the practical mechanisms and instruments for the establishment of a favourable international system is the alliance of Islamic countries and unity within the Muslim world. Therefore, the Islamic Republic of Iran, following Islamic teachings and its Constitution, is duty-bound to make efforts to create a unified Islamic Ummah. To quote the Constitution of the Islamic Republic of Iran: 'All Muslims form a single nation, and the government of the Islamic Republic of Iran has the duty of formulating its general policies towards cultivating the friendship and unity of all Muslim peoples in order to bring about the political, economic and cultural unity of the Islamic World' (Article 11).

The unity of the Muslim world is possible and imaginable in three ways. In the first model, it will be realized within the framework of solidarity and cooperation of

Islamic countries in different fields, especially in the area of foreign policy and at the international level by upholding the interests of the Islamic world. In the second model, it will be attained through economic and political integration of Islamic countries, forming an integrated and convergent politico-economic bloc like the EU. These two stages could prepare the ground for the eventual political unity of Islamic countries and societies, a united Islamic Ummah, under a united political sovereignty. Such an Islamic super state will signify the final stage: union of the Islamic world.

Formation of an anti-hegemonic coalition

The third mechanism for changing the present international system and bringing about the formation of a desirable international system is to make an anti-hegemonic coalition comprising those countries and players opposed to hegemony. Although the present order and system of domination does throw up opposition, the realization of anti-hegemonic aspirations demands intentional cooperation and the coalition and unity of all the anti-hegemonic government and non-government forces. To this end, the Islamic Republic of Iran is trying to form such an opposition from among the revisionist and revolutionary countries.

Such an aim has always been pursued in the foreign policy of the Islamic Republic of Iran as an external balance against hegemonic forces. For example, Imam Khomeini has defined one of the aims of Muslim unity as confrontation with colonialist powers: 'Our cause is the unification of Muslims and Islamic states against colonial powers' (Khomeini, [1360] 1981, pp. 83–85). He also underlined the alliance and then uprising of oppressed people as a means to fight those powers. 'It is hoped that a worldwide popular revolution would be staged against inhumane imperialist forces' (Khomeini, [1361] 1982, pp. 113–115).

Based on this, the administration of President Ahmadinejad has announced one of the goals of the IRI foreign policy to be 'enforcement of the multilateralism strategy at the international level and confrontation with unilateralism on the international scene' together with 'the expansion of cooperation with independent and non-aligned countries'. Within the framework of such a strategy, it has been stipulated by the foreign minister: 'One of the axes of foreign policy of the 9th administration ... is diversification of Iran's international relations by putting emphasis on logical confrontation with the present order of world domination and unilateralism and maintenance of national interests and national security of the Islamic Republic of Iran through formation of a coalition from all over the world' (Mottaki, [1385] 2006). The most evident example of Iran's attempts to form a coalition is the emergence of Third Worldism and Latin Americanism in the foreign policy of the country (Delghani, [1387] 2008).

Conclusion

The Islamic Republic of Iran as a revisionist state is discontented with the present international order and system and is trying to change and replace it with a more suitable one. According to the IRI this would entail an Islamic world society, an

Islamic international society and a just international system. Although its ideal is the formation of an Islamic world society, the country is more intent on a just international system on the basis of principles of equality of states, rule of law and common human interests that are free from domination and structural violence, an international system within which all countries, having nothing to do with power relations, could maintain their own national interests and the interests of humanity in general on the basis of mutual respect. Therefore, contrary to some analysts, the IRI does not negate the Westphalian order based on the nation-state system; rather it seeks the reform and change of its principles according to a notion of justice.

Revisionism in the foreign policy of the Islamic Republic of Iran originates from three discourses, namely Islamism, Third Worldism and the quest for justice, all of which are against the power-based hierarchical system, recommending instead a just system that is free of domination. Therefore, one of the goals of the foreign policy of the country is the establishment and creation of a just and desirable international system. The most important mechanisms and instruments for the establishment of such a just system is deconstruction of the present system, unity of the Islamic world, coalition and unity of anti-hegemonic players at an international level, as well as the reform and launch of independent and efficient international organizations.

Bibliography

Adib-Moghaddam, Arshin (2005), 'Islamic Utopian Romanticism and the Foreign Policy Culture of Iran', *Critical Middle Eastern Studies* 14(3): 265–292.

Ahmadinejad, Mahmood [1384] (2005), http://www.president.ir/ahmadinejad/cronicnews/ 26 June 1384.

Ahmadinejad, Mahmood [1385] (2006), http://www.president.ir/Farsi/Ahmadinejad/cronic-news/1385/06/29/index-F.htm.

Bromley, Simon (1994), *Rethinking Middle East Politics: State Formation and Development*, Cambridge: Polity Press.

Bull, Hedley (1977), *The Anarchical Society: A Study of Order in World Politics*, London: Macmillan.

Bull, Hedley (1988), 'The Revolt Against the West', in Hedley Bull and Adam Watson, eds., *The Expansion of International Society*, Oxford: Clarendon Press.

Dawisha, Adeed (1983), *Islam in Foreign Policy*, Cambridge: Cambridge University Press.

Dehghani F., Seyed Jalal (2005a), 'Societal Sources of Iranian Foreign Policy', *Discourse: An Iranian Quarterly* 6(3–4): 33–58.

Dehghani F., Seyed Jalal [1384] (2005b), *Tahvol Goftmani dar Syasat khareji Jomhoorie eslami Iran* [Discursive Evolution in the Islamic Republic of Iran's Foreign Policy], Tehran: Entesharat Rooznameh Iran.

Dehghani F., Seyed Jalal [1386] (2007), 'Hoviat va mnfaat dar syasat kharejie Jomhoori eslami Iran' [Identity and Interest in Islamic Republic of Iran's Foreign Policy], in Davood Kiany, ed., *Manafe Mellie Jomhoorie eslamie Iran* [National Interests of Islamic Republic of Iran], Tehran: Pajooheshkadeh motale'at rahbordi.

Dehghani F., Seyed Jalal (2008a), 'Emancipating Foreign Policy: Critical Theory and IslamicRepublic of Iran's Foreign Policy', *The Iranian Journal of International Affairs* 3(xx): 1–26.

Dehghani F., Seyed Jalal [1387] (2008b), 'Syasat Khareje Dolat Nohom' [Ninth Administration's Foreign Policy], *Rahyafthaye Syasi va Binolmelali* 13(1).

Doyle, Michael W. (1983), 'Kant, Liberal Legacies, and Foreign Affairs', *Philosophy and Public Affairs* 12(3).

Doyle, Michael W. (1986), 'Kant Liberalism and World Politics', *American Political Science Review* 80(4): 1151–690.

Ettelaat, Newspaper [16 January 1361] 5 April 1982.

Galtung, Johan (1964), 'Editorial', *Journal of Peace Research* 1(1).

Galtung, Johan (1969), 'Violence, Peace and Peace Research', *Journal of Peace Research*, 3: 167–192.

Halliday, Fred (1995), *Islam and the Myth of Confrontation*, London: I. B. Tauris.

Halliday, Fred (1999), *Revolution and World Politics*, London: Macmillan Press.

Holsti, Kalevi (1988), *International Politics: A Framework for Analysis*, 5th edn. Englewood Cliffs, NJ: Prentice Hall.

Kelsen, H. (1966), *Principles of International Law*, New York: Rinehart and Winston.

Keohane, Robert O. and Lisa L. Martin (1995), 'The Promise of Institutionalist Theory', *International Security* 20(1).

Keohane, Robert O. and Joseph S. Ney (1989), *Power and Interdependence*, 2nd edn. New York: HarperCollins.

Khamenei, Ali (Ayatollah) [1386] (2007), *Rooznameh Iran*, 31 May 1386 [Iran Newspaper].

Khatami, Seyed Mohammad [1379a] (2000a), *Ettelaat*, 5 April 1379.

Khatami, Seyed Mohammad [1379b] (2000b), *Ettelaat*, 17 June 1379: 2.

Khomeini, Rouhollah (Imam) [1360] (1981), *Sahifeh Noor*, vol. 1.

Khomeini, Rouhollah (Imam) [1371] (1992), *Sahifeh Noor: Majmooeh rahnemoodhaye emam Khomeini* [A Collection of Imam Khomeini's Guide lines] vol. 21, Tehran: Sazman Madarek Farhangi Enghelabe Eslami.

Khomeini, Rouhollah (Imam) [1374] (1995), *Aeen Enghelab Eslami* [The Manner of the Islamic Revolution], Tehran: Moasseh tanzim va nashre Asare Emam Khomeini.

Malley, Robert (1996), *The Call From Algeria: Third Worldism, Revolution, and the Turn to Islam*, Berkeley, CA: University of California Press.

Mojtahedzadeh, Pirouz [1383] (2004), 'Rouhieh edalatkhahi va Jaygah an dar Hoviat Melli Iranian' [The Spirit of Justice–seeking Spirit and Its Position in Iranian National Identity], in Davood Mirmohammadi, ed., *Hoviat melli dar Iran* [National Identity in Iran], Tehran: Motale'at melli, 231–244.

Moshirzadeh, Homeira (2007), 'Discursive Foundations of Iran's Nuclear Policy', *Security Dialogue* 38(4): 521–543.

Mottaki, Manouchehr [1385] (2006), *Syasat khareji dolat Nohom* [Foreign policy of the Ninth Administration], Tehran: Markaz Tahghighat steratejik Khavaremianeh.

Mottaki, Manouchehr [1386] (2007), *Rooznameh Iran*, 30 May 1386 [Iranian newpaper].

Neuchterlein, Donald E. (1979), 'The Concept of National Interest: A Time for New Approaches', *Orbis* 23(1).

Philpott, Daniel (2002), 'The Challenge of September 11 to Secularism in International Relations', *World Politics* 55, October: 66–95.

Ramazani, Rouhollah K. (1990), 'Iran's Export of Revolution: Politics, Ends, and Means' in John Esposito, ed., *The Iranian Revolution: Its Global Impacts*, Miami: Florida International University, 40–62.

Rohani, Hassan [1384] (2005), 'Paybandi ma beh regimhaye adam eshae az moze'e bavarmandi mast' [Observing Non-Proliferation Regimes is Based on our Beliefs], *Rahbord* 36: 7–15.

Schmid, Herman (1968), 'Politics and Peace Research', *Journal of Peace Research*, 3: 217–232.

Tibi, Bassam (2000), 'Post-Bipolar Order in Crisis: The Challenge of Politicized Islam', *Millennium, Journal of International Studies* 29(3): 843–859.

Van Dyke, V. (1966), *International Politics*, New York: Appleton – Century Crofts.

Vatikiotis, P.J. (1987), *Islam and the State*, London: Routledge.

Zubaida, Sami (1989), *Islam, the People and the State*, London: Routledge.

Zyaee-Bigdeli, Mohmmad Reza [1368] (1988), *Eslam va Hoghooghe Bainolmelal* [Islam and International Law], Tehran: Scherkat Sahami Enteshar.

4 Peace and security in the international system

An Iranian approach

Asghar Eftekhary

Introduction

> A definition of national security based on the production of wealth and people's creativity is the basis of a country's foreign policy ... (in modern times)[1]

This simple but thoughtful definition proposed by Mahmoud Sariolqalam on the future structure of the international system shows that many foreign policy analysts are concerned about this issue. The key question is, 'What are the basic trends which determine the outcome of peace and security in the international arena?' As outlined by Ruhollah Ramezani, new conditions have emerged in which all the rules, discourse and strategic methods have changed. Therefore, we are faced with a new world order whose strategic equations cannot necessarily be solved by using old principles and regulations.[2]

If this idea, whose truth cannot be doubted,[3] were accepted, new peace and security structures must be discussed and the most important international political matters should be delineated. The result will be important in that it will determine the centre of gravity (of political developments), on which security structures will be based. Naturally, our understanding of this issue can determine the direction of theoretical studies and practical proposals regarding national security.

To do this, firstly, major scenarios on the structure of global security and their important components should be identified. Then, by analysing tension-creating trends in each of these scenarios, the most important issues related to international peace and security in the 21st century could be delineated and an Iranian approach to solve problems and establish international peace and security proposed.

Future outlook of the international order from Iran's viewpoint

> Scenarios are a tool with which to make the intuitions and understandings of leaders and managers more orderly. Defining scenarios ... is aimed at adopting strategic decisions which would be wise and stable enough for 'all believable futures'.[4]

As Alizadeh has correctly noted, 'generating scenarios' can be a good way to speculate about a future situation which would pave the way for the formulation of a long-term national strategy for political actors under changing conditions of international peace and security. Two major scenarios can be discerned in relation to the structure of the 'international order', which is the source of knowledge about the main security issues in the 21st century.

The American scenario

Zbigniew Brzezinski in *The Grand Chessboard* in 1997 noted that the collapse of the Soviet Union provided the United States with a unique opportunity in the international hierarchy of power.[5] Thus far, a lot of texts and viewpoints have been presented, whose content is based on this main argument: the United States, as the world's sole superpower in the 21st century, is capable of playing an effective role in managing and leading both issues and trends of international order. From this outlook, strategic assessment of US power in terms of such hardware components as technology, the economy and, above all, the military indicate that no other power has the potential to vie with or confront the United States:[6] America has undisputed superior economic power as well as, to some extent, military might. On the other hand, the idea of a 'soft power' put forth by Joseph Nye has introduced another perspective in power equations in the international system and this approach indicates another angle of US superiority in the international system. Nye's interpretation of soft power, which is based on 'an actor's capacity to encourage and persuade others to do as he wishes' goes beyond 'coercion' and denotes 'legitimization' by other actors of the measures taken by the initiating actor.[7] With this viewpoint in mind he takes a critical approach to the application of soft power by the United States.[8] However, this concept has been taken as a positive approach by such thinkers as Rosemary Foot, who relies on such experiences as the US invasion of Afghanistan and the war on terror and/or welcoming liberal democratic values in the global expanse to conclude that America's soft power has reached its peak at the beginning of the 21st century and, like hard power, has brought about some kind of supremacy to this country.[9] As Henry Kissinger points out, the United States is in such a superior position at the beginning of the 21st century that there has been no precedence, even among the largest ancient empires. The US has become an indispensable part of international stability in all fields.[10]

Therefore, the structure of the international system is a combination of the following categories all of which are defined on the basis of 'hegemony' and, thus, will lead to a negative form of peace and security for the international system (see Figure 4.1).

First category: allies

As David Lake has shown, these actors are the closest satellites to the hegemonic power and are characterized by the following features:

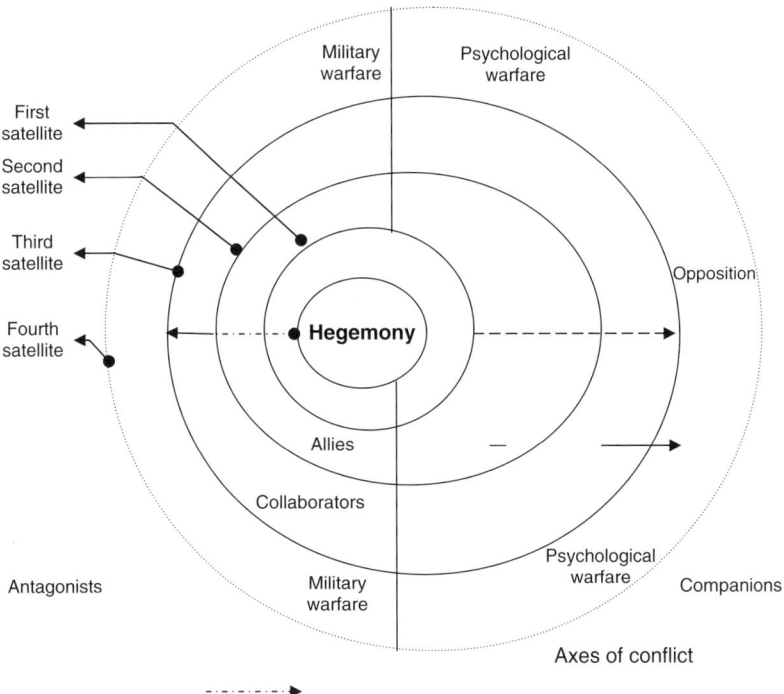

Figure 4.1 Structure of international peace and security: the American scenario axes of conflict.

A) They have their own domains of influence and the hegemonic power avoids violating and interfering in their specific fields, which include their vital interests.
B) They have critical interests in other areas where they should also play an effective role.[11]

Their operational logic is to protect their critical interests in their specific regions and cooperate and bargain with the hegemonic power to secure their vital interests elsewhere. The European Union, Russia and China are major actors in this regard.[12]

Second category: collaborators

The second orbit includes a number of actors in good strategic positions, yet for many reasons they avoid being pitched against the hegemonic power. According to David Lampton and Richard Ewing, they seek to achieve their goals through 'beneficial cooperation' with the hegemonic power.[13]

Third category: antagonists

Although in the international system, 'opposition' is different from 'antagonism' in terms of operational meaning, that difference is not prominent in hegemonic conditions and according to Henry Kissinger's analysis, prevalence of the 'with us or against us' logic causes any opposition to be naturally looked upon as antagonism. The third orbit includes actors 'opposed' or 'antagonistic' to the hegemonic power.[14]

Fourth category: companions

Besides the actors within the above-mentioned categories, there is also a fourth orbit on the sidelines of international security equations within the international system. Edwin Feulner has characterized those actors in the following way:

Firstly, they are entangled in their domestic issues and are not capable of orchestrating an effective international presence.
Secondly, they seriously avoid opposing the hegemonic power and suffering the consequences.
Thirdly, they are subject to the rationale of attunement with the international community.

They try to weather security developments by remaining silent until the direction in which global trends are moving are clarified and then accept them (explicitly or implicitly)[15] (see Figure 4.1).

The European scenario

Richard Kugler maintains that the United States has numerous and acceptable reasons to welcome a united Europe. But that idea may give birth to a new rival power for the United States. Such a Europe may cause problems for the United States.[16]

As Kugler also comments, the European scenario is based on the willingness of the EU to play a more effective global role. In other words, the two main pillars of its foreign policy are as follows (see Figure 4.2).

First pillar: strategic union with the United States

According to the security assessment of the independent working group of Stockholm International Peace Research Institute (SIPRI), security arrangements in Europe cannot be considered an outcome of war. The security system of the EU, however, has gradually come about from negotiations and agreement on norms, establishing common and broad-based legal organizations. Therefore, the security arrangements of Europe have been traditionally and historically safeguarded by making an alliance with the United States, and most European-American analysts maintain that Washington is willing for this situation to continue.[17] Also, major probable security threats posed to Europe (such as ethnic–religious conflicts, probable social tensions from the expansion of the Union, environmental problems and so on) could be checked and thwarted through effective cooperation on the part

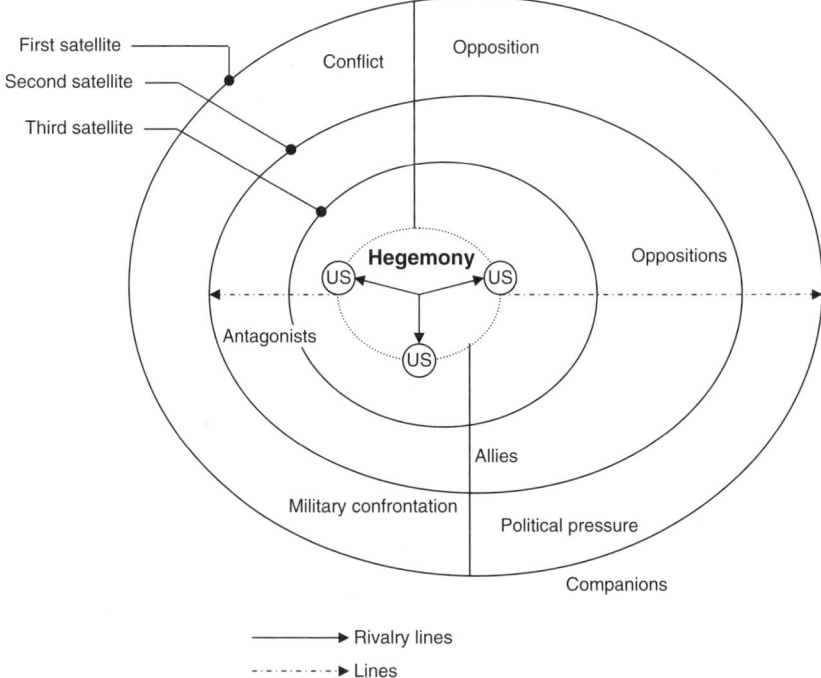

First satellite

Second satellite

Third satellite

Conflict

Opposition

Hegemony

Oppositions

Antagonists

Allies

Military confrontation

Political pressure

Companions

⟶ Rivalry lines

- - - - - - - - -▶ Lines

Figure 4.2 Structure of international peace and security: the European scenario.

of the United States.[18] In this respect, one can point to the common philosophical foundations between these two actors,[19] the emergence of common threats to them,[20] and awareness by both sides of the untoward effects of any divergence between Europe and the United States for their interests in different parts of the world,[21] all of which lead both actors to create the strongest power alliance of the future world, which will be based on the common strategic interests of both the United States and Europe.[22]

Second pillar: Getting out from under the US hegemonic umbrella

Despite the above-mentioned logic, it seems that after the collapse of the Soviet Union, the European Union is no longer interested in a continuation of past strategies based on the unrivalled leadership of the United States. What follows is a compendium of major factors which encourage the European Union to correct its previous situation and to enter global equations as an independent and effective leader.

Economic interests are very important to the European Union and, as outlined by Robert Gilpin, they are the driving force behind many basic relationships and developments in the 21st century.[23] From this standpoint, the growing need for energy, industrial development, consumer markets and global capital flow will become the main factors in forming international power bases and, being aware of these issues, the European Union is not willing and cannot forgo this dimension of power.[24]

Another issue deals with promoting the strategic capability of the European Union as, following Andrew Rathmell's argument, the global enthusiasm for Europe to play a more important role is a reaction to US unilateralism.[25] Therefore, world demand has been effective in changing the EU's foreign policy model and the Union will try to correct to some extent the post-World War II imbalance in its own favour. Following on from this one can assess the best effective move as strengthening the role of the European Union in international policies.

When these two pillars are combined, the result would be a strategy based on the rationale of 'competition for partnership'. The essence of that strategy can be explained as follows.

The EU is not against a world hegemonic power

The viewpoints of analysts reflected on the NATO website in response to how collective security can be guaranteed in the future indicate that ending the chaotic situation will not be possible except through the effective role of a powerful centre whose decisions will be supported by adequate executive guarantees.[26] Therefore, security policy will be tied to executive strength and the European Union will not basically oppose the application of pressure aimed at establishing the security desired.

The European Union does not intend to replace the US

Following the collapse of the former Soviet Union, some countries sought a replacement (such as Russia, China or the European Union) as a buffer against the United States.[27] Under these circumstances, the EU was the most appealing option. However, as mentioned earlier, it has neither the strength nor the motivation to accept that role. On the contrary, according to the argument of the participants at the conference on 'Future Outlooks of European Foreign and Security Policies', the powerful presence of the United States is in fact a major pillar of the EU's security policy because it both blocks criticism of Europe's totalitarianism and can also help create a suitable atmosphere for a critical presence (in economic, political and communication spheres) in other parts of the world. A powerful US can also serve as an efficient executive guarantee for the realization of an optimal legal model desired by the European Union, which would be based on European human rights.[28] Such considerations denote that the presence of a United States with superior military power, and even one with militaristic tendencies, can be assessed to be in line with the long-term interests of the European Union.

The EU sees itself as part of the world hegemonic system

The complexity of security matters on the international scene, their high cost, the limitations faced by the superpowers, development of the world network, the emergence of new powers and ultimately the increased capabilities of the European Union all indicate that the United States is not capable of establishing a world order by itself. As Michael Randle sees it, global problems cannot be solved unless through a global will.[29] Paul Rugers and other researchers have concluded that although realization of a global will is not possible in the short term, the minimum requisite for it is the participation of influential and vested powers which will encourage others to follow suit.[30] Mention should be made of the idea that was brought up in two conferences related to future security in Europe (which took place in Brussels on 14 November 2002 and 11 June 2003) whose participants generally maintained that the European Union was entitled to emerge as a world hegemonic power and believed that the EU's strategic appraisals give it the 'right' to be effective in determining international policies, just like the United States.[31]

The EU considers protecting UN status a necessity

Due to the philosophy of the United Nations and its role in generating 'legitimacy' in international politics, the European Union believes that no hegemonic power will be able to maintain stability without assistance from the UN as a common humanitarian organization. In other words, although unilateralism can be effective in the beginning, historical experiences have shown that it is not capable of giving 'legitimacy' and will face problems in the establishment phase.[32] Peter Feaver and Christopher Gelpi have tested the above idea in the course of the US invasion of Iraq and have shown how the marginalization of the United Nations caused problems for American security policy, both in domestic and foreign contexts. Therefore, more enthusiasm to use military instruments indicates weak legitimacy and will help make a crisis of legitimacy more profound. This phenomenon was witnessed in the Iraqi crisis in the form of a delayed launch of the invasion, a lack of international consensus, together with problems in the political management of occupied Iraq.[33] Many analysts maintain that the UN presence in that case could have changed its direction, forming international alliances that would have much reduced the costs of development in Iraq.[34] From this point of view, Muhammad Ayyoub has noted that it would be impossible to guarantee US leadership through short-term unilateral measures adopted by the Bush administration because such measures might destroy the opportunity for continuing the legitimate superiority of the United States in the international system in the long run.[35]

The conclusion of the above-mentioned four considerations is that the European Union defines world hegemonic power as a phenomenon comprising three elements, each with its own role in international politics and division of labour (see Table 4.1).

Table 4.1 Role: to provide executive guarantees.

Role: to provide executive guarantees	US	1. Military arm
Role: to spur on diplomatic developments	EU	2. Political arm
Role: to give legitimacy to requested developments	UN	3. Legal arm

After the European Union moves into the core of the world hegemonic system, other layers can be defined as follows:

1st layer: Allies – actors who confirm the hegemonic powers' policies on the grounds of their common interests.
2nd layer: Opponents/antagonists – actors standing against the hegemonic power.
3rd layer: Companions – actors on the margins of the international system.

Critical assessment: Iran, US, Europe

Although there has been no consensus on the causes of 9/11 terror attacks in scientific, operational and security terms,[36] few thinkers are in doubt about its profound consequences.[37] Therefore, what Ahmad Yousof Ahmad and Mamdouh Hamza have said about the emergence of new issues in peace and security arrangements of the contemporary world can be considered to the point. Within the framework of this analysis and in view of the said scenarios, major criticisms of global peace and security plans in the 21st century can be listed as follows.

Hegemonic tendencies in the US and Europe

Although there are operational differences between the two scenarios, as witnessed in the security policies of the US and the EU in Afghanistan and Iraq, it seems from a strategic standpoint that said differences are more tactical in their nature than strategic. In other words, there is a kind of positive rivalry[38] between the two main actors that is more similar to 'partnership' than 'substitution'.[39] Therefore, countries like the Islamic Republic of Iran, which do not agree with the hegemonic principle and its negative consequences, cannot accept and attune to this scenario. Of course, the European scenario seems to be much more appealing than the American one. So the following propositions can be taken into account:

First proposition: In case of weakness emerging inside the European Union and the empowerment of US unilateralism, militarism against actors who are antagonists to the hegemonic power will be on the rise.
Second proposition: If the American scenario were realized, the United Nations would be marginalized and direct contacts among actors would increase.[40]
Third proposition: If the EU ended up as a world hegemonic power, diplomacy would be used in parallel to military methods (modification of military methods in favour of diplomacy).
Fourth proposition: If the American scenario prevailed, US exclusionism would be strengthened to the detriment of other international actors, especially weak countries.[41]

Despite its great importance in understanding international peace and security in the 21st century, the 'axis of rivalry' has not been fully analysed and is generally overshadowed by security considerations related to conflicts in Iraq and

Afghanistan. Moreover, the idea of conflict between Europe and the US in international politics, and claims about taking advantage of that conflict in favour of national interests (as they did in the Cold War period), were among other factors adding to the complexity of the true concept of this security axis.

This concept means that the EU has adopted said strategy in order to convince the United States to accept EU partnership in establishing a complex world hegemonic power, and although this measure is of security and tactical importance to other countries it is considered to be a positive strategy.

Expansion of conflicts

We will witness an escalation of political tensions under both scenarios of a hegemonic order in world security. This is because a hegemonic power will have to, firstly, eliminate actors at odds with its policies and, secondly, manage long-standing international political problems in order to prove its superior position to the rest of the world. Obviously, both those policies require an application of force, which proves that the following propositions will be raised in the 21st century:

First proposition: Due to the power-based nature of international peace and security equations, the conceptual border between 'antagonism' and 'opposition' will fade and those opposing the hegemonic power will be considered 'antagonists'.[42]

Second proposition: Since the hegemonic power needs to demonstrate its authority, considerations of axial powers have increased and the rules of international politics and even the philosophy of international organizations have been subject to redefinition.[43]

Third proposition: A new generation of modern wars gradually emerges, which is totally in favour of the hegemonic power.[44]

Fourth proposition: As a result of the assimilation of the European Union into the world hegemonic system, basic tenets such as 'war is an alternative to diplomacy in another way' and 'diplomacy is a continuation of war in another language' will be reassessed. This means that US military might and its unilateral policies will be considered a new executive guarantee for the realization of the goals of the new complex hegemonic power.[45]

Conclusion: towards a new order

It seems that after going through such major upheavals as the 9/11 attacks, the international system has distanced itself from the ambiguous atmosphere that prevailed at the end of the Cold War. We are witnessing the emergence of new principles, which are to be a feature of international politics in the future. Therefore, an answer to the question about international peace and security can be given with more certainty.

According to this author's analysis, there are common realities in both scenarios that will be pursued by big powers (that is, American and European scenarios, which respectively seek to establish an international hegemonic power or a complex hegemonic power), which can be mentioned as pillars of a peace and security plan for the 21st century. In other words, beyond oppositions and conflicts that can be seen on the global power chessboard, there is a single trend that seeks to establish the world hegemonic system. So an international peace and security plan will comprise of the following two axes:

The first axis is an expansion of international conflicts, which are seen by Iran as fostering insecurity and not to the benefit of the international system and regional order.

The second axis, which is more important, is 'rivalries between the European Union and the United States' on the nature of hegemony.

Although international politics at the beginning of the 21st century have been familiar with objective developments and wars emanating from the first axis, this author believes that the future trend of those developments is towards the second axis. Therefore, discussing US–EU relations will not only present a more logical interpretation of global developments after the collapse of the Soviet Union, it can also be used to plan national strategies for countries and assess world trust in this actor. In other words, the international security agenda will include two items in the years to come, which will indicate the direction in which developments will move. The first item is positive rivalry between the EU and US, with the second item being treatment of antagonist actors by the world hegemonic power.

In view of the above two axes, the Islamic Republic of Iran is willing to distance itself from the hegemonic order because of its negative consequences for Iran and other Third World countries. Iran's proposed scenario is based on regional orders in which, instead of a hegemonic core, a group of actors positively interact with one another in the form of power regions. This model both greatly reduces the intensity of conflicts (since there is no hegemonic power in the international system) and is also realistic. It conforms to a definition and acceptance of rivalries at regional level and paves the way for positive dynamism in the international system together with the establishment of positive peace and security.

Notes

1 Sariolqalam, Mahmoud, 'Constant Principles of National Wealth Generation', in *Developmental Foreign Policy*, Tehran: Center for Strategic Research, 2008, p. 83.
2 Ramezani, Ruhollah, *An Analytical Framework for Assessment of the Islamic Republic of Iran's Foreign Policy*, Tehran: Nei Press, 2001, pp. 159–162.
3 Although there are differences in this regard, it seems that security community is unanimous about basic changes that followed the disintegration of the Soviet Union. See Eftekhary, Asghar, 'Leviathan Security', *Rahbord Quarterly*, no. 24, summer 2002, pp. 31–47.
4 Alizadeh, Aziz *et al.*, *Writing Scenarios or Making Plans Based on Scenarios*, Tehran: International Energy Studies Institute, 2008, p. 58.
5 Brzezinski, Zbignew, *The Grand Chessboard: America Primacy & Its Geostrategic Imperatives*, Basic Books, 1997, p. 10.

6 Brzezinski has written that the United States is superior in four aspects and is a world power. It is a leading military power and no other player can measure up to it. In economic terms, the United States is still the world's driving force and it is also superior in technology and culture; ibid., p. 24.

7 The commission in charge of formulating US national security strategy, *US National Security Strategy in 21st Century*, Persian translation by Jalal Dehmeshki *et al.*, Tehran: Abrar Mo'aser Tehran Institute for Cultural Studies and International Research, 2001, Chapter 1.

8 Joseph Nye has offered critical views based on the differentiation between soft and hard power. Strategic assessment of US power holds true for hard power, but not necessarily for soft power. Therefore, while accepting US supremacy in hard power, he has doubted its continuation due to shortages in soft power and maintains that the importance of soft power prevents one from hoping that the United States will be unrivalled in the 21st century. For more information see Nye, Joseph, 'Us Power & Strategy after Iraq', *Foreign Affairs*, July–August, 2003.

9 See Foot, Rosemary, *et al.* (rdis), *U.S. Hegemony & International Organization*, available at http://www.oup.usa.org/isbn=0199261431.html.

10 Kissinger, Henry, *US Diplomacy in the 21st Century*, translated by Abolqasem Rahchamani, Tehran: Abrar Mo'aser Tehran Institute for Cultural Studies and International Research, 2002, p. 11.

11 See: Lake, David, *Entangling Relations: American Foreign Policy in Its Century*, available at http://www.pupress.princeton.edu/titles/6638.html.

12 See Mead, Walter, *Special Providence*, Routledge, 2002.

13 See Lampton, David and R. Ewing, *U.S.–China Relations in a Post-September 11th World*, available at http://www.nixoncenter.org/special/press-relase china.Mono.html.

14 See Kissinger, Henry, *Does America Need a Foreign Policy?* Available at http://www. amazon.com/exec/obidos/detail/0684855674.

15 See Feulner, Edwin (ed.), *Leadership For America: The Principles of Conservatism*, available at http://www.heritage.org/about/bookstor/leadership for america.cfm/2003.

16 Kugler, Richard, 'The European quest for unity' in *The Global Century: Globalization And National Security*, ch. 39, pp. 16–20.

17 See *A Future Security Agenda For Europe*, Stockholm, International Institute for Peace Research, 1999.

18 See Claes, Dag Harald, 'The Process of Europeanization – Norway and the Internal Energy Policy', *Journal of Public Policy*, vol. 22, September–December 2002, pp. 229–323.

19 See Hunt, Michael, *Ideology & U.S Foreign Policy*, available at http://www.amazon. com/exec/obidos/tgdetail/030043694.

20 See Danzig, Richard, Big Three: The Greatest Security Risk & How to Address Them, available at http://www.ndu.edy/inss/books/big.20three/dancont.html.

21 See Lord, Cames, *The Modern Prince*, available at http://www.yale.edu/yup/books/ 100078.html.

22 Huntington, S., *The Clash of Civilizations*, New York: Simon & Schuster, 1996, ch. 2.

23 See Gilpin, Robert, *The Challenge of Global Capitalism: The World Economy in the 21st Century*, Princeton, NJ: Princeton University Press, 2000.

24 Smil, Vaclav, 'Energy resources & User: A Global Primer for the Twenty-First Century', *Current History* (March) 2002, pp. 126–132.

25 Rathmell has put special emphasis on the EU's role in the Persian Gulf. See Rathmell, Andrew, *et al*, *A New Persian Gulf Security*, available at http://www.rand.org/publications/ IP/IP284.

26 See *NATO Today: Building Better Security & Stability For All*, 2002, available at http:/// www.nato.int/docu/him.html/intro.

27 See Gruber, Lioyd, *Ruling the World: Power Political and Rise of Supranational Institutions*, available at http://www.pupress.princeton.edu/titles/6869.html.

28 See: http://www.isis-europe.org/isiseu/conference/conference-1/Conference.html; also see Ikenberry, John and T. Inoquchi (eds), *American Democracy Promotion: Imputes, Strategies & Impacts*, Oxford: Oxford University Press, 2000.

29 Randle, Michael (ed.), *Issues in Peace Research 2002: Challenges to Nonviolence*, available at http://www.brad.ac.uk/acad/pubs.html. This project continued from 1994 to 1999; a group of experts, journalists, and academicians identified and proposed solutions for the most important international problems. Their solutions were based on a determination beyond a single international player.

30 See Tansey, Geoff, Kath Fansey and P. Rugers (eds), *A World Divided*, available at http://www.brad.ac.uk/acad/pubs/reports.html.

31 For the text of the papers see: http://www.isis.europe.org/isiseu/conference/conreports.html.

32 Franck, Thomas, *Fairness in International Law & Institutions*, available at http://www.oup.usa.org/isbn=0198267851.html.

33 See Feaver, P. and C. Gelpi, *Choosing Your Battles: American Civil – Military Relations & the Use of Force*, available at http://www.pupress.edu/litles/7662.html.

34 Brilmayer, Lea, *American Hegemony: Political Morality in a One – Superpower*, available at http://www.Yale.edu/yup/books/068530.html.

35 Ayyoub, Mohammad, 'War against Iraq: Normative and Strategic Consequences', *Defense Strategy Quarterly*, 1st year, no. 1, fall 2003, p. 144.

36 Ahmad, Ahmad Yousof and Mamdouh, Hamza, 'al-Arab wal Imrika: Minal Inbihar bil Hilm ila Uqdatil Kirahiya', *Jama' minal Muallifin, Sina'atil Kirahiya fil Alaqiyat il-Arabiya – Imrikiya*, Beirut: Dirasat Wahdat il-Arabi Center, 2003, p. 40.

37 See Eftekhary, Asghar, 'Security Impact of 9/11: Viewpoints and Analyses', *Strategic Studies Quarterly*, fall and winter, no. 17–18, 2002, pp. 654–637.

38 See Reiter, Dan and Allan C. Stam, *Democracies At War*, available at http://www.pupress.plinceton.rdu/titles/7292.html.

39 See Rose, Gideon and J. Hoge, *America & The World: Dictating The New Shape of International Politics*, available at http://www.cfr.org/publication.php?id=5174.

40 See Kagan, Robert, 'The World & President Bush', *Survival*, vol. 43, (spring) 2001.

41 See Lockhart, Charles, *The Roots of American Exceptionalism Institutions*, available at http://www.palgrace-Vsa.com/catalogue/index.asp/?isbn=1403961964.

42 See Pfaff, William, 'The question of hegemony', *Foreign Affairs*, vol. 80, (January–February) 2001

43 See Slater, David *et al.* (eds), *The American Century*, Malden: Blackwell Publishers, 1999; Chesterman, Simon, *Just War or Just Peace?*, available at http://www.oup.usa.org/isbn=019925799x.html.

44 See Kugler, Richard, *Military Strategy and the Situation of US forces in the 21st Century*, Ahmad Reza Toqa and Davoud Olamaei, Tehran, Islamic Revolution Guards Corps, High Course on War, 2001.

45 Buzan, Barry, 'New patterns of global security in the twenty-first century', *International Affairs*, vol. 67, no. 3, (July) 1991.

5 The Islamic republic of Iran and the international system

Clash with the domination paradigm

Manouchehr Mohammadi

Introduction

In the aftermath of the collapse of the Soviet Union and with the end of the bipolar hegemonic system, scholars and policymakers in the West sought to find a substitute, and great efforts were made with the aim of stabilizing and defining the continuation of the hegemonic Western-oriented system. Before long, the creation of a New World Order with the remaining superpower from the Cold War playing the pivotal role was raised and presented to the US Congress as the doctrine of George Bush, Sr.

Nevertheless, the inefficiency of such a unipolar system and the rejection of other world powers very soon proved that there was no room for the hegemony of a superpower. Therefore, Western scholars and theoreticians, especially in the United States, by presenting other theories such as the 'End of History' (Francis Fukuyama) and the 'Clash of Civilizations' (Samuel Huntington) tried to further underline Western sovereignty and hegemony and view the world from a Western domineering and hegemonic perspective. However, now that two decades have passed since the demise of the bipolar system, the world is still in a transitional period. Not only has no stable system come forth or stabilized to fit the previous bipolar one, but a kind of anarchism is now ruling over international relations so that Western theoreticians are unable to define a clear justification or stable regulations for it. Recently, Richard Haas admitted that the world is entering 'an era of non-polarity'.

Among these developments what was ignored by Western scholars was the movement of Imam Khomeini in the early 1960s in Iran followed by the success of the Islamic Revolution in 1979 and the ever increasing consistency and strength of the newly born religio-political system, despite anything the Western powers could do. The author, who has personally witnessed these developments, believes that such a phenomenon has had a great effect on the future world order and will continue to do so. The movement not only destroyed the monarchical autocracy in Iran that had been in place for several thousands of years, but had major repercussions in the region and seriously challenged the hegemonic system left over from the Peace of Westphalia.

Furthermore, through Islamic vigilance and the awakening of the colonies of the imperial nations, Islamic Iran has undertaken the leadership of a new camp of what can be called Counter-Autocrats and is set to shape the future of international relations by opposing the hegemonic system of the West. It aims to lay new foundations for such relations, which in structural terms or in terms of context and concept would have no similarity with what has so far been defined in the literature of political sciences and international relations. With regard to such an important development and its subsequent events, this chapter will present a new paradigm called 'the clash with domination'. We believe that what Huntington has tried to observe within the framework of the Clash of Civilizations is, in fact, not a clash of civilizations as such but a clash of counter-autocratic regimes resulting in the domination of hegemonic states, which this chapter will try to review.

Concepts

Definition of paradigm

A paradigm, basically a Platonic term, has been translated as 'an example' and 'a pattern' and was first used by Thomas Kuhn for the elucidation of scientific developments and philosophical aspects of science. A paradigm is a concept for elaborating on the roots of science. In Thomas Kuhn's view, a paradigm is the recognized scientific achievements that will provide a model and example of the issues and social solutions of professional agents of science for some time to come. In other words, a paradigm contains a series of undisputed presumptions, which are the basis for and contain any scientific activity. These presumptions include philosophical and metaphysical expressions on which they are based.[1]

In another definition, a paradigm is 'a collection of assumptions, theories, plans, models and cases of test and value which are common in a specific circle of scientists who are working in a specified area'.[2]

Definition of international system

An international system is an environment in which political units are active, so that the behaviour, orientations, intentions and demands of said units are subject to the influence of the international system, on the basis of the definition offered by Morton Kaplan: 'The system is comprised of a collection of variables which are dependent on each other and any change in any element constituting the system will spread to its other sectors and will affect them.'[3]

Another definition introduces the international system as the pole and gravitational centre for international policy in an era of human history. In another definition, the international system is considered as an environmental concept in which a multitude of countries, regional and international organizations and the like are present to such an extent that the behaviour, orientation and demands of said countries are subject to the influence of the international system.

It seems that, in fact, the international system embodies both the above definitions because, on the one hand, it is a gravitational centre affecting regional and global policies and strategies and, on the other, it is comprised of a group of countries. And although the international system consists of a group of countries, its structure is different from that of individual countries, because the internal society (country), contrary to the global society (international system), enjoys additional unity, structure and institutionalization with a unified rule and three branches of government.

Historical trend of the international system

How the international system affects countries and to what degree has not been the same throughout history, due to the structure and nature of that system. To further clarify this issue, we will review the international system historically from the Westphalia Treaty onwards. The reason for selecting this historical juncture is that after the Treaty of Westphalia the international system took shape in its present form.

At the end of the Thirty Years War in 1648 between the principalities under the sovereignty of the Holy Roman Empire and the kings of France and Spain in Europe, the Treaty of Westphalia was signed, the most important outcome of which was that for the first time the independence and territorial integrity of European countries, (and therefore respect for them) were officially recognized. It was also stipulated that only sovereign countries could conclude treaties with each other and an institution under the title of nation-state was set forth for the first time, replacing the previous feudal system.

- **First juncture of the international system**: Since the Treaty of Westphalia was signed – irrespective of any short anomalous period up to World War I, the system governing international relations was based on the balance of power. Such a system meant that the power that existed at world level was distributed evenly among powerful European governments through joining one another or separating from each other. This established a balance of power among countries and thus prevented the domination of any one country over any others. Such a system dominated for a period of 250 years despite the problems involved in dividing up other countries of the world under the name of colonialism. However, the expansionist tendencies of some of these countries (such as Germany) prepared the ground for the downfall of this system and the emergence of a new one.
- **Collective security system**: In the aftermath of World War I and the defeat of Germany, a new arrangement known as 'the Collective Security System' was set up by the then US president, Woodrow Wilson. Following this, all countries (not only the big powers) were to choose a type of cooperation strategy for the realization of world peace. Furthermore, in order to achieve peace, an international organization called the League of Nations was founded, which was expected to mobilize all countries against violation. There was no trace of some of the defects of the balance of power in the new system, but due to the dissatisfaction of some of the members (such as Germany and Italy) with the prevailing situation and the refusal of the US to join, as well as the absence of enough support by other members, this system was broken up with the premature outbreak of World War II in 1939.
- **Bipolar system and the Cold War**: With the failure of the collective security system in establishing and maintaining world peace, after World War II the

triumphant and powerful countries, relying on the theory of the then US president, Franklin Roosevelt, undertook responsibility for shaping the post-war international system and formed the United Nations and the Security Council. The victors of World War II, whom Roosevelt termed 'the Big Brothers', had the right of veto in Security Council resolutions. Meanwhile, the military supremacy of both the US and Russia pushed the world towards a bipolar system and gradually the policies and strategies of these two countries came to openly oppose each other. There were several reasons for this confrontation, but it could be summarized as the preservation and enhancement of power, which brought about some type of balance of power – or balance of terror.

The above, known as the bipolar system, exhibited characteristics such as dividing the world into two blocs and two regions of influence, and founding multilateral military and economic institutions (such as the North Atlantic Treaty Organization [NATO] and its counterpart the Warsaw Pact), and followed a status of no war/no peace, replacing non-confidence with understanding in determining the military, political and even economic and cultural policies of members of the bloc, for each bloc needed to supervise and control the strategies of countries within its own bloc in order to balance the other.

The Cold War refers to an era that began with the end of World War II, from the middle of the 1940s, up to 1988 and the collapse of the former Soviet Union. The characteristics of this period were the open and hidden political, economic, military and cultural rivalry and struggle of the Western bloc, led by the United States, against the Eastern bloc, under the leadership of the Soviet Union. The struggle had spread its heavy and dark shadow over the international atmosphere and was determining the fate of mankind.

Transition period

The transition period is a temporary phase in which an international system or structure dies away before it has been replaced by any new system or structure. Such a process has no definite deadline but is not endless either, as it will eventually be replaced by a new structure.

In his book *Transitions* William Bridges considers a passage as the transfer of one stage to another stage and defines three stages for it:[4]

1.   The termination stage of the old system
2.   The stage of indifference
3.   Building a new infrastructure.

Theories presented in the West

The end of the Cold War is without any doubt among the most important developments of the late 20th century, for it diversified international policy and created new mental challenges, resulting in many different theories on the process of shaping the future international system. In the second half of the 1980s, the socialist Soviet Union underwent such drastic changes and fundamental and extensive evolution that not only did its inner structure collapse in an unexpected manner but, by terminating the bipolar era, it presented the international community with a highly important and decisive question: what type of future world system will replace the present one and on what criteria and standards will it be based?

The new world order theory

Following the collapse of the Soviet Union, which triggered the defeat of Marxism-Leninism ideology, the fall of its apparent unconquerable power and its pullout from the leadership of the Eastern bloc prepared the most fertile ground for the other superpower to occupy the resulting vacuum by trying to expand its now unrivalled world authority. Some of the American theoreticians considered the end of the Cold War a highly appropriate reason for promulgating the idea that world order and peace demanded the establishment of a dominant power which, by relying on its financial resources and absolute might, claimed to maintain and safeguard public security and welfare in the world. Following this ideology, American theoreticians presented the doctrine of George Bush, Sr. as the New World Order, which was based on the premise that the United States, the remaining superpower from the Cold War era, in order to impose an effective influence in the world, still needed to preserve a considerable part of its military forces. The theory in question attracted the attention of several international policy thinkers at American universities, who began to justify and defend it.

The conditions for the continuation and consolidation of the new order could be based on two main principles: firstly, the US administration would have the power and authority that goes with the leadership of the hegemonic system in military, economic, political and social terms; secondly, the remaining members of the world community would accept obedience to this system and submit to US demands and, in case of mutiny and disobedience, the US would have the means to punish and quell the insurgent state.[5]

The existence and enforcement of the said double standards, constituting the basis for the continuation of the New World Order – a unipolar or hierarchical system – seemed impossible, for the US community was not ready in economic, political or social terms nor did it have enough impetus to lead the world, and the other hegemonic powers were not prepared to accept its leadership and give unconditional obedience. As a result, in the early 1990s the world witnessed a number of US efforts at stabilizing the system and the refusal of other countries to accept it. This eventually resulted in the US failing to realize the new world order. It was at this point that other countries such the People's Republic of China proposed the formation of the multi-polar system, which is not favoured by the US and which it has so far refused to accept.[6]

In a multi-polar system, economic interests play a determining role in international relations and replace military power – which in the transient stage of this international system has no meaning in the absence of attention of major Asian powers, especially China and Japan – as the new poles. In the past the United States and Europe had used their military might to exert a checking influence over Asia, especially on Japan. Thus, under the new status quo in which China as an economic power has experienced outstanding growth on an almost daily basis, a new choice has been provided for these regions while the US is still drowning in a crisis of confusion.

The clash of civilizations paradigm

Meanwhile, the American theoreticians and policymakers were pursuing new theories while preserving the continuation of the US hegemony, hoping they could set a guideline for the US and Western policymakers. In line with this, the renowned American political scientist Samuel Huntington proposed his controversial theory of the Clash of Civilizations.

Huntington, contrary to some analysts who view the end of the Cold War as the termination of ideological disputes, considers it a prelude to the new era of the Clash of Civilizations. Huntington interprets and comments on many contemporary events and occurrences in the world that would further support the assumptions of his new theory.

He divides the existing civilizations of the world into seven or eight major categories[7] and believes that the fault lines between them are sources of future conflicts and substitutes for the old nation-state unit.

In Huntington's view, the confrontation of civilizations will constitute the dominant world policy and the final stage of completion of clashes in the contemporary era, because in his ideology the following are present:

– Differences among civilizations are fundamental.
– Self-awareness of civilization is on the rise.
– Revival of religious life is a means for filling the growing identity gap.
– The hypocritical behaviour of the West has caused a growth of self-awareness of others' civilizations.
– Cultural characteristics and differences are unchangeable.
– Economic regionalism and the role played by cultural commonalties are growing.
– Existing fault lines among contemporary civilizations have replaced the political and ideological borders of the Cold War era and these lines are ready to spark crises and bloodshed.
– The 1400-year hostility between Islam and the West is growing and relations between the Islamic and Western civilizations are so bad that it is likely that bloody events will ensue.

So, based on this ideology the paradigm for the Clash of Civilizations has overshadowed other global issues and in the new era fresh alignments are taking shape, finally the Islamic and Confucian civilizations are standing alongside each other against Western civilizations. In brief, the main centre of future conflicts is between

Western civilization and an alliance of Confucian societies in East Asia and the Islamic world. In fact, the clash of civilizations would be the final stage of clashes in the new world.[8] What is apparent here – although critics of this theory have paid little attention to this – is that Huntington's intention in offering such a theory has not been in putting forward a new 'paradigm' but rather presenting a solution or justification of contradictions that have emerged in the aftermath of the collapse of the bipolar system.

Theory of the end of history

Francis Fukuyama, by revising Hegel's ideology on the End of History, reaches the conclusion that the 'true course of history' found its moral perfection in 1806 and that, following the emergence and defeat of fascism and Marxism, it finally resulted in the spread of liberal democracy, also reaching its financial perfection.[9]

In his point of view, the only real and creditable alternative for fascism and communism is liberalism, all of which have collapsed, but he does not believe that there is no existing ideology. Rather, he feels that in the end some societies have become successful liberal ones and the rest ignore the claim of offering different and superior forms and patterns on human organization. In fact, liberalism becomes dominant in the world because there is no other mobilizing ideology to confront it. This is regarded as the end of the ideological evolution of mankind and the spread of Western democracy as the final form of government, with its capitalist system of living and its tendency towards a consumer society that ends up in economic and political liberalism. He termed this stagnation of conflict and probe of thoughts as the End of History, an era in which enthusiasms have faded away and centuries of inconvenience and discomfort are to come. The characteristics of the past centuries, that is to say, the campaign for exploration, readiness for devotion to completely abstract and isolated ideals, world ideological struggles that necessitated bravery and powerful imagination, have all changed place with a more frugal economy, an endless probe for technical solutions, environmental concerns and the satisfaction of complicated consumer expectations! In the interpretation of this theory, the following points should be cited:

1. Such an approach does not yield anything new and is similar to the theory of Daniel Yale/Bell 30 years ago on the end of ideologies and to Marxism's historical theory on reaching the final stage of human life (the End of History).
2. Fukuyama's view is indicative of the termination of historical narratives and the severe crisis of progress ideology and is based on the presumption that history has only a linear movement (linear expansion), whereas it revives in central, collective or meaningful forms.
3. The common point of communism and capitalism is a kind of imagination and futile thought and is about the prior importance of 'economy' in the hierarchy of basic human issues.
4. The defeat of communism has come about because of its weakness and not the strength of Western liberalism, yet it is not clear whether liberalism could have

resisted and become victorious when faced with a more powerful rival. Communism sacrificed freedom for equality. However, liberalism is faced with basic challenges that could push it towards annihilation.

Islamic revolution and the future world order

From the end of the 19th century Iran found itself in a precarious strategic situation, especially after it had been weakened following defeats in wars with Tsarist Russia, and was unable to resist the military, political and cultural assaults of hegemonic powers of that time; this situation continued up to the victory of the Islamic Revolution (1979).

Prior to World War I, Iran had been the scene of competition for influence between Britain and Tsarist Russia and between the two world wars it accepted the undisputed domination of Britain. Following World War II the US as the new superpower acted out its superior role in political and social developments in Iran. It is interesting to note that anti-imperialistic and anti-colonialist movements in Iran which took shape and became victorious at that time, such as the Constitutional Movement of 1906 or the Oil Nationalization Movement in 1950–1951, were not devoid of the interference and support of some foreign powers: in the Constitutional Movement, Britain supported the constitutionalists in order to gain more influence over Tsarist Russia, while in the Oil Nationalization Movement, the Americans supported the National Front in order to gain a share in Iranian oil.

The first spark of a movement independent of foreign influence was the Islamic Movement under the leadership of Imam Khomeini, which was formed in 1960–1961 during the peak of the Cold War and the unchallenged sovereignty of the bipolar system in the world. With these famous sentences: 'The US is worse than Britain; Britain is worse than the US; the Soviet Union is worse than both'[10] and, 'We are at war with international Communism to the same extent that we are at war with Western world mongers led by the US',[11] Imam Khomeini uttered his cry against the tyrannical world system as he saw it, a system that had considered the distribution of booty more important than serving the interests of other nations. In fact, the Islamic Movement was the first popular movement to rise up as the representative of oppressed people of the world, ignoring contradictions and rivalries among the world superpowers. The more interesting point is that both world superpowers as well as other big powers in the East and the West, despite their rivalries and hostilities that were only too obvious on the international scene, unanimously considered the Islamic Movement a 'reactionary move' and, especially after the uprising on 5 June 1963, condemned it and lined up against it.

With the Islamic Revolution reaching its climax in 1978–1979 and with its slogan of 'neither East, nor West, only an Islamic Republic', the movement continued its independent strategy, opposing the world hegemonic system. It triumphed at a time when no government in the world supported it, certainly not the major players of the time (which included the big Eastern and Western powers, including the Soviet Union and the People's Republic of China), who had upheld the dictatorial regime of the Shah.

This stance continued until the collapse of the Soviet Union, which brought with it the end of the Cold War, and especially during the war with Iraq, following its aggression against Iran – the main players of the hegemonic system still continued their confrontation with the Islamic Republic of Iran, fully supporting Iraq with all the political, military and economic means at their disposal.

With the collapse of the bipolar system and faced with the possibility of a new hierarchical unipolar system, the Islamic Revolution maintained its uncompromising stance vis-à-vis the status quo and was labelled as the first 'rogue' state in the new system. The US administration employed ceaseless efforts to punish Iran in order to prove its undeniable supremacy to the international community, through consolidating and stabilizing the newly institutionalized system it had created.

It seems that the theory of the Clash of Civilizations was not only an admission of the premature defeat of the unipolar system but an attempt to affect world public opinion and conceal the controversy that Imam Khomeini and the Islamic Revolution had exposed: highlighting the hegemonists, imperialists and colonialists against the plight of the dominated, oppressed, colonized and wronged nations and communities of the world. In brief, it was a confrontation between the oppressors and the oppressed throughout the world and the Islamic Revolution and the Imam, as the mastermind of this theory and supporter of the oppressed, took up the banner of this struggle and rose up against all world oppressors.

> The imperialists through their political agents who have become dominant over the people have imposed a tyrannical economic system as a result of which the people were divided into two groups, of oppressors and the oppressed ...[12]

In other words, the Islamic Revolution not only triumphed over the oppressive monarchical regime but launched a world movement for crushing the systems that had hitherto dominated the world by relying on vigilance and the uprising of the oppressed and tyrannized nations.

The Islamic Revolution, as a religious uprising, with its special worldview and its origins in the Islamic school of thought, acted not only in the national dimension with the revival of its special projects, plans and philosophy for the government and state officials but in the global dimension too, as the cosmopolitan nature of the Islamic school of thought has its own philosophy and offers its vocabulary. Like any revolution with its own specific goals, it carries with it its special concepts, terms and terminology, for example 'the oppressed', 'oppressors', 'the imperialist world' or 'sovereignty of the oppressed'. The Islamic Revolution and its leadership not only rejected the dominant views on international relations and the prevailing hegemonic system of the world, originating from the thoughts of Machiavelli, Hobbs and Hans Morgenthau, who considered moral obligation together with force, but moved towards the view that:

> Safety and peace in the world depends on the collapse of the oppressors; as long as uncultured hegemonists live on earth, the oppressed will not reach the

inheritance that Almighty God has bestowed upon them … Rule of the bare-footed is righteous.[13]

With the success of the Islamic Revolution and its awakening influence on Lebanese Shiites, a wave was created so that following the blasts at the US embassy and American military bases, France and Israel evacuated Beirut in 1982 and the last remnants of the Zionist forces withdrew from South Lebanon in 2000. The combatants of the Lebanese Islamic Resistance showed for the first time that by reliance on faith, jihad and martyrdom one could dominate the world hegemonic powers, at the same time demonstrating the inefficiency of Western hardware, ineffective against the newly emerging power of Islamic nations, no matter how small they may be in size.

Formation of two camps

With regard to what has been discussed – some of the events and developments in the world of Islam, the Third World and even the developed world, are indicative of the awakening and uprising of the popular masses and the blows dealt to the main players in the hegemonic system who had repeatedly failed in their confrontation with 'vigilant' nations – it could be stated that the reason for the long-lasting transition period following the Cold War and the lack of success of the big powers in the formation and stabilization of new systems compatible with their own philosophy, was a result of the emergence of new anti-hegemonic movements and subsequently the victory of the Islamic Revolution in Iran. Such movements have snowballed with an increasing velocity and all the efforts of the hegemonic powers at halting them have backfired, resulting in further authority and vigilance of the oppressed and tyrannized nations. Meanwhile, it has caused the hegemonists to plunge into even deeper quagmires of their own creation. Thus it could be asserted that the period of sovereignty of the Westphalia system has reached its end and the world will witness the turn of a new page in the history of international developments, bringing new criteria and standards in international relations:

1. The world community is witnessing a continuous trend in the formation of two opposite camps, one of which contains 'domineering governments' and their lackeys while the other includes nations, social groups and governments that have emerged from within the masses who have launched their struggle against the hegemonic system and are expanding its dimension. In other words, such a trend could be interpreted as an encounter between the two domineering and counter-domineering camps, each of which has its own characteristics and groupings, has created new definitions of international relations and seeks different goals.
2. While, in the domineering camp, players are trying to preserve the tyrannical and unjust Westphalia system and its rules of the game, the counter-domineering camp is trying to break the hegemonic system that has been in place for over one hundred years and explain to the world community new plans, goals and regulations of the game.

3.   The ideals and goals of these two camps have no similarities and are in serious confrontation and contradiction with each another, to such an extent that there is no possibility for reconciliation and compromise between them. In other words, any blow dealt to one of them will strengthen the status and power of the other.

Arrangement of forces and players

Domineering camp

In the aftermath of the Cold War and collapse of the Soviet Union in the transition period, the world is witnessing a new arrangement of the main players in the global scene among governments who are questioning the authority and motivation of the big powers. It could be claimed that the leadership of the hegemonic system in this era is in the hands of those who govern the United States, a country that enjoys both the dominant military might and has the required motive for being in such a position. In the meantime, there are other players who, despite having serious differences with the US, have accepted such provisions and agreed that the US government should be placed in the frontline of confrontation against the anti-domineering countries that pay the price in this new dispute. If the United States cannot undertake or is not capable of leading such a movement to confront this new process, no other country would volunteer to accept such a responsibility. In the event of the United States confessing to its inability or refusing to accept responsibility, the domineering camp would break up and thus strengthen the counter-domineering camp.

The second ring of the hegemonic camp comprises governments who are members of the European Union, especially those powers who enjoy the right of veto, such as Britain, France and, to some extent, Germany. Europe, considered the political, economic and cultural centre of the world in the 19th century, is now trying to present a unified identity in an effort to turn itself into a dynamic and active international body. Such a trend in the 1990s, following the collapse of the Soviet Union, has further expanded regional interaction in Europe; on the other hand, with the requirements of Cold War groupings having come to an end, the presence of Europe as an independent player has gained a new momentum.

In the next circle, non-Western developed governments, such as those of Russia, Japan and China, are observed. After the collapse of the socialist system, the Soviet Union once again joined Western society and in cultural terms considers itself a Western country. It expects European countries to accept it as part of Europe. However, the historical background of clashes with Russia over the years, the geographical position of that country – partly in Asia, partly in Europe – and its past capabilities, together with concerns over its ambitions, would leave no room for such a welcome on the part of European governments. As a result Russia, together with Japan and China, stands in the third circle of this camp.

In the next circle there are subservient governments who are among the developing nations and see their survival and sustainability in supporting and backing the domineering system and thus act like tools in the hands of the dominators.

Counter-domineering camp

In this camp both the conditions and the players are fundamentally different from those in the domineering camp. The foundation for movement into this camp is the uprising of the masses, who have been oppressed and colonized for centuries and have suffered injustice; people who favour peace and justice and, thanks to the development of communications and advancement of technology, are aware of the conditions of others in different societies; people who have harboured grudges against hegemonic governments and revolted against them and, thanks to the victories they have gained, have been encouraged to surpass fear and feel that there is the possibility at last for predominance and victory over the hegemonic system, even barehanded.

Today a serious convergence has been forged among all these people irrespective of racial, ethnic, religious and linguistic differences that are expressed in words and sentiments. With the speed of communications and development of public awareness, any possibility for deviation of thoughts and brainwashing of the masses through promotional and media bombardment have been removed and hegemonic systems are no longer capable of dragging the dominated masses towards warmongering goals while portraying their enemies as evil.

The Muslim Iranian nation, having launched this movement to defeat the hegemonic system, was naturally placed at the forefront of this great world movement. The Islamic Revolution did not only set its targets for the overthrow of its own tyrannical monarchical regime but from the very beginning held the banner of struggle and confrontation with the entire hegemonic and dictatorial world, under the title 'campaign against world imperialism and support for the world's oppressed'. It has been clearly stipulated in the Constitution of the IRI, inspired by the teachings of Islam, that Iran has the potential and actually has in its possession the required mechanism to lead such a global campaign against the present hegemonic system.

The world's Shiites constitute the second circle of this front, as Shi'ism itself originated from protest and confrontation with hegemonic systems. They are adherents of imams who never submitted to arrogant systems and generally sacrificed their lives in this way and attained martyrdom. The actual manifestation of this is crystallized in the historical uprising of Imam Hussein (AS) against the hegemonic system of the Umayyads, which not only provided a lesson in devotion and the sacrifice of lives, property and households to all those struggling for justice and freedom but set an example, not only for the Shiites, but for all Muslims and freedom-seekers of the world throughout history.

In the third circle of this front are located other Muslims of the world, numbering over 1 billion and living in an expansive area of three old continents, from Mauritius in the West to Indonesia in the East. They not only enjoy a special status from a strategic and geopolitical point of view but possess huge God-given sources of wealth, especially energy. In the light of the success of the Islamic Revolution in Iran, the Muslims of the world have attained a degree of vigilance and collective awareness that has set them on the path of not following Western culture and beliefs but in returning to their genuine Islamic beliefs and ideologies. All other

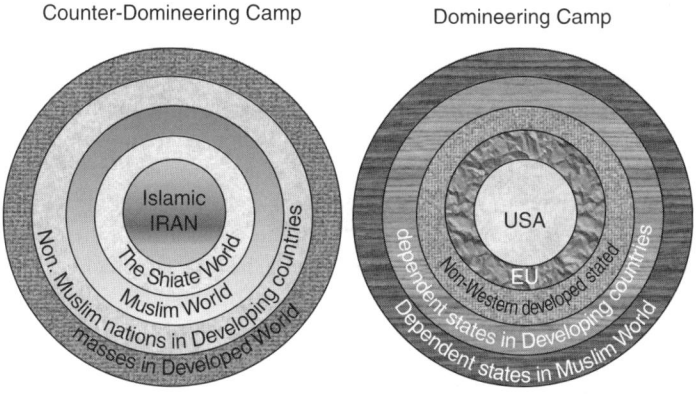

Counter-Domineering Camp   Domineering Camp

Figure 5.1 The formation of the clash with domination paradigm in two camps.

groups and liberation movements that were based on materialistic thoughts and ideas such as Marxism, socialism and liberalism have suffered a setback in the Islamic world and have been forced to close down their institutions and agencies. In the meantime, Islamic attitudes have developed and expanded rapidly, for seeing that Shi'ism was free from political and structural advantages, reforming movements have come to power within the framework of present systems and through the existing democratic process and thus have established the rule of Islamic laws and criteria. Despite the victory that Muslims gained in the elections in Algeria, they were harshly suppressed, but in Turkey, irrespective of confrontations, military intervention or efforts at coups, they have gradually taken hold of power by drawing on past experiences and are trying to increase their influence through carefully considered planning.

In the fourth circle of this front are the oppressed non-Muslim people of the Third World, nations who have tasted imperialism and the slavery of the hegemonic system throughout the past five centuries. Masses of people in Africa and Latin America will never forget the eras of slavery and imperialism and consider all their underdevelopment and misery to have originated from the oppressive and predatory policies of the 'civilized' West.

In the fifth circle are the masses of people in developed countries who are abused in order to satisfy the requirements of the hegemonic governments. The formation of these two camps can be observed in Figure 5.1.

Characteristics of the two camps

These two camps have fundamental differences and distinctions. In fact, it can be claimed that the distinctions of the two camps highlight deep contradictions and levels of irreconcilability that make any possibility of reconciliation, peace and compromise between the two not only difficult but impossible. What is considered by one side as of value is certainly not so for the other side; what is right for one side is false for the other; each goal one side pursues is in contradiction to the goals of the other. Such contradictions have produced different and, in some instances, contradictory definitions in common understandings in both international relations and political sciences; fundamentally they stand opposed to one another.

The domineering system believes that right is accompanied by force and maintains that the one who is powerful is righteous as well. This belief reaches the point where gaining power becomes the target – to the extent that in their definition of man they go as far as describing him as one having an inherent passion for insatiable power. They have based their school of thought, called realism, on such pillars and have managed to lay the foundations of the hegemonic system throughout history. They bring all living creatures under the domain of their power under this tyrannical title. They proceed in this direction, considering governments to be the representative of their power or, in other words, the power itself. Thus they regard politics as a science of power and equivalent to the science of government.

Yet those among the counter-domineering group and the oppressed consider 'right' to denote respect for human dignity, justice, kind treatment, mutual assistance, equity and fraternity.

Ideologies hailing from the West that are built on materialistic foundations have generally aimed at justifying the hegemonic system and even if they have experienced confrontations with some form of hegemony, nevertheless they are still aimed at substituting a different kind of hegemony. The West, like the Italian Renaissance writer Machiavelli, considers politics to be based on hypocrisy, dissimulation, deception and immorality and does not refrain from expressing such views. The politics of power, or realpolitik, have been built on this foundation. As a result, political, social, economic and cultural relations have evolved according to such principles and, therefore, there are no grounds for establishing such relations on the basis of sincerity and transparency together with ingenuity.

Warmongering is an inherent habit of hegemonists; they set about it with three objectives in mind. It is either for the expansion of the realm of their power, for competition with the hegemony of their rivals or for obtaining yet more reserves and interests to further enhance the men of power and wealth. Yet those fighting against hegemony in the counter-domineering group do so on the basis of new values, compatible with their human and theistic nature and are in serious confrontation with the values of the hegemonists. In this camp the oppressed masses have right on their side; power belongs to these people, for their beliefs and faiths are based on human dignity and are superior to the military might of the other camp. Social, political and economic relations are defined on the basis of justice, close association, affection and serving those who are oppressed. Wealth and natural resources are considered to belong to all human beings and goals of campaign have been determined for the liberation of the masses from oppressors and monopolists. It wholeheartedly welcomes devotion, sacrifice and faithfulness for the Divine cause and for the sake of humanity and serving ones fellow creatures. It considers revolt against oppressors and resistance against violators its own duty. Fear, frailty, turning one's back on the enemy and escaping from the war fronts have no place in this camp.

In summing up, it can be said that confrontation between the camp of the domineering and that of those fighting against hegemony, the counter-domineering group, is like playing the zero-sum game, that is to say what one side is losing the other side will gain, and what one is winning the other will lose.

Prospect of a clash with the domination paradigm

Although the camp of the domineering is equipped with special attributes, given its background and performance during past centuries, its internal and external actions and reactions are understandable and predictable for the world community. However, the camp of those fighting against domination is in its early stages of formation and has a long way to go in order to become more consolidated and be accepted by the world community. Of course accelerating elements should not be forgotten. The developments already mentioned have created the serious belief among world nations that new players who are powerful on the international scene have a role to play and could heal the old wounds sustained during the imperialist and colonialist era through resistance, steadfastness and forgiveness and deal blows to the strong hegemonic system. Any effort made by the hegemonic system to confront this world movement and to strengthen and stabilize its own stance has produced the opposite result: it has been forced to leave its aggressive plans unfinished and has thus failed.

The development of communications and the wide access to media networks with their massive information and speedy data transfer have adversely affected any promotional policies and one-sided arguments propagated out by the hegemonic system. The previous Western monopoly over the mass media today, through multiple and non-monopoly satellite channels or the Internet, has confined the area of activity for the media monopolists to such an extent that in order to keep their viewers and listeners some of them are forced, however reluctantly, to transmit the world messages of their enemies: remarks made by such people as Dr Ahmadinejad (IRI president) or Seyed Hassan Nasrallah (leader of the Lebanese Hezbollah) who generally attack the West.

Islamic thoughts and ideologies as a school of campaign are swiftly expanding. Given that Islam promotes fraternity, affection, peace and friendship irrespective of race, nationality and colour and given that many societies are fed up with war, bloodshed, injustice, hostility and enmity, they are open to receiving the message of this righteous religion. The great expansion of Islam in recent years has caused concern and is seen as a threat by the West, which seeks to spread Islamophobia or misrepresent Islam as being synonymous with terrorism. However, this serves to attract the attention of more people to this life-enhancing school of thought.

As the bonds between popular governments and the masses become strengthened, unified and consolidated, fronts form for defending themselves and confronting any extravagance on the part of the hegemonists. The relationships within these

Muslim communities are not only stabilized on the basis of common interests but also on affection and convergence, terms that have no meaning in materialistic terminology. The influence of Islamic Iran on those fighting against hegemony is being further expanded and accepted by other nations, and as a pioneering and progressive country Iran is attracting the attention of most Muslim and non-Muslim nations as an applicable model and pattern.

Governments in both the Muslim and the Third World that are subservient to the hegemonic system are likely to become pressurized by their citizens and be forced to finally either surrender to the will of their people and gradually delegate power to them or face uprisings and popular revolutions, while the hegemonic system would gradually lose power in supporting them.

Generally speaking, it could be said that hegemonists would be faced with three types of challenges and confrontations in this era:

1. Differences and a clash of interests among hegemonic governments, which would continue as they would not reach agreement over the division of interests in the world community over the limitation of resources and competition for access to them, and each would try to gain a better status and more benefits. Of course, such contradictions and challenges would not result in an armed confrontation among them.

2. With regard to the growing awareness of the masses within the hegemonic countries, not only has their mobilization by a one-sided propaganda effort favoured by their governments become more difficult, but ever-increasing serious bottlenecks have been created preventing the implementation of their aggressive policies, which result in the defeat of their ruling governments – as has already been witnessed in Spain, Italy, Britain and the US.

3. The extension of resistance against hegemony, accompanied by the overthrow of lackey governments and their replacements by more popular ones, would increasingly present the hegemonic system with serious challenges, which could well drive them to extremes.

     Therefore, it is predicted that the hegemonic system would not be able to simultaneously confront these three types of challenges and would gradually lose influence, and that a day will come when nations celebrate the absolute victory of the counter-domineering camp – of course at a high cost – and this would be the realization of Almighty God's promise, as has been expressed by the late Imam Khomeini.

Since the beginning of the Islamic Movement and especially after the victory of the Islamic Revolution, Imam Khomeini used to make references in his remarks and writings to an appropriate world system in the eyes of Islam and the Islamic Revolution. Being inspired by those materials, we have defined the framework for such a system:

1. Contrary to Marxists who believe in the constraints of history and consider sovereignty of the labouring class an inevitable event, Imam Khomeini

believed that only through vigilance and awareness can the oppressed attain their rights and become victorious.

> The oppressed should rise up against the oppressors; the oppressed people in all cities and countries should gain their rights with clenched fists and should not wait for the restoration of their rights, as the oppressors would not give anyone their rights.[14]

2. While the awareness and general uprising of the oppressed for gaining their sovereignty over the world is necessary and inevitable, by relying on verses of the Holy Quran he feels that their victory is certain and definite.

> You the oppressed nations of the world, rise up and attain your rights and do not fear the brawling of the powers, as God is with you and the earth is your inheritance and God's promise could not be violated.[15]

3. Preservation of the safety and revival of world peace is neither dependent on the establishment of the balance of power nor other systems on offer by Western scientists and policymakers: it is only possible through the destruction and defeat of the hegemonic powers.

> This movement of the oppressed against the oppressors should be expanded throughout the world. Iran is the starting point, the ultimate destination and pattern for all the oppressed nations in all parts of the world; Muslims should rise up, even the oppressed should rise up. God's promise embodies the oppressed and He says He would grant his mercy to them to make them leaders and inheritors in the world. Leadership is the right of the oppressed. Inheritance is the right of the oppressed. The oppressors are usurpers. The oppressors should be expelled from the scene.[16]

4. The oppressed are not confined to the Muslim or the Third World nations but are the masses that live under tyranny and imperialism throughout the world, whether under Eastern or Western oppressors. Therefore, neither geographical and cultural factors nor nation-state classifications could be considered as demarcations between the oppressed and the oppressors. Therefore, the theory of the Clash of Civilizations or clash of cultures or even world polarization merely serve to perpetuate the present system of hegemony over the oppressed, or competition and contradiction among the oppressed in distributing resources and coloniz-ing and oppressing different societies and nations of the world.

> You should know that people (of the world) even those nations who are not Divine, are all part of the oppressed of the world who have always remained under the domination of the oppressors.[17]
> Both the superpowers are prepared to destroy the oppressed nations and we should support the world oppressed; Islam makes no difference

between Muslim or non-Muslim countries and is a supporter of all the oppressed in the world.[18]

5. Contrary to former systems, which had been formed on the basis of secularist and humanistic thoughts and were promoting enjoyment, pleasure and consumerism as patterns for a satisfactory life, this system is based on a return to religion and the sovereignty of God, and considers a prosperous life to be one devoted to further commitment to establishing justice, piety, ethical rule and spiritual and divine beliefs, thus negating the whimsical and wealth-plundering culture practiced by the oppressors.
6. Muslims in general and the Muslim people of Iran in particular, who have been able to triumph over oppression for the first time, thanks to the life-giving and educating philosophy of Islam, have been bestowed with the role of guiding this immense world, and bringing about the rise and expansion of the Islamic Revolution in line with the world struggle against oppression and support for the oppressed.

> God willing, with the expansion of the Islamic Revolution of Iran, diabolic powers would be driven to isolation and the rule of the oppressed would prepare the ground for the world sovereignty of Mahdi (may God hasten his reappearance), the last of all.[19]

Conclusion

What is evident in the writings and theories of Huntington, Zbigniew Brzezinski or other Western theoreticians, is that the theories and planning of the domineering powers still preserve their domination over the world. Meanwhile, out of their theories a halo of concern is obvious from the growing awareness of the oppressed nations of the world, signalling further unity and consolidation, free from any type of cultural, racial and religious differences in their confrontation with hegemonic and imperialist governments.

Therefore, it could be predicted that in the 21st century the world community, after passing through a transitional period, would enter a new era not resembling any of the past, and that would be the formation of two camps. In one of the camps oppressive powers with all their military and economic capabilities would be present, while in the other camp the oppressed nations, especially the oppressed Third World nations under the leadership of vigilant and aware Muslims of the world, would rise up and bring the oppressors to their knees.

Although the oppressor governments enjoy outstanding military and economic means and potential, they are forced to enter into a relentless struggle with the vigilant and aware masses, for all their might would be of no avail for God has promised the final victory will go to the oppressed who are the inheritors of the earth.

> We have placed the people who were oppressed as inheritors of the East and the West of the Earth.[20]

Notes

1 Thomas Cohen, *Structure of Scientific Revolution*, translation by Ahmad Aram, Soroush Publications, 1990.
2 Therese Baker, *What is Science? A Prelude to Schools of the Philosophical Study of Sciences*, translation by Saeed Ziba Kalam, Scientific and Cultural Publications, 1995.
3 Kaplan, M., *System and Process in International Relations*, New York: John Wiley, 1977.
4 William Bridges, *Passages*, Press Quality Progress, April 1997.
5 The framework for the new unipolar system was provided for the US in the event of the occupation of Kuwait by Iraq: the US could, by resorting to aggression, prepare the ground for the implementation of the new system under its leadership. Although Saddam's government, prior to the American invasion in the Second Persian Gulf War, had announced its readiness to withdraw from Kuwait, the US paid no attention and launched its war through aerial and surface attacks. The costs of the war were undertaken by the oil-rich Persian Gulf states and some Western European countries as well as Japan.
6 For further information on the world systems, see Mohammadi, M., 'The New World Order' in volume 28 of the publication of the Faculty of Law and Political Sciences of Tehran University (November–December, 1992).
7 These civilizations include Western, Confucian, Islamic, Indian, Slavic, Orthodox, Latin American and, on the sidelines, African.
8 Samuel P. Huntington, 'The Clash of Civilizations', *Foreign Affairs*, (summer 1993).
9 The deputy of Japanese origin at the US Foreign Ministry for Political Planning, summer 1989.
10 *Sahife Noor*, vol. 1, p. 105.
11 Ibid., vol. 12, p. 19.
12 Imam Khomeini, *Velayat Faqih* (Rule of the Jurisprudent), Kaveh Publications, Tehran, p. 42.
13 *Sahife Noor*, vol. 11, p. 262.
14 Ibid., vol. 11, p. 259.
15 Ibid., vol. 15, p. 212.
16 Ibid., vol. 6, p. 168.
17 Ibid., vol. 15, p. 213.
18 Ibid., vol. 12, p. 19.
19 *We are in Search of the Way*, from the Imam's remarks, p. 15.
20 *Qessass Surah*, verse 5.

6 Transnational culture and international relations of Iran

Mohammad Javad Nateghpour

Introduction

International relations are a product of transnational culture, which plays an important role in the evolution of global society. Transnational culture brings people together from all parts of the world without any national, ethnical and religious boundaries, thereby encouraging relationships between diverse groups of people. The transnational influence of many different cultures and the resulting cultural cross-pollination has prompted many countries to take into account the identity provided by 'transnational culture' in order to close the gap between expatriates and people living in their home countries.

Despite the efforts of Iranians to present themselves positively on the global stage, it seems that the international policies of the Iranian government have not been as successful in fostering cultural traffic between itself and other countries. Consequently, there is a lack of effective engagement with transnational culture within Iranian foreign policy. This has resulted in many ambiguities not only for those outside Iran trying to understand its political policies and actions, but it has also created a vacuum in the minds of the new generations of Iranians living abroad regarding the socio-political, economic and cultural situation of Iran.

Given this context, several questions arise. To what extent do we appreciate the effect/presence of our culture at the international level? Does it still make sense to talk about Iranian culture on a global scale? To what extent is 'transnational culture' a focus of contemporary Iranian foreign policy? And last but not least, to what extent does Islam encourage global relations and the growth of transnational culture? The answers to these questions lie in the explanation of the following sub-questions that form the basis of the content of this chapter.

- Does the 'transnational culture' exist?
- How does 'transnational culture' change society on a global scale?
- To what extent has 'transnational culture' played a role in Iranian foreign policy?

Transnationalism: an overview

During recent decades, the concept of 'transnationalism' has occupied a crucial place within the terminology of the social sciences, particularly in the lexicon of immigration studies and also the new migrant communities that have been developing rapidly in Western industrial countries.[1] The study of immigration has produced some important work such as Randolph Silliman Bourne's (1886–1918)[2] early work on the subject and Ann Lambton's *Qatar Persia* (1912–2008).[3] The latter describes immigration in Iran during the 19th century. There are some theories which suggest that the root of 'transnationalism' is the worldwide economic system of corporate capitalism. The rise and development of capitalism has resulted in significant changes within socio-cultural, political and economic realms leading to the emergence of transnational NGOs and dual citizenship in a 'post-national' era.[4] It is said that the term 'transnationalism' has emerged and evolved during a period of mass migration in which migrants have left various less developed countries (LDCs) to live in more developed countries.[5] It has also been asserted that the massive wave of political immigrants from communist and Third World countries towards Western liberal and democratic societies should be considered another cause of the emergence of 'transnationalism'. Schiller and Basch believe that transnationalism is a product of world capitalism.[6]

Peter Kivisto criticizes some understanding of transnationalism by examining the use of the term itself, particularly to describe and analyse new immigrant identities and communities. According to Kivisto the term transnationalism is widely used by three groups of social scientists, each with a different understanding of what it signifies. Kivisto identifies anthropologists as the first group to promote the concept of transnationalism.[7]

In the second group there are some notable sociologists who have used this term to describe the second generation of migrants in a host society. The third group, which represents the most recent usage of transnationalism, is comprised of political scientists who have used the term 'transnational culture' to describe the political situation of migrants in new societies and their relationship with politics in their country of origin.[8]

Immigration: past and present

Historically, some scholars such as Basch *et al.* (2000) have found notable differences between past and present generations of immigrants. They consider the earlier generations of immigrants to have broken off all social relations and cultural ties to their countries of origin, locating themselves within the socio-cultural, economic and political circulation of their host society.[9]

In contrast, 'today's immigrants are distinguished by their networks, activities and patterns of life, encompassing both their host and home societies. Their lives cut across national boundaries and bring two societies into a single social field.'[10] Kivisto asserts: 'From this historical comparison, Glick Schiller *et al.* offer a rationale for a new analytic framework, making a case for the introduction of two new terms: "transnationalism" and "transmigrants". The former refers to "the process by which immigrants build social fields that link together their country of origin and their country of settlement", while the latter refers to the "immigrants who build such social fields" by maintaining a wide range of affective and instrumental social relationships spanning borders.'[11]

Despite the difference emphasized between the two types of immigrants by Schiller *et al*, other scholars consider such ideas dubious and have suggested dramatic similarities between both kinds of migrants, such as a common interest in saving the culture of their homeland.[12]

Cultural exchanges

Basch *et al*. believe that the new generations of migrants bring positive benefits not only to the inhabitants of their countries of origin, but also to the inhabitants of the countries in which they settle. These benefits are derived from the migrants' ability to influence friends and relatives who have remained in their homeland, and also the impact they have on economic and political decisions in their host society. Basch *et al*. also point out that homeland governments are particularly happy to accommodate expatriate communities when they are economically beneficial.[13]

The cultural phenomenon of transnationalism should be seen as an alternative to assimilation or cultural pluralism. This notion also confirms that 'assimilation' denotes the adoption of a second national identity for migrants who are interested in using the socio-economic and political opportunities of a host country in connection with their homeland. Additionally, ethnicity and race are important determinants regarding the assimilation of an immigrant into a new society.[14]

'Cultural pluralism' should also be considered one of the most significant factors in fostering cultural relations between immigrants and the populations of host societies. 'Cultural pluralism' can refer to the structural and cultural tenacity of ethnic groups that determines new forms of social relationship between migrants and their host society. The terms 'assimilation and cultural pluralism' both signify long-term socio-cultural cooperation and the social evolution of a host society.[15]

Early migrants frequently sought connections with their host society in order to secure benefits and advantages for themselves. Recent generations have a greater appreciation of, and inclination towards social cooperation, as means of identifying and protecting mutual interests within a diverse society, particularly with regards to establishing and maintaining links between their countries of origin and their host society. With particular reference to the notion of cultural transnationalism, it is possible to say that earlier immigrants underwent a process of assimilation, while the new generation of immigrants is representative of integration within a more pluralistic society. This, some suggest, is why the early generations of migrants were so conservative in exhibiting their culture, in comparison with the new generations of immigrants.[16]

Politically, migrants have retained significant involvement in their countries of origin. Many immigrants aspire to return to their homeland having accumulated substantial wealth in their host country.[17] Indeed, for those immigrants who accrue sufficient wealth in their adopted countries, returning home is often the first choice, particularly from middle age onwards.

Kivisto believes that Portes was one of the pioneers in expanding the term 'transnationalism' through his studies on post-1960 American immigration. According to Kivisto, Portes provided a new understanding of the different ethnic groups living in America as immigrants, and in particular their involvement in business and other economic activities. Portes also used the term 'second generation' instead of 'immigrant generation' to describe the new generation of immigrants.[18]

Kivisto draws attention to the three different types of transnationalism that Portes identified: economic, political and socio-cultural. Economic transnationalism involves entrepreneurs whose network of suppliers, capital and markets crosses national borders. Kivisto asserts that Portes' formulation ignores members of the professional middle class – the so-called 'brain drain' immigrants.[19] This type of immigrant is an important component of many contemporary migrant communities. Kivisto also believes that this imperfect definition limits the number of migrants whose economic activities can be considered transnational.[20]

Political transnationalism focuses on involvement in political activities either as party officials or governmental staff; community leaders whose main goals are to achieve political power may also have significant influence in their countries of origin and their host countries. The socio-cultural aspect is the third type of transnationalism that Portes asserts relates to activities oriented towards the enforcement of national identity abroad or the collective enjoyment of cultural events and phenomena. In this regard the terms 'national identity' and 'ethnic identity' are considerably important. Because, by analysing these terms, it might be possible to establish a framework for improving the relationship of immigrants with the countries they have left and those to which they migrate.[21]

It is noteworthy that new immigrants seek to retain ties with their homeland. This might sometimes affect the decision of immigrants to refuse to become a citizen of their host society or at least to give preference to dual citizenship.

Steven Vertovec describes the concept of transnationalism in socio-cultural and political terms such as: social morphology focusing on the new types of social formation; diasporas of consciousness; various modes of cultural reproduction; an avenue of capital for transnational corporations; the form of remittances sent by immigrants to family and friends in their homelands; a site of political engagement both in terms of homeland politics and the politics of homeland governments vis-à-vis their émigré communities, and in terms of the expanded role of international non-governmental organizations; and a reconfiguration of the notion of place from an emphasis on the local to the translocal.[22]

Culture and transnationalism

The term transnationalism encompasses component concepts such as 'transnational culture'; this term has been used to describe global diasporic communities and their role in reducing the cultural gap between host and origin societies which began in the early twentieth century and has been a remarkable phenomenon in global politics during the last two decades. However, the concept of transnational culture remains indistinct within contemporary public discourse and remains open to various interpretations. Williams states that 'the concept of culture is fascinating but often puzzling because it has been used in several distinctive ways'.[23] He suggests that the way to remove this ambiguity is to demonstrate the process by which the meaning of culture has changed over time.[24]

Chaney tries to remove any ambiguities from the definition of culture by focusing on the relationship between culture and everyday life. He points out that 'although the term culture, used in its sense of a way of life as well as the content of libraries, museums, galleries and so on, has become one of the common terms of descriptions of social life, it has retained a quality of privilege'.[25] He goes on to say that 'it is through culture that everyday life is given meaning and significance'.[26]

Chaney suggests that changes in the meaning of the term 'culture' and the gap between modern and traditional cultures is in part the result of mass communications industries, which profoundly affect the nature of a culture. Chaney states that 'a loss of faith in traditional order and values intensified for many intellectuals as it became apparent that new industries of masses communication and entertainment would increasingly threaten traditional forms of stratification between elites and the masses'.[27]

In order to clarify the meaning of culture, Hall refers to the ideas of Harper (1987), Biggart (1989), Denison (1990) and Meyer and Scott (1992) suggesting that each microcosm within a society consists of its own unique culture, therefore 'a broad approach is necessary because, for example, businesses have their own distinctive cultures of the office, the shop, the enterprise'.[28] Hall explains that culture within an economic framework encourages people to look beyond national boundaries. He points out that 'culture has become an important product of economic activity and an important source of jobs'.[29] The notion of culture also extends beyond this framework and is important in the realms of business and politics. This provides a new understanding of the significance and functions of culture within a society. Hall believes 'if we must recognise the cultural aspects of politics and business, the politics and business of culture also seem important'.[30] Referring to Mills (1959), Hall describes the relationship between politics and culture as being more specifically a relationship between power and culture, and points out as a result that 'even in the United States in the years after Mills wrote seem to have confirmed his views about the relationship between culture and power'.[31]

Hall offers the following understanding of culture 'culture is more than a set of artefacts, codes or signs to be catalogued by cultural archaeologists of our own era. Culture gets produced, one way or another, and at least some of it come into our times in ways that may change our experience and how we live.'[32]

Geertz also sought to clarify the ambiguous meaning of the term 'culture'; he defines culture as 'historically transmitted pattern of meaning embodied in symbols, a system of inherited conceptions expressed in symbolic forms by means of which men communicate, perpetuate, and develop their knowledge about and attitudes towards life'.[33]

Culture is a key concept for Geertz when describing a social system. He accepts that a 'cultural system' provides shared meaningful symbols by which various social actors communicate.[34] In this regard culture plays a crucial role in constructing and preserving the history of a society and also in facilitating the integration of past and present generations of a society. This practical function helps in understanding the significance of transnational culture and its function in social policy.

Norms and values are key concepts in understanding transnational culture. In order to close the cultural gap between societies, norms and values play a crucial role. A culture's norms and values reflect the dynamic relationship between a host society's culture and that of its immigrant community. Any foreign policy that fails to consider these key factors would be forced to confront socio-cultural barriers on a global scale. Parsons explored the role of norms and values in social communications and as essential elements of a social system. Norms and values are represented in social conduct and communications as well as cultural heritage. As Parsons suggests, norms and values should be considered the essential nucleus of a society.[35]

Culture has long been considered the main tool with which to analyse social change and movement. This important position makes culture extremely important in policymaking at an international level. Long believes that culture has been the main preoccupation of sociologists in studying the modern world. She points out that 'Sociology has been centrally, if ambivalently, concerned with culture from the field's inception. Both responses seem conditioned by the context of sociology's formation in the crucible of the "great transformation" of modernity in the west.'[36] Long also emphasizes culture as the core element in social change and points out that 'culture has been crucial in accounting for social change, whether explaining the pull of tradition, or the emergence of new forms of social life and new register of social experience'.[37]

The importance of culture in social analysis is emphasized by the fact that Marx, Durkheim and Weber based their work on the platform of culture; as Long states 'Marx's analysis of ideology, consciousness, and commodity fetishism, Weber's concern with the values of traditionalism and the gradual emergence of a more "rational" religious validation of this – worldly asceticism (the Protestant Ethic), and Durkheim's discussion of anomie and collective representations, register the attempt of early social thinkers to grasp various aspects of what we would call culture.'[38]

Transnational culture and beyond

Skelton and Allen suggest three reasons for conceiving of the modern world as truly 'global', these are summarized as 1) the lack of any alternative way of representing the whole world, 2) the need to describe worldwide events and processes, 3) world integration.[39] Some scholars believe that a substantive effect of globalization will be to gradually reduce localization; these scholars suggest that the process of globalization will lead to the dominance of global capitalism, as 'transnational corporations' take the place of national integration, and the consequent decline of the power of nation-states. That is why the idea of globalization has been criticized by some scholars.[40] Meanwhile, Cvetkovich and Kellner believe that 'global' and 'local' are both cultural constructs and should be discussed and developed in the context of cultural development. They assert that 'is important to note that both the global and the local are cultural constructs and thus subject to discussion, debate, and development'.[41]

The slogan 'think globally, act locally' promotes a *glocal* outlook that combines 'global and local' to suggest a practical conceptual framework for immigrants who retain strong cultural links to their homeland. Ferguson believes that everybody is local. However, some are more local than the others. He points out 'even if it is true that all social processes are in some sense "local", it is also clear that, in normal anthropological practice, some problems, some research settings, even some people, seem to be more "local" than others. Unsurprisingly, it is the least "developed" who are generally understood to be the most "local".'[42]

It is important to understand that there are commonalities in human society that provide a platform for all peoples to engage in dialogue relating to their common interests, in relation to common aspects of national and local identities. This kind of dialogue is vital to the smooth functioning of our diverse global community.

Dialogue among civilizations: culture and international relations

After a long cold war between Iran and the USA, which caused a lot of political and economic difficulties for Iran, it was surprising that reformist president Khatami could change the international attitude towards Iran from mutual intimidation to mutual respect. Khatami believed in a transnational culture that was to be created gradually through the establishment of a new cultural and political platform within the international arena vis-à-vis Iran. His first major step in this direction was the doctrine of Dialogue among Civilizations,[43] which was a response to Huntington's dominant Clash of Civilizations paradigm.[44] The idea soon received a warm welcome from politicians and social theorists; particularly intellectuals and politicians who desired greater global integration, peace and friendship. Khatami's initiative was a direct challenge to Huntington's theory.[45] This was the first time after the Islamic Revolution of 1979 that a political leader encouraged politicians and intellectuals worldwide to revise their understanding of the Islamic Republic of Iran and also Iranian people.

Khatami expounded an Iranian foreign policy based on transnationalism; he was certain that transnational culture was capable of integrating both the parent and adopted societies of Iranians abroad. In fact, he encouraged Iranian migrants to develop a peaceful relationship between Iranian and Western societies and cultures. Therefore his foreign policy emphasis on subjects such as human rights, international peace and friendship, joint scientific and academic endeavours, and interfaith dialogues, must be regarded as the embodiment of the Dialogue among Civilizations that he promoted.[46]

Given the number of Iranians living abroad, the concept of 'transnational culture' should be used to provide a bridge between national identity and the culture of adopted societies by Iranians who live abroad permanently; this is particularly important for the generations born and raised outside Iran. The scale and speed of migrants leaving Iran during last three decades confirms a significant change in

Iranian society; it is no exaggeration to say that almost every Iranian family has one relative living as a migrant abroad.[47] In this context, it is vital to consider the role of 'transnational culture' in Iranian foreign policy.

Immigration and rapid communication technologies such as the Internet and satellite technologies have affected the speed of information diffusion and gradually changed the nature and meaning of private and public spheres. This transformation is evident in the cultural realm as well as economic and political areas. In the economic sphere transnational trade was the logical consequence of transnationalism, while in the political arena the foreign policy of numerous nations had to evolve accordingly. It is inevitable today that international policy must adjust to the exigencies of transnationalism. For example, about 6 million Iranians are living outside of the country, but are nevertheless capable of participation in the socioeconomic and political development of the motherland.[48] To take advantage of this influential diaspora it is necessary to understand the new global language represented by 'transnational culture'.

Today, new generations of Iranian migrants living abroad are in a position to combine the two cultures of their homeland and adopted societies in order to create a new culture beyond national and ethical boundaries, which consists of both national and international culture. This is, as Tomlinson asserts, a 'transnational culture'. He points out that transnational culture is a new form of global culture that closes gaps between nations by creating new global relations without any national, geographical, ideological and political boundaries.[49]

Tomlinson refers to 'global culture' as a new form of international culture which plays a crucial role in bringing nations together. Global culture could also be considered as an application of the idea of Dialogue among Civilizations. However, as well as 'transnational culture' there is another term, 'globalized culture', which has been used in the political sphere. 'Globalized culture' refers to a new culture that contains no sign of the national cultures of immigrants. In other words, while 'global culture' encourages migrants to retain their own national cultures while adapting to their host society's culture, 'globalized culture' tries to introduce a dominant universal culture without any consideration for local and national cultures.

Despite the idea of 'globalised culture' there exists an alternative paradigm of societal and cultural interaction that emphasizes cultural exchange. Instead of the limitations of 'west and the rest' the global approach advocates the concept of 'us amongst others' as the essential foundation of 'transnational culture'. This concept paves the way for global cultural participation, which is needed to facilitate understanding between nations today.

Thus, as Tomlinson points out, global culture is an opportunity for all cultures in the world to orientate themselves in a global context. As a result, 'global culture' will lead to cultural interdependency and mutually beneficial relationships between cultures, encouraging equal opportunities and also emphasizing the common ground between various cultures instead of highlighting their differences. This notion will provide opportunities for different cultures to develop a mutual understanding of democracy, human rights, social norms and values. Therefore, 'transnational culture' is a productive means to close gaps between nations by creating new global relations without any racial, national, geographical, ideological or political boundaries.

Transnational culture: obstacles and impediments

Historically, globalized culture is an extension of the 18th-century Eurocentric world, the outlook that believes in dichotomous divisions of culture in the world: West and the rest. This idea emphasizes 'cultural hegemony, national boundaries and exclusive culture' in one hemisphere, and 'cultural isolation' in the other.[50] In fact, Eurocentrism sees Western culture as the only cultural example that all non-Western nations and societies should take into account with reference to their own societies. This idea has been one of the main obstacles to mutual cultural exchange during last two centuries. Such ideas have also contributed to the misunderstanding of 'modernization' as 'Westernization', which Turner and Hulme pointed out.[51]

Transnational culture raises an important question concerning national identities: To what extent will transnational culture lead to the demise of people's national identities? In order to explore this question, it is necessary to appreciate that transnational culture is essentially dualistic, consisting as it does of national and international identities. This character has led to the creation of 'global' culture, a combination of the words 'global' and 'local', which acknowledges the dual identity of transnational culture.

The cross-cultural relationships that define transnational culture enable it to accommodate and resolve potential confrontations between different cultures. Toleration of culture allows the modification of a nation in loose harmony with others, making possible the integration and coexistence of various nations and different ethnic groups. Additionally, a pluralistic identity facilitates the understanding of different cultures by a nation. This quality of transnational culture enables a 'humanistic' approach to alien cultures instead of an approach based on its 'racial and ethnic' identity.

Despite the need for politicians to understand transnational culture, there are still some barriers that lead to clashes between cultures and civilizations instead of dialogue among them. For instance, the humiliation of other cultures, through the exposure and questioning of their most fundamental taboos, such as the case of the Danish cartoon depicting the prophet Mohammad, and also so-called 'Islamophobia', which presents Islam as a threat to the world. This sort of conduct, which vilifies a particular culture and presents it primarily as a threat to other cultures, should be considered to be one of the main obstacles to the development of transnational culture.

The consequence of such actions will be to push the harassed culture to defend itself, and this will potentially amplify threats such as war, restrictions on the movement of natural and human resources and also civilizational clashes. Such approaches also lead to 'cultural resistance' instead of 'cultural tolerance'. In addition to the obstacles mentioned, it is important to consider xenophobia as another impediment to transnational culture. Xenophobia will lead to the externalizing of internal problems, and the location of their supposed triggers in external factors/ cultures. This sort of thinking on culture will increase profound misunderstanding between different cultures, a factor responsible for much of the current cultural hostility in the world. The dichotomy coined by George W. Bush that you are 'either with us or against us' also increased cross-cultural antagonism.

I suggest that the reasons already mentioned are adequate to encourage policy-makers to consider global culture as the basis of foreign policy. This is particularly relevant to contemporary Iranian foreign policy, given the approximately 6 million Iranian migrants in the world today.

Culture and new wave: Iran in a global world

Many post-revolution events in Iran, including the vast protests of Iranians living abroad following the result of the last presidential election in Iran, once again confirmed the remarkable role of Iranian migrants in the political realm, and in the social movements of their homeland. A brief glance at Persian weblogs, Iranian Internet sites and also Iranian media abroad, highlights the importance of Iranian migrants in closing the gap between their adopted societies and their homeland. This relationship is acknowledged by the government of Iran, who allocate five TV channels of the Islamic Republic Broadcasting organization to Iranian expatriates. In addition, the government has planned annual official gatherings, with selected Iranian migrants being invited to stay in Iran for a week and discuss topical issues relating to the country.

Trade, and the economic and cultural activities of Iranians living abroad, has motivated the Iranian government to keep in touch with migrants for political purposes. However, there is still a degree of ambiguity concerning the relationship of the Iranian government with Iranians living abroad. For example, due to the rapid turnover of Iranian officials and the resulting disconnection between the outgoing officials and those who enter office in their place, there is no stable and long-term Iranian foreign policy; despite this, reformist president Khatami focused on Iran's international relations, leading to a more prominent position for Iran following the revolution of 1979.

During Khatami's presidency many Iranian expatriates were attracted to partici-pate in Iranian development programmes.[52] Furthermore, because of his peaceful programmes and conduct on an international level, the integration of migrants opposed to the government gradually declined and many began to reassess their opinion of the Iranian government.

In particular, Khatami and his reformists tried to promote the positive aspects of Islamic civilization[53] and specifically Shi'ism as a peaceful and tolerant school of Islamic thought, which seeks a more secure and cooperative existence for all the people of the world through respect for others based on the humanistic, pluralistic and tolerant socio-cultural and political principles of Islam.[54]

The reformist approach of engagement with the modern world stems from its interpretation of Islam, which directly affects its decision-making and socio-political and cultural planning. For example, the radical interpretation of Islam that informs the current political conservatism in Iran normally neglects to consider global culture in international relations. In order to understand this interpretation, it is necessary to compare the two kinds of Islamic interpretation that affect ordinary people, intellectuals, officials and statesmen. While Islam encourages all believers to have fruitful and respectful relationships with other cultures, radical conservatives ignore these obligations in the context of international cultural relations.

Iran's response to transnational culture

During last three decades some remarkable changes have taken place in Iran that should be considered the results of the expansion of transnational culture, which gradually permeated Iranian society after the end of the war between Iran and Iraq. This was a primary cause of socio-political engagement by Iranians, which crystallized in the emergence of the reformist government in Iran in 1997.

Transnational culture has led to the emergence of a new socio-political and cultural atmosphere in Iran, characterized by factors in public, social, religious, political and youth spheres, as follows:

> In the public sphere a rapid and significant change occurred with regards to gender issues. Social attitudes towards gender issues gradually changed from a radical understanding of the role of woman in society to a more democratic view. As a result of this, many women participated in socio-political and cultural activities in Iranian society. For instance; an analysis of the list of NGOs in Iran confirms that a remarkable number of educated Iranian women have been involved in these organisations.[55]

The changes in the gender situation in Iran have also led to new socio-cultural and political phenomena such as female participation in administrative affairs, with a consequent increase in their political activities, including females occupying more seats in the Islamic assembly during last decade. The increased involvement of Iranian women is also evident in digital media, particularly weblogs. During the last presidential election the weblogs of Iranian women played a crucial role in information diffusion. The emergence of a new political movement in Iran, known as the Green Movement is mostly due to Persian weblogs and also mobile communication technologies.

At the same time the ideological tendency among young Iranians was towards an adoption of a democratic society, which led to massive migration towards Canada, the UK and Australia. This group of Iranians, who also identify with the Islamic culture of Iran, represent a new generation who seek to bridge the gap between the culture of their host society and their country of origin by emphasizing the common elements of both cultures.

In order to achieve a 'global' culture under the umbrella of transnationalism, Iranian youth have been responsible for a great change in arts such as music, fine art and cinema. Transnational culture was also encouraged by the Iranian population who sought to maintain their connection with Iranians living abroad. Communication between Iranians and foreigners also led to the exchange of information concerning the culture of both sides. As a result, many long-held misconceptions propagated by various media and political propaganda were gradually challenged. This in turn led to stronger international relations and paved the way for cultural participation between Iranians and foreigners.

The desire of Iranian youth to seek new employment opportunities, to communicate with foreigners and to pursue higher education abroad resulted in a significant increase in young Iranians learning English. As a result of this, many English language institutes were established in Iran, and these attracted a vast intake of Iranian youth in keen pursuit of the goals described above. Familiarity with a new language allows far greater integration with a new culture and this remarkable social change led to the rise of a new generation of Iranians who paid significantly more attention to foreign media in forming their opinions of world events.

Politically, a remarkable change took place in Iran as a result of the emerging global culture. For instance, by the time of the 1997 presidential election there was some social mobility in Iran, which confirmed that the sizeable latent interest in changing the political atmosphere of the country was the main basis for socio-cultural change. The reformist movement made a tactical error during the presidential election of 2004 that resulted in the triumph of radical conservatives, however the conservative victory not only failed to remove many of the social reforms initiated under Khatami's stewardship but it also unwittingly empowered the emergent Green Movement, as was seen in the aftermath of the election in June 2009. However, the assumption of power by the new radical conservative government increased the political engagement, particularly of the Iranian youth, who voiced their opinions through the Internet, short-lifespan newspapers and silent demonstrations.[56]

The socio-cultural and political actions of the radical conservative government brought together Iranians living abroad with those living inside the country who held the common goal of socio-cultural and political change in the country. Reformists Sheikh Karrobi and Mousavi unified many political activists, intellectuals, university students and young people under the banner of the so-called 'Green Movement', which represents a new reformist voice in Iran.

Declarations by Karroobi, Mousavi and also the military commander Mohsen Rezaei, confirm their enthusiasm for global culture that has the potential to bring great cultural changes to Iran. In brief, some of their presidential propaganda included: resolving the ever-present tensions with the United States; promoting the social capital of Iran; changing the political atmosphere towards the establishment of civil society in the country; changes in the state structure, such as Constitutional law (Karroubi was a particularly vocal advocate of this reform); proposed changes in international relations towards peaceful relations; economic growth; improvement in the position of women in government; the promise of social welfare and security; and the creation of a more open social atmosphere, particularly for Iranian youth.

How is it possible for these candidates to propose such modern reform in the radical conservative atmosphere of present-day Iran? Particularly when, less than ten years ago, they advocated politics that today would be considered fundamentalist and radical. Is it true to say that this kind of transformation represents a primary function of global culture in contemporary Iranian politics? Government officials and political activists should appreciate that transnational culture can make a profound contribution to the creation of successful political structures, particularly in the field of international relations. It is a matter of fact that the tendency towards 'transnational culture' in Iran is not only symptomatic of external movements towards greater integration, but is representative of a silent but powerful voice from inside the society itself. Under the radical conservative government this fact has normally been neglected and, instead, the administration has tried to resolve its problems by condemning alleged foreign governments' interference in national affairs.

Islam and transnational culture

The last part of this chapter considers the relation between the various interpretations of Islam and the resultant inclination (or otherwise) towards transnational culture. At the time of the Islamic Revolution there were two main outlooks in Islam, which were later used by the state to legitimize the socio-cultural, political and economic programmes of the government.

During recent decades many religious individuals including clerics, theological scholars, officials and administrators gradually called the dominant political ideology of Iran into question. This questioning was a response to the emerging radicalism of 'Islamic politics'. The reformist movement's challenge to radicalism in Iran was catalysed by the election of the radical conservative Ahmadinejad in 2005. The political policies and performance of the current radical conservative administration suggest a dismissive posture towards transnational culture, as the concept appears entirely absent from the foreign policy of the current conservative government.

The possible growth of transnational culture in Iran is heavily dependent on various interpretations of Islamic paradigms that are represented in the two primary types of 'Islamic' politics, namely reformist and conservative.

It is worth remembering that according to the reformist leaders in Iran, the present-day 'Islamic Revolution' differs profoundly from the revolution of 1979 in its aims, socio-cultural, political and economic tendencies. Reformists believe that the main aim of the 1979 Islamic Revolution was to establish human rights for all people through justice, a respect for global culture, social freedoms, equality and cooperation in international relations, all of which they consider fundamental to Islam.

Prominent reformists in Iran assert that these objectives were originally defined by Ayatollah Khomeini.[57] They believe that the radical conservatism of modern Iran is not in accordance with Islam, and also that it deviates significantly from Ayatollah Khomeini's vision of the Islamic Revolution.

Under the present radically conservative government, it seems unlikely that any concessions will be made towards the idea of mutually beneficial transnational culture.

Conclusion: dramatic change on the way

The rapid development of communication technologies, changing job opportunities and socio-political crises in LDCs, have all contributed to remarkable changes in migrant communities. During last two decades vast numbers of migrants have left their homelands in search of a better life in Western countries. This constant movement is key in the emergence of so-called 'transnational culture'. Transnational culture has played a crucial role in strengthening the connection of migrants to their homeland, the end product of which is increased global cultural exchange. Today, productive international relations are often due to the appreciation of transnational culture as the cornerstone of foreign policy.

Because there are so many Iranian migrants in Western countries, and because Iran itself receives numerous immigrants from its neighbours, it is a primary example of the emergent 'transnational culture'. From the moment the reformist government of Khatami took office, global transnational culture became the focus of Iranian foreign policy.

Theoretically, there is not any contradiction between Iran's Islam-centric political direction and greater cross-cultural exchange. Moreover, Islam encourages people to travel and to familiarize themselves with other societies in order to benefit from their cultures and thereby improve their own lives. The reformist appropriation of social democratic rhetoric is based on a contemporary interpretation of Islam, in contrast the radical conservative interpretation is more rigid, fundamental and controversial.

The aftermath of the Iranian presidential election in June 2009 was symptomatic of a fundamental social change, brought about by powerful communication technology in the hands of the Iranian youth. Many supporters of reformism in Iran are Internet users, which means they are familiar with the modern cultural language of the world. This new global cultural language is now used in houses, universities, offices and family gatherings in Iran. This language has reduced the cultural gap between Iran and other nations and has paved the way for transnational culture, which represents the new form of knowledge transfer on a global scale.

The concept of 'transnational culture' signifies an aspiration towards change, peace and friendship within the framework of 'global culture'.

Notes

1 Wimmer and Schiller, 2002; Faist, 1998 and 2000; Kivisto, 2001.
2 Randolph Silliman Bourne, 1916. In his article 'Trans-National America', Bourne argued that the US should accommodate immigrant cultures into a 'cosmopolitan America', instead of forcing immigrants to assimilate to Anglophilic culture. In this article Bourne rejects the melting-pot theory and does not see immigrants assimilating easily to another culture. See Lasch, 1997, cited in: http://en.wikipedia.org/wiki/Randolph_Bourne#cite_ref-0 (accessed 28 April 2011). See also: http://randolphbourne.org/ (accessed 28 April 2011)

  3 Lambton, 1987. Ann Katharine Swynford Lambton, PhD, FBA, OBE (1912–2008) was a British historian and leading figure on medieval and early modern Persian history, Persian language, Islamic political theory, and Persian social organization. She was an acknowledged authority land tenure and reform in Iran, Seljuq, Mongol, Safavid and Qajar administration and institutions, and local and tribal histories. Cited in: http://en.wikipedia.org/wiki/Ann_Lambton#cite_ref-1 (accessed 28 April 2011) See also: http://www.timesonline.co.uk/tol/comment/obituaries/article4379464.ece (accessed 28 April 2011).
  4 Appadurai, 1996, Hannerz, 1996, cited in Kivisto, 2001; Appadurai, 2000, Castells, 1997, Castells, 2010.
  5 Less-developed countries
  6 Glick Schiller *et al.*, 1992, cited in Kivisto, 2001, pp. 550–551; Sklair, 2000, 2001; Basch *et al.*, 2000
  7 Kivisto, 2001, p. 551; Basch *et al.*, 2000.
  8 Kivisto, 2001, Portes, 1995, cited in Kivisto, 2001. Faist, 1998.
  9 Basch *et al.*, 2000.
 10 Glick Schiller *et al.*, 1992, 1997, cited in Kivisto, 2001, p. 552.
 11 Kivisto, 2001, p. 552.
 12 Kivisto, 2001; see also Daniels, 1990.
 13 Basch *et al.*, 2000, Kivisto, 2001
 14 Appadurai, 1996, Hannerz 1996, cited in Kivisto, 2001, pp. 553–554.
 15 Glick Shiller *et al.*, 1992, cited in Kivisto, 2001, p. 554.
 16 Kivisto, 2001, pp. 554–555, for more information, see Castes and Miller, 1993; Kivisto, 1984.
 17 Kivisto, 2001, see also Jones, 1976; Daniels, 1990.
 18 Kivisto, 2001, p. 556.
 19 Ibid.
 20 Ibid.
 21 Kivisto, 2001, p. 560–563.
 22 Vertovec, 1999, cited in Kivisto, 2001.
 23 Williams, 1976.
 24 Williams, 1976; also Chaney, 1994, p. 2.
 25 Chaney, 1994, p. 3.
 26 Ibid., p. 7
 27 Ibid., p. 8
 28 Hall *et al.*, 1993, p. 2.
 29 Ibid.
 30 Ibid.
 31 Hall *et al.*, 1993, p. 2.
 32 Ibid., p. 3.
 33 Geertz, 1973, p. 89
 34 Ibid., see also, Parsons, 1951.
 35 Parsons, 1951.
 36 Long, 1997, p. 2, See also, Polanyi, 1957.
 37 Long, 1997, p. 2
 38 Ibid., pp. 2–3.
 39 Skelton and Allen, 2000.
 40 For more information see Featherstone, 1990, King, 1991; Robertson, 1996; Wilson and Wimal, 1996; Held, 1995.
 41 Cvetkovich and Kellner, 1997, p. 15.
 42 Ferguson, 2002, p. 159.
 43 Mohammad Khatami's idea of Dialogue among Civilizations became known more widely after the United Nations adopted a resolution to name the year 2001 as the year of Dialogue among Civilizations. See: http://www.un.org/Dialogue/ (accessed 28 April 2011).

44 Huntington, 1996.
45 For more information see Nateghpour, 2006.
46 Ibid.
47 During the period of war between Iran and Iraq it was said that almost every Iranian family had one martyr in the war, today it is said that almost every Iranian family has at least one immigrant living out of the country.
48 See: http://www.migrationinformation.org/feature/display.cfm?ID=424; also see: http://www.topiranian.com/news/archives/002454.html (accessed 28 April 2011).
49 Tomlinson, 2000.
50 For more information on Eurocentrism see Amin, 1989, also Said, 1994.
51 Hulme and Turner, 1985.
52 For more information regarding Khatami see Khatami, 2000, also, Ansari, 2007, Nateghpour, 2006.
53 Concerning Islamic civilization see Nasr, 2003.
54 Ali ibn Abutalib, the fourth caliph of Islam and the first *Imam* (leader) of Shia Muslims, gives advice to his son Hussein (the third Imam of Shia Muslims), which confirms the Islamic thought concerning cultural exchange with the host society. He asks his son to respect the other cultures (norms and values) while he lives in the other society. The Arabic text of his word within the form of his poem is as follows:

حسين اذا كنت فى بلده غريبا فعاشر بآدابها

Poems of Ali bin Abu-Talib, Najafi (trans.), p. 8.

(ديوان اشعار على عليه السلام، ترجمه محمدجواد نجفى، صفحه 8)

Also, a number of references confirm the peaceful mind of Shia in regard to socio-cultural relationship with other societies. For instance, Molla Mohsen Feiz-Kashani, the leading Shia clergyman during 19th century points out in his major book *Risale Ulfat* (The Thesis of Love, Friendship, and Peace) that the final purpose of the majority of Sharia rituals is to achieve love, peace and friendship, things that will appear in a fruitful social relationship.
55 Nateghpour, 2006.
56 For more information regarding the radical conservatism in Iran see Ansari, 2008; Ehteshami and Zweiri, 2007.
57 Ayatollah Sanei, Ayatollah Bayat-Zanjani, Khatami, Karroobi, Mohtashamipour, Mohsen Kadivar and other reformist clergies, and also Mir Hossein Mousavi and many religious intellectuals believe what they are pursuing is what Ayatollah Khomeini was looking for as well.

References

Amin, S. (1989), *Eurocentrism*, Moore, R. (trans.), London: Zed Books.
Ansari, A.M. (2007), *Iran, Islam, and Democracy: The Politics of Managing Change*, Washington DC: Brooking Institution Press.
Ansari, A.M. (2008), *Iran Under Ahmadinejad: The Politics of Confrontation*, London and New York: Taylor & Francis.
Appadurai, A. (1996), *Modernity at Large: Cultural Dimensions of Globalisation, Public World*, Vol. 1, Minneapolis, MN: University of Minnesota Press.
Appadurai, A. (2000), Grassroots Globalization and the Research Imagination, in: *Public Culture* – Vol. 12, No. 1, Winter 2000, pp. 1–19.
Basch, L. *et al.* (2000), *Nations Unbound: Transnational Projects, Postcolonial Predicaments and Deterritorialized Nation-States*. Routledge, fifth printing, 1st published in 1994, New york: Gordon and Breac Sciences Publisher.
Biggart, N.W. (1989), *Charismatic Capitalism: Direct Selling Organisations in America*, Chicago, IL: Chicago University Press.

Castells, M. (1997), *The Power of Identity*, Oxford: Blackwell.

Castells, M. (2010), *The Rise of the Network Society,* the first volume of *The Information Age: Economy, Culture, and Society*, Oxford: Wiley-Blackwell.

Castes, S. and Miller, M.J. (1993), *The Age of Migration: International Population Movements in the Modern World*, Houndmills, Basingstoke and London: Macmillan.

Chaney, D. (1994), *The Cultural Turn: Scene-Setting Essays on Contemporary Cultural History*, London and New York: Routledge.

Cvetkovich, A. and Kellner, D. (1997), *Articulating the Global and the Local*, Boulder, CO: Westview Press.

Daniels, R. (1990), *Coming to America: A History of Immigration and Ethnicity in American Life*, New York: HarperCollins.

Denison, D. (1990), *Corporate Culture and Organisational Effectiveness*, New York: Wiley.

Ehteshami, A. and Zweiri, M. (2007), *Iran and Rise of its Neoconservatives: The Politics of Tehran's Silent Revolution*, London: I. B. Tauris & Co Ltd.

Faist, T. (1998), 'Transnational social spaces out of international migration: evolution, significance, and future prospects' *Archives Europeennes de Sociologie*, 39 (2), 213–247.

Faist, T. (2000), *The Volume and Dynamics of International Migration and Transnational Social Spaces*, Oxford: Oxford University Press.

Featherstone, M. (ed.) (1990), *Global Culture: Nationalism, Globalisation and Modernity*, London: Sage Publications.

Ferguson, J. (2002), 'Development', in: *Encyclopaedia of Social and Cultural Anthropology*, Barnard, A. and Spencer, J. (eds), London: Routledge.

Geertz, C. (1973), *The Interpretation of Cultures: Selected Essays*, New York: Basic Books.

Glick Schiller, N. (1997) 'The situation of transnational studies', *Identities*, 4(2), 155–166.

Glick Schiller, N. *et al.* (eds) (1992), 'Transnationalism: a new analytic framework for understanding migration', *Towards a Transnational Perspective on Migration: Race, Class, Ethnicity, and Nationalism Reconsidered*, New York: New York Academy of Sciences, pp. 1–24.

Hall, J.R. *et al.* (1993), *Culture: Sociological Perspective*, Englewood Cliffs, NJ: Prentice Hall.

Hannerz, U. (1996), *Transnational Connections: Culture, People, Places*, London: Routledge.

Harper, D. (1987), *Working Knowledge: Skill and Community in a Small Shop*, Chicago, IL: University of Chicago Press.

Held, D. (1995), *Democracy and the Global Order*, Cambridge and Palo Alto, CA: Polity Press and Stanford University Press.

Hulme, D. and Turner, M. (1985), *Sociology of Development*, Manchester: Manchester University Press.

Huntington, S.P. (1996), *The Clash of Civilizations*, New York: Simon & Schuster.

Jones, M. (1976), *The Old World Ties of American Ethnic Groups*, London: Macmillan.

Khatami, M. (2000), Human the combination of the rise of sprit and the fall of intellect (*Ensan Moltaghaie Mashregh-e Jan va Maghrebe Aql*), Centre for Documents and Diplomatic History, Ministry of Foreign Affairs, I.R.IRAN.

King, A.D. (ed.) (1991), *Culture, Globalisation and the World System: Contemporary Conditions for the Representation of Identity*, Binghamton: SUNY Art Department.

Kivisto, P. (1984), *Immigrant Socialists in the United States: The Case of Finns and the Left*, Rutherford, NJ: Fairleigh Dickinson University Press.

Kivisto, P. (2001), 'Theorizing transnational immigration: a critical review of current efforts', *Ethnic and Racial Studies*, 24(4), July 2001, 549–577.

Lambton, A. K. S. (1987), *Qajar Persia*, London: I. B. Tauris & Co. Ltd.

Lasch, H. (1997), *The Radical Will: Selected Writing of Randolph Bourne*, New York: Urizen Books.

Long, E. (1997), *From Sociology to Cultural Studies: New Perspectives*, Cambridge: Blackwell.

Meyer, J. W. and Scott, W. R. (1992), *Organisational Environments: Ritual and Rationality*, Beverly Hills, CA: Sage Publications.

Mills, C. W. (1959), *Sociological Imagination*, New York: Oxford University Press.

Nasr, S. H. (2003), *Islam: Religion, History, and Civilisation*, San Francisco, CA: HarperCollins.

Nateghpour, M. J. (2006), 'The cultural dimensions of Anglo-Iranian relations'. Working Paper, University of Durham, Centre for Middle Eastern and Islamic Studies, Durham.

Parsons, T (1951), *The Social System*, New York: Free Press.

Polanyi, K. (1957), *The Great Transformation: The Political and Economic Origins of Our Time*, Boston, MA: Beacon Press.

Portes, A. (ed.) (1995), 'Children of immigrants: segmented assimilation', *The Economic Sociology of Immigration*, New York: Russell Sage Foundation, pp. 248–280.

Randolph, B. (1916), 'Trans-national America', in: Peter B. Levy (ed.), *100 Key Documents in American Democracy*, Westport, CT: Greenwood (1994), pp. 303–309.

Robertson, R. (1996) *Globalization: Social Theory and Global Culture*, London: Sage Publications.

Said, E. W. (1994), *Culture and Imperialism*, New York: Vintage Books.

Sklair, L. (2000) Social Movements and Global Capitalism, in: Roberts, J. Timmons and Sklair, L. (2001) *The Transnational Capitalist Class*, Oxford: Blackwell.

Skelton, T. and Allen, T. (2000), *Culture and Global Change*, London and New York: Routledge.

Tomlinson, J. (1999), *Globalization and Culture*, Cambridge: Polity Press.

Vertovec, S. (1999), 'Conceiving and researching transnationalism', *Ethnic and Racial Studies*, 22(2), 447–462.

Wilson, R. and Wimal, D. (1996), *Global/Local: Cultural Production and the Transnational Imaginary*, Durham, NC: Duke University Press.

Williams, R (1976), *Keywords: A Vocabulary of Culture and Society*, London: Fontana.

Wimmer, A. and Glick Schiller, N. (2002), 'Methodological nationalism and beyond: nation-state building, migrations and the social sciences', *Global Network*, 2(4), 301–334.

Quran, Chapter 3, Verse: 200.

Najafi, M. J. (n.d.), Poems of Ali, Adibiyeh publisher, Tehran.

محمدجواد نجفی (مترجم)، دیوان امیرالمومنین علی علیه السلام، کتابفروشی ادبیه، تهران، ناصرخسرو، بی تا .

http://en.wikipedia.org/wiki/Ann_Lambton#cite_ref-1

http://www.timesonline.co.uk/tol/comment/obituaries/article4379464.ece.

http://www.telegraph.co.uk/news/obituaries/2524891/Professor-AKS-Lambton.html

http://www.un.org/Dialogue/

http://www.migrationinformation.org/feature/display.cfm?ID=424

7 Two different faces of Iran–West relations

Incompatibility of official levels with everyday life

Vahid Shalchi

Introduction

In a world that has been condensed by globalization, not only does confrontation among civilizations and cultures increase in time, but also the quality of that confrontation becomes different. One difference is the multiplicity of contact points. Therefore, an analysis of the relationship among countries and civilizations will no longer be effective on the basis of the relationship among states. The same is true about reducing that relationship to political and economic relations. Analysing relations between two civilizations solely on the basis of interstate relations or official political levels will be unacceptable reductionism both in terms of epistemology and policymaking. The importance of this point can be better understood when analysing the relationship between the important civilizations of Iran and the West.

Following a post-structuralist viewpoint influenced by Derrida, we have to deconstruct the concept of 'relationship'. This will be done through attention to a growing field of studies that is 'everyday life'. In a time of nation-states, relationships among cultures, civilizations and nations are mostly considered within a framework of relationships among states. Since, according to a conventional definition, every state has a good command over its people within its own territory, relationships among states are of the utmost importance. That importance will be considered on two levels. Firstly, the relations between higher and lower levels (like a transnational civilization or within two communities in a society), and secondly, various aspects of that relationship (economic, social and cultural) under the political influence of states.

In a time of 'late modernity', although nation-states still exist, the state is no longer taken as a good theoretical basis to analyse the efficiency of relations. At present, levels of relations and channels of contact have not only moved beyond official frontiers but have also moved beyond the control and supervision of governments. 'Everyday life' is a subject for discussion among many others. This chapter maintains that attention should be paid to everyday life when analysing relations among countries and civilizations. Attention should not be limited to admission of the role of everyday life in the totality of relations, but it should be taken into account when formulating macro policies, because actions taken by different actors in the complex situations of everyday life contain a trove of 'implied knowledge', which can offer politicians more possibilities. As Goffman indicates, this knowledge is a form of implied knowledge that is not usually talked about, and it includes solutions to problems that actors face in dealing with structural limitations, which draw on structural facilities and cultural resources.

Another point is that interactions among countries is not affected by interests, but is influenced by the image they have in mind of their interests. Therefore, we witness many ups and downs in the history of political relations, some of which result from objective changes in interests. However, the importance of 'defining' interests should not be ignored. Since 'interests' have been derived from a post-structuralist viewpoint, we are faced with 'different definitions of interests'. We have no such thing as interest; we have different narratives of interest. The consequences of different narrations are a good criterion, which can be important in this viewpoint.

Through such epistemological understanding, we will not be faced with a conflict of interests among civilizations, but there is a conflict of narrations between two civilizations. Thus, conflict results from two narrations. This is not rejection of the objective world outside the language, but it means that understanding of the real is the root cause of friendship, rivalry, unity, conflict and dispute. Therefore, new languages create new ways. This approach gives rise to many possibilities, which are logically unlimited and influenced by new discourses. In this new configuration of relations among states and cultures, since the type of relationship, whether it is either friendly or hostile, is a result of 'discourse', then new ways of narration can lead to basic developments.

This chapter will use two epistemological and theoretical considerations when analysing relations between Iran and the West – relations that, in the past three decades, have never been normal and have had many up and downs when fundamental evaluations have taken place in the world order, but have not officially been outside their framework. Many states on both sides of that relationship have changed, but challenges still exist. This chapter will try to pay attention to ongoing relations that are either ignored or interpreted in meaningless ways, to highlight another possibility that is not merely theoretical, but is also ongoing.

Relations between Iran and West in the past three decades have been affected by the West's efforts to promote its own interests or that of its regional allies without paying any attention to Iran's interests, the cultural structure of the region and any discourse-based resistance on the part of Iran. The Iranian government has tried through the anti-discourse of the Islamic Revolution, which offers a new configuration of cultural and civilizational resources in the region, to protect its specific interests. This has been going on for 30 years and any change in it depends on the creation of new narrations. Measures taken by some Western groups to eliminate the Islamic Revolution discourse have not been unsuccessful so far because the discourse is based on a deep-rooted culture, and it seems that the West's efforts to eliminate a discourse through political and economic pressures and by presenting a monster-like picture of the opposite side and introducing itself and its values as a myth is not a good way to overcome conflicts.

Therefore, this chapter aims to find other possibilities in Iran–West relations out of four presumed theoretical domains[1] and focus on the everyday life because that domain is believed to be useful for the official domain. Out of two domains of Iranian and Western everyday life, it focuses on Iran.[2] Thus, the main question of this chapter is: how is the interaction with 'the West' different in everyday life and the official level in Iran? And what binary oppositions in its semantic sense can explain that difference better.

Political importance of everyday affairs and special awareness of it

'Everyday life' is a difficult concept in sociology. Everyday life is associated with known affairs and general knowledge. Social theoreticians of the past considered everyday life as the product of structural forces that work beyond awareness of social actors. In two major approaches to everyday life, which were presented by two classical theorists, social actors were nothing but cultural puppets who passively internalized social roles and norms. The only difference was that, in one theory, those roles and norms were based on unity while the other theory saw them as reflecting the interests of the ruling class. However, both of them considered everyday life as an arena for domination over individual subjects.

Weber and Mead were the first theorists who noted that the internalization of social norms by individuals was not simply passive, but created a capacity for self-motivated action. In late 20th and early 21st century, another development occurred in the concept of everyday life, which was more dynamic and more controversial. Impressed by developments of modernity, everyday life was not a homogeneous concept, but a pluralistic and controversial area that could be understood in the context of 'cultural division' of later modernity. Thus a controversial field of everyday life's experiences has come into being due to increased social dynamism. In this new approach, everyday life is a dynamic and interactive process that takes shape through dynamic application of media and consumer products by actors who aim to construct identities and implement lifestyle projects.

Michel de Certeau was one of the most important theorists, influential through his book *Everyday Life Action*, to present such a picture of everyday life. He aimed in his research to show methods through which texts and pictures are applied by actors who have not created them. He mentioned analytical differentiation between 'strategies' and 'tactics' as a substitute to be used for differentiation between the elite and the public.

The strategy is used by people who are powerful and live in self-made circumstances. In contrast, there are people who cannot make such changes, and live under circumstances that have been imposed on them. Less powerful people use tactics. They use commodities and signs of the consumer society in such a way as to meet their own interests. In fact, they act in a domain that has been imposed on them by an external force. Therefore, they should act differently; they should meet their needs by manipulation of the circumstances made by those who sway monopoly over strategies.

De Certeau started to muse over everyday life following developments in 1968 as a new method of thinking about political action and historical changes came to the fore. Also, Moran has written in his book *Reading the Everyday Affair* that we can see realities and changing historical potentials in most ordinary phenomena. Now, everyday life is a growing field of study in cultural theories as well as political discussions. Auge has mentioned everyday life developments as a criterion to differentiate simple events from basic changes and calls it the driving force behind social changes.

Therefore, the main issue is politicization of everyday life. Politicization of everyday life has been consistently ignored through the willingness of media and political discourse to see the public sphere as a threat. In recent years, neoliberal ideology has greatly succeeded in depoliticizing everyday life and connecting it to the neutral environment of the market. In this context, the relative popularity of policies and ideologies has been less related to their public acceptance as part of the outlook of everyday life.

Moran has noted in his book how cultural material has represented everyday life in recent decades and has been willing to ignore the potential of true social change. He has noted that if we want to initiate changes in everyday life aimed at improvement, we may need to closely observe everyday life and not consider it as a commonplace leftover of contemporary life, but as a real place in which our real life goes on.

Lefebvre, a prominent theorist of everyday life who has come up with an avant-garde sociology of 'everyday life', has criticized revolution as a complete action and radical dissociation and emphasizes that true change should take place through places and actions of everyday life. He maintains that the boring nature of everyday life is a support both for radicalism and adaptation. Lefebvre maintains that no simple differentiation can be made between everyday life and the discovery of lofty plans or truth. Lefebvre also believes that plural approaches and critical interdisciplinary frameworks are needed to diversify everyday life.

John Fiske is another important theorist who has theorized about the dynamic and innovative nature of everyday life in order to demonstrate people's role in building social order. He did not intend to reduce the value of studies on the influence of power block, but claimed that any explanation of social affairs and cultural systems that ignore people's positive role could not be a complete theory because people can disrupt supervisory and information mechanisms, something that was called mechanisms of power by Foucault. Fiske also criticized the gap between everyday life and the academic methods used to explain the world. Therefore, when discussing large-scale issues attention should be also paid to the role of everyday life, and signs of profound changes at this level should be followed. This level represents a dynamic domain of society, which can be a source for new institutions and languages. Of course, attention should be paid to the dominant form of knowledge in that domain.

The British theorist Anthony Giddens has presented one of the best explanations in this regard. Giddens has shown the importance of 'agency' in his theory of 'structuration'. He maintains that neither motivation (as Freud believed), nor meaning (as Weber said) nor profit (which is mentioned in logical selection theories) can be considered as the main feature of a social actor. Giddens starts with the assumption that a social actor knows how to enter the game.

He believes in three forms of awareness. They are topped by discursive consciousness, followed by practical self-awareness in the middle and unconsciousness at the bottom. Discursive consciousness is the ability to describe things in words and requires the ability to describe actions using words. However, practical self-awareness, which plays the most important role in everyday life, is of higher importance in his theory of structuration. This form of awareness is materialized through words and an actor's subconscious actions. This form of awareness is a level of implied or obvious knowledge. Also, this implied and obvious level has more relevance to everyday activities of life and plays an important role in Giddens' theory.

Practical self-awareness is of theoretic importance because it refers to knowledge about the quality of action. Knowledge of quality of action is not verbal and most of it is gained without learning and is considered obvious; examples include where, when and how we should say hello to our friends.

Most of us do that without even thinking about it. Such skills can be quite intelligent or simple. Social actors frequently guide their conduct for protracted periods of time by relying on practical self-awareness. As long as that process keeps going, the person pays no attention to the motivation and meaning of that behaviour.

Binaries indicating two different aspects of Iran–West relations

This chapter focuses on the binary opposition of official levels versus everyday life to analyse the relationship between Iran and the West and will try to explain the fundamental binaries that are indicative of the above binary opposition. The main cause of that difference is not the subject of this chapter and questions will be answered at a descriptive level. In their everyday lives, Iranians have understood Western affairs in all areas of life and have reacted to them. Of course, different groups show different reactions, but there are also common points in the average society, which will be discussed in this chapter.

Before discussing different reactions shown by Iranians at official levels and everyday life, attention to a similarity is important. Iranians at both levels share common concerns and values. At both levels, they consider themselves as heirs to a civilization that is not in its own deserved position and should be restored to that position. Other common concerns include independence and cultural and civilizational distinction, the undeniable colonialistic past of Western countries, severe damages to Iranian interests in the contemporary era from the West, the basic importance of political and economic interests for the West and the marginalization of ethics in Western politics. Although public opinion in Iran is compatible with the official opinion on the above subjects, the reactions shown at the two levels are different.

Universalism/particularity

The first binary opposition is that of universalism versus particularity. 'General principles' are taken as a basis of action at official levels and those principles are followed in all forms of political, economic and other relations. At the official level, there are a number of generalities, some of which are evitable and others which are not.

The first generalization pertains to the image of the West. Here, some features are imagined to be basic, profound, stable, fundamental and determining while others are less important, superficial, minor and temporary. In addition to the necessity of paying attention to some issues and ignoring others, this form of knowledge may be afflicted by two forms of implications: simplification and 'essentialism'.

The first implication causes complexities to be ignored in favour of a simple image of the West. Clichés are determining factors in this case whether they are justified or not. For example, there is a common belief that the West does not care for spirituality. The second implication is essentialism. For the West, essence is assumed as the Greek philosophy: an essence that is permanent and explains behaviours that emanate from it. Today, considering essence for social phenomena is in doubt both from philosophical and sociological viewpoints.

Another generalization, which is sometimes seen at official levels, is generalization of time. It means that less importance is attached to changes. This generalization is also applied to the quality of the West and is intensified in essentialist approaches because changes in the West do not necessarily change its nature and are of secondary importance. Therefore, changes in governments and statesmen are considered too trivial to lead to a serious change in the West.

Such generalizations at a cognitive level will certainly lead to generalizations in practice. Therefore, the need for changing actions or the dominant discourse is not felt at the official level. There are 'unshakable general principles' that should be taken as a guide. If our understanding of 'we' is confirmed by its 'compatibility' to the 'real thing' and if our understanding of others is also 'correct' as such and both civilizations have a constant 'essence', then reflections and flexibility will be limited to the tactical, and not strategic, level. Such a viewpoint on both sides (even when it has nothing to do with epistemological fundaments) can lead to the reproduction of an objective state. Such an approach to the West can be justified in view of the injustice done to Iran by the West.

Such generalizations at another level will lead to a similar understanding of the other party's conduct in various fields. In this generalization, they either see practical logic of the opposite side to be the same in all fields, or don't care for it. The other side, firstly, enjoys an integrated self and there is no difference in terms of political factions or parties, and secondly, a single fundamental practical logic is applied in all fields from sports to economy and from the elite down to ordinary citizens. This form of generalization is also of importance at official levels.

Alternatively, we see particularity in all the above-mentioned aspects at the level of everyday life. In this sphere, where Iranians interact with 'the West' in their daily life, Iranian persons or communities find themselves faced with 'the

West' in all fields; from economy to culture, from political affairs to social ones, from technology to climate changes, from being located on the path of drugs to the West to Western artefacts, from sanctions to different values and from lifestyle to modern medicine. Therefore, it would be a mistake to think that interaction of Iranians with the West is less limited at everyday life level compared to the official level.

The mainstream of everyday life takes a different approach to many of the above issues. When it comes to knowledge, there is no uniform judgement that considers all aspects of the West to be the same. They believe in the plurality of understandings, and judgements about different aspects of the West are not uniform. Here, the West is grey in colour, neither black, nor white. They do not treat 'the West' in an essentialist manner and there is less sign of general principles that can be applied in all cases. Judgements are usually case by case and may even be conflicting. There are inorderly interpretations, which are related to the context of the action.

Unlike the official level, here we are not dealing with the West, but with a number of 'Wests'. There is no generalization to be applied to all economic, political, scientific, cultural and social fields and even if there is, it will not remain constant in time. A general question may arise as to quality of the West. This understanding of the generality of the West may arise momentarily, but will rapidly lose ground in another situation in the face of practical self-awareness logic. Here, there is more possibility to pay attention to different Western affairs. At this level, Western politics are not unrelated to Western football, arts or aesthetics, but correctly or incorrectly, they are not considered to be the same. This is why despite negative attitudes to foreign British politics, which has caused people to see British hands behind all plots, they still love Manchester, Liverpool and Arsenal football clubs.

Particularity is also evident when it comes to reactions. There are few fixed principles that you may apply in relation to the West. Iranians react to the West in a very intelligent 'selective' manner. Goods and objects are not only chosen selectively, but are mixed to make new combinations and articulation. Thus, they are given new meanings and are used to serve the Iranians' purposes.

In garments, for instance, this is quite visible. One day, a combination of green American coat and other garments are used as an anti-imperialistic symbol while the next, a Western suit minus tie is considered as a sign of being Hezbollah (a euphemism for a revolutionist person in Iran). Selective adoption of Western elements is also seen in foods. Many Western foods have been combined with new Iranian foods and have entered Iranian homes.

This 'selective' and 'innovative' way of dealing with the West, not only covers its objective aspects, but also includes Western values. At the level of everyday life, Western values are dealt with not in a general manner, but in a selective manner that depends on the situation. Here again, what is Western is not simply rejected or accepted, but rejection or acceptance depends on the context. For instance, democratic values of the West are treated in a specific and active manner as is the case with the new definitions of femininity and masculinity.

Table 7.1 Universalism/particularity

	Epistemological level	*Practical level*
Official level	Essentialist: the West as an integrated whole	Following suit with general, unshakable principles
Everyday life	Wests, varieties of the West	Selective treatment, new combinations and articulation, bricolage

Authenticity/hybrid

Another binary that can indicate differences in how Iranians deal with the West at official and everyday-life levels is the binary of authenticity/hybrid. At the official level, they try to base their efforts on 'authentic' and not 'hybrid' methods. There is a constant sense of suspicion at the official level towards whatever is considered 'other', whether commodities, ideas or methods. Alternatively, there is always a positive attitude towards whatever is 'local'.[3] This approach covers everything from social and political thoughts to products and architecture.

Conversely and at the level of everyday life, they act in a 'hybrid' manner; from customs and rituals to foods, garments, and principles governing social relations. The most important example is the hybrid lifestyles that have been reviewed in studies carried out by Chavoshian, Shahabi, Zokaei, Shalchi, Goushbor and others. At this level, even ideological affairs are protected in a hybrid manner. For example, family is of the highest importance in Iran, but flexibility towards new family values is shown in order to reconstruct a traditional family structure by applying new values and methods. This binary is related to the next binary.

Continuity/flexibility

The binary of continuity versus flexibility also indicates differences in how Iranians relate to 'the West' both at official and everyday life levels. The political approach of Iranians towards the West at the official level has not greatly changed in the past three decades, which seems to be due in part to the West's unfriendly attitude. However, a totally different dynamism governs everyday life,[4] both over the course of time, and among different social groups.

'Spatial flexibility' is quite evident. The city walls throughout the city reflect that change. For a decade, advertisements related to Western products were erased from walls and gave way to anti-imperialistic slogans. In the next decade, the same walls were covered with advertisements for diverse Western brands. In parallel, changes in lifestyle can be observed from prejudiced avoidance of Western elements to …

Interestingly, flexibility in everyday life does not mean giving up past concerns, but is an effort to address those concerns commensurate with new conditions. Iranian parents still have the same concerns, but are also flexible enough to meet the conditions of their time. That flexibility results from acting according to 'situation logic'. Intelligent reactions of the Iranian family to environmental changes are the best example of safeguarding the past while being flexible.

Simplicity/complexity

Simplicity/complexity represents another binary. Here, we must review some presumptions about action in everyday life. Everyday life theorists like Garfinkel, Goffman and Bourdieu have shown that at the back of the 'commonplaceness' of everyday life, there is a hidden intelligence. One of the instances that may reveal that complexity, is how Iranians act in the face of 'the West'. Special field studies are needed here to show how the people of Iran have intelligently treated a complex reality like the West despite their emphasis on safeguarding their 'historical self' in a way that is much more complex than usual groupings at the official level – even where, as put by De Certeau, they cannot avail themselves of strategy and they maintain their identity by using tactics. Being predictable or unpredictable is a suitable criterion to demonstrate this binary.

Self/other

Another binary is self/other. This binary is quite evident in Iran's relations with 'the West' and has even been generalized to cover cultural and other fields. However, in the everyday life of Iranians it is not prominent. Also, at an official level, 'we' versus the other binary is reduced to Iran versus West. In other words, 'other' is reduced to the West and different challenges with non-Western 'others' are of secondary significance. At the level of everyday life, however, the borders are more fluid and multiple and cannot be reduced to an Iran versus West binary. At this level, the temporal situation and the context of the action determines who is the real 'other' of the Iranian 'we'. Sometimes, even neighbouring countries are the real 'other'.

Cold/warm

These binaries lead to the cold/warm binary in Iran's relations with the West. During the past few decades, relations have been cold at the official level, but at the level of everyday life they have been quite warm and vital. Warmth here denotes the intensity and dynamism of the relationship or the fact that it is positive. In their everyday life, Iranians are experiencing warm confrontation with the West, with regard to which they adopt active tactics. An 'imbalance' in power, which willingly or unwillingly leads to 'imposition', is among everyday life challenges that Iranians are facing with regard to the West. However, despite such challenges the overall atmosphere is one of dynamism, innovation and creativity. Despite difficulties and structural limitations, Iranians are actively trying to benefit the most and suffer the least through their confrontation with the West. It does not seem as if Western sanctions or a power imbalance could have or will reduce the intensity of that relationship or dampen the 'active' presence of Iranian 'agents'.

Discursive consciousness/practical consciousness

If the cold versus warm binary is used to describe the current situation of Iran–West relations on the basis of the official/everyday life binary, the discursive consciousness/practical consciousness binary is indicative of two different forms of practical logic or two types of different consciousness that are used at two official and everyday life levels. Here, we will take advantage of three levels of consciousness, which Giddens has mentioned on the strength of 'sociological methodology'. As stated in the section on theoretical bases, it is practical consciousness that plays the main role at the level of everyday life. Therefore, Iranians experience two kinds of consciousness, which act differently towards the West at the two levels of official and everyday life. We are not discussing the discursive consciousness of Iranians in general, but comparing dominant discursive consciousness at the official level.

Conclusion

This chapter has tried to cast a new look at an issue that is usually discussed from the viewpoint of political sciences and international relations. This chapter has taken a post-structuralist approach and has discussed Iran–West relations from a cultural viewpoint in order to prove the importance of the everyday life level. Therefore, using a method derived from semantic binary opposition, it has first engaged with the Iran/West binary at two levels: official and everyday life. To explain the differences in Iran–West relations at official and everyday life levels, several other binary oppositions have been discussed and the issue has been reviewed within a framework of ten such binaries (see Table 7.2).

The realist/constructional binary were explained at the epistemological level and it was proved that adoption of a constructional epistemology highlights the importance of language and discourse. Then discursive consciousness/practical consciousness was elucidated in order to shed light on differences in consciousness at two levels, of everyday life and officialdom.

The universalism/particularity binary is one of the most important opposition binaries when dealing with the West at the two above levels. The simplicity/complexity binary shows another aspect of differences between those two levels. The important point is that despite some presumptions, Iranians' dealings with the

Table 7.2 Binaries' opposition indicating different reactions shown to the West by Iranians at two levels

Iran	West
Official level	Everyday life
Discursive consciousness	Practical consciousness
Realistic epistemology	Constructional epistemology
Universalism	Particularity
Authentic	Hybrid
Continuity	Flexibility
Simplicity	Complexity
Self	Other
Cold	Warm

West in their everyday life are accompanied by special complexities. Another useful binary in this regard is the binary opposition of continuity/flexibility – flexibility is important both in terms of time, and in terms of the field of action. Another difference in dealing with the West at official and everyday life levels is reflected in the binary opposition of self/other. At the official level, it is reduced to the Iran/West binary and the rest of the 'others' are of secondary importance. At the level of everyday life, however, other binary oppositions may be more important than the Iran/West one.

Those binaries will finally lead to a different situation in relations at the two levels, which is reflected by the cold/warm binary opposition. The main purport of warm relations at the level of everyday life is the intensity of the relationship and its dynamism according to the conditions of the time. This is an active situation, which is not necessarily positive, and it indicates serious differences in the consciousness of Iranians in relation to the West at official and everyday life levels. In other words, the practical consciousness of Iranians with regard to the West at the level of everyday life is very different from the consciousness that prevails at the official level. That difference becomes more interesting when we note that concerns about safeguarding the country's independence and national interests are similar both at the official level and in everyday life and there is even a similar judgement about the post-colonial aims of the West.

These differences do not necessarily prefigure conflict, yet herald complexity of action by Iranians because at both levels its aims are similar. This difference demonstrates two logic actions and necessity as we have not observed that the nation/state fusion in the previous decades in Iran and the Islamic Republic has gained wide support from a range of people. The unfriendly attitude of the West to Iran has had an important role in constituting Iranian politics at the formal level. Therefore, change in the West's foreign politics when dealing with Iran can be a determining factor.

It seems that when dealing with important relations between Iran and the West, on which the resolution of many global challenges depends, attention should always be paid to the possibility of the application of new language and discourse. Also, everyday life should be considered much more important than before. Iranians have tried in this area to draw on their cultural resources and interact in a creative manner with the West, despite structural limitations such as the imbalance of power. They have endeavoured, through selective and flexible adoption of Western elements, to keep their different historical identity alive.

Notes

1 Iranian and Western official domains as well as Iranian and Western everyday lives.
2 The reasons include study limitations, more political understanding of everyday life in Iran, and a much higher importance of 'Western affairs' in the everyday life of Iran compared to the importance of 'Iranian affairs' in Western everyday life.
3 The main issue here is the image of being 'domestic' or 'foreign'; the correctness or falseness of a claim of authenticity is not an issue.
4 See studies by Azad Armaki, Chavoshian, Shahabi and Shalchi.

Bibliography

Abazari, Yousef, and Neda Milani (2005), 'Representation of the West in Student Periodicals', *Nameh Olum Ejtemaei*, No. 26, winter 2005, pp. 97–122.

Ahearne, Jeremy (1995), *Michel De Certeau: Interpretation and its Other*, Cambridge: Polity Press.

Alikhah, Fardin (2008), 'Political Consequences of Consumerism', *Iranian Cultural Studies Quarterly*, No. 1, spring 2008, pp. 231–256.

Armaki, Taqi Azad (2007), *Everyday Life in Iran: Power and Culture*, Tehran: Jihad University Institute.

Armaki, Taqi Azad, and Vahid Shalchi (2005), 'Two Iranian Worlds: Mosque and Coffee Shop', *Iranian Society of Cultural and Communication Studies Quarterly*, 1st year, No. 4, fall and winter.

Bennett, Andy (2007), *Culture and Everyday Life*, translated by Leila Joafshani and Hassan Chavoshian, Tehran: Akhtaran Press.

De Certeau, Michel (1988) *The Practice of Everyday Life*, translated by Steven Rendall, Los Angeles: University of California Press.

Fazeli, Mohammad (2008), 'An Image of the Cultural Lifestyle of an Academic Community', *Iranian Cultural Studies Quarterly*, No. 1, spring 2008, pp. 175–198.

Fazeli, Ne'matollah (2008), 'Modernity and Housing: An Anthropological Approach to the Concept of Home, Rural Lifestyle, and its Modern Developments', *Iranian Cultural Studies Quarterly*, No. 1, spring 2008, pp. 25–63.

Fiske, John (1992), 'Cultural Studies and Culture of Everyday Life' in L. Grossberg (ed.) *Cultural Studies*, New York: Routledge.

Fokouhi, Nasser (2008), 'Minority Subcultures and Lifestyle: Trends and Outlooks', *Iranian Cultural Studies Quarterly*, No. 1, spring 2008, pp. 143–174.

Hajiani, Ebrahim (2007), *Lifestyle Models in Iran*, Tehran: Strategic Studies Research Institute.

Hamidi, Nafiseh, and Mehdi Faraji (2008), 'Women's Lifestyle and Cover in Tehran', *Iranian Cultural Studies Quarterly*, No. 1, spring 2008, pp. 65–92.

Highton, Ben (2002), *Everyday Life and Cultural Theory: An Introduction*, London: Routledge.

Ian, Kribe (1999), *Modern Social Theory: From Parsons to Habermas*, translated by Abbas Mokhber, Tehran: Agah Press.

Kazemi, Abbas, and Mohammad Rezaei (2008), 'Dialectics of Differentiation and Removing Differentiations: Sauntering and Lifestyle of Lower Urban Classes in Tehran Shopping Malls', *Iranian Cultural Studies Quarterly*, No. 1, spring 2008, pp. 1–24.

Moran, Joe (2005), *Reading the Everyday*, New York: Routledge.

Reiters, George (1997), *Theory of Sociology in Contemporary Times*, translated by Mohsen Salasi, Tehran: Scientific Press.

Shahabi, Mahmoud (2003), 'Subcultures of Youth in Iran: Readings and Consequences', *Iranian Sociological Letter*, No. 4.

Shahabi, Mahmoud (2006), 'Youth Subculture in Post-Revolution Iran: An Alternative Reading', in Nilan, Pam, and Carlos Feixa (eds), *Global Youth? Hybrid Identities, Plural Worlds*, UK: Routledge.

Shalchi, Vahid (2008), 'Coffee Shop Youth Lifestyle', *Iranian Cultural Studies Quarterly*, No. 1, spring 2008, pp. 93–115.

Sohrabzadeh, Mehran (2008), 'A Comparison Between Generational and Intergenerational Mentality in Academic Generations after the Islamic Revolution', *Institute for Cultural and Social Studies*, Ministry of Science, Research and Technology.

Stevens, Rob (2000), *Great Sociologists*, translated by Mehrdad Mirdamadi, Tehran: Markaz Press.

Zokaei, Mohammad Saeed (2007), 'Youth, Globalization and International Immigration: A Study on Young Elites', *Iranian Journal of Sociology*, Vol. 7, No. 2.

Zokaei, Mohammad Saeed (2008), 'Youth, Body and Fitness', *Iranian Cultural Studies Quarterly*, No. 1, spring 2008, pp. 117–141.

Zokaei, Mohammad Saeed, and Seyed Ayatollah Mirzaei (2006), *Young Boys and Manliness Values*, Vol. 5, No. 3.

8 Domestic politics and foreign policy in contemporary Iran

Anoushiravan Ehteshami

Introduction

More than 30 years on from Iran's Islamic Revolution, which ended the reign of monarchs, the country continues to fascinate, worry and excite outsiders in equal measure. Though unique in so many ways, Iran also has key features in common with other revolutionary regimes. This revolution, like so many others before it, though essentially domestic, caused a tear in the very fabric of the prevailing international system. Revolutions, furthermore, disrupt and change the balance of power and with it the normal flow of diplomacy, and again Iran's was no exception in this regard. Iran's religious-inspired revolution undid the intricate international web of relationships that the Pahlavi monarchy had spawned and sustained, and it also brought forth a series of new initiatives more consistent with the values and outlook of the new emerging elite and their ideological commitments. So, as we take stock of Iran's foreign relations, and the ebb and flow of its policies, we would be well advised to examine its external role with its unique revolutionary origins in mind. The revolution may be little more than a historical curiosity today, but the political regime it spawned has been anything but. Iran has played a significant part in shaping the Middle East region, and the revolution did everything to accelerate Tehran's interaction with its hinterland. Regional and global powers alike have had little option but to contend with Iran, and despite efforts to isolate or 'contain' it, the country has made huge strides towards becoming a considerable regional player. Indeed, while in the 1990s the discussion was more about Iran as a regional *actor*, since 9/11 the more common analytical currency has been about understanding Iran as a regional *power*.

Furthermore, I made the assertion in 2004 that in the case of Iran it is often the interaction between the domestic tensions and the complex external conditions that provide the matrix for assessing its foreign policy.[1] Events since the end of the Cold War, and in particular post-9/11 Western interventions in the region have very much amplified this relationship. Indeed, since the election of President Ahmadinejad in 2005, and his re-appointment as president following the June 2009 elections, my conviction is that this relationship has, if anything, become even more organic.

Given Iran's regional weight and its presence in so many regional theatres, it has been grabbing the headlines for some time. Of interest to the outside world are the consequences of its apparent political influence and geopolitical weight in the broader Middle East region; the intensity of its nuclear (and related military) programme; the diplomatic crisis and economic and political stand-off with the international community that its nuclear intentions sparked; the antics and diplomatic conduct of its neoconservative president; and, last but not least its tenth presidential race in June 2009 in which the incumbent was facing a strong challenge from three other candidates for his second and final term in office. The election was of immediate international concern because of the consequences of its outcome for Iran and also for the country's policy priorities for the next few years. The outside world was keenly interested in the election for it provided the first chance to see beyond the neocon-servative Ahmadinejad. Let us recall that with the overwhelming victory of Mahmoud Ahmadinejad in Iran's June 2005 presidential election, Iran had entered new and uncharted waters in both its domestic politics and foreign relations. Elected on an anti-corruption and religio-populist platform, Ahmadinejad's (second round) success in the June 2005 ballot enabled him to take office on 3 August as the clear champion of the conservative tendencies in Iran.[2] His platform was unashamedly populist and his outlook increasingly neoconservative.[3] President Ahmadinejad soon began implementing policies consistent with his new priorities, moving beyond the established interests of the state as drawn by the two previous administrations of Rafsanjani and Khatami. Ahmadinejad's policy positions (for example, his vitriolic attacks on Israel and Zionism and his denial of the Holocaust) unsettled nerves at home and abroad, and raised suspicions of Iran's motives and strategic objectives in the region. Iran, arguably, entered a new era of post-détente after August 2005.[4] Ahmadinejad has drawn considerable support from the Revolutionary Guards (Sepāh) and the large paramilitary Basij force, and in the relationship with this military elite his administration has been different from all previous ones. His election victory in 2005, one can argue, for the first time brought into the political mix the powerful Sepāh and has given them a strong political voice in both the domestic and external affairs of the republic. For all intents and purposes, the Ahmadinejad administration marked a break in both policy terms and outlook from its predecessors.

Indeed, given the outcome of the June 2009 election, interest in contemporary developments in Iran could not be greater. Iran has continued to hog the limelight. But allegations of fraud in the 12 June presidential race, followed by brutal suppression of protesters, allegations of torture and Soviet-style show trials of prominent reformists for their alleged conspiracy to carry out a 'velvet revolution' in the country, have not only tarnished the republic's image but have also exposed the deep cleavages in the country's political elite about the future direction of the country. Credibility abroad and legitimacy at home have emerged as two new and important commodities for Tehran to reacquire as it has tried to reassess its relationship with the world.

Iran before the tenth presidential poll

It is worth underscoring the fact that before the June election Iran could not have been more assured of its standing in the region – it had, for one, penetrated the heartland of the Arab world and in both Iraq and Palestine it had established a strong presence. It also had successfully strengthened its links with Syria and presence in Lebanon. It had established strong links with Islamist groups in Palestine, with Hamas in particular, and built a series of relationships with political forces in post-Taliban Afghanistan. In post-invasion Iraq, moreover, it had emerged as the new Baghdad's trusted friend and partner and, to the chagrin of Iraq's Sunni Arab neighbours, had also created enclaves of Iranian presence all across the country, in Iraqi Kurdistan as much as in the Arab-dominated parts of the country. Also, with regard to its nuclear programme, Tehran had declared the negotiations over its uranium enrichment activities closed, and by snubbing the 5+1 July 2008 package of incentives it had effectively rejected any compromise on this matter. Indeed, in the June election campaign President Ahmadinejad was to boast about his administration's great success in defeating the West's efforts to undermine Iran's nuclear ambitions, stating that he had achieved all of Iran's goals without any compromise or concession. Iran, in his eyes, had emerged stronger and more influential as a consequence – unlike the period in which Khatami had been in charge he emphasized. As he put it, Iran had managed to join the select nuclear club of countries with ease and in spite of Western efforts to deny it the fundamentals of nuclear technology and power. On this front too, Iran apparently was worlds apart from so many of its neighbours, for it had single-mindedly developed the country's scientific base and also the means to defend it. Ahmadinejad argued that for all these achievements, therefore, Iran was in a better position than virtually all of its neighbours.

With oil prices at historically unprecedented levels too, for much of Ahmadinejad's first term in office (2005–2009) he truly must have felt blessed and incapable of doing anything wrong. In sum, going into the elections, Iran's regional role and influence post-9/11 was apparently assured and its power unassailable. It was now a great regional power with a finger in every pie, and it was a power that was making rapid and eye-catching advances in the nuclear field as well as in the field of defence and military industries. All that it had to do now, to ensure its place as an international player of some significance, was to show the world the power and authenticity of its democratic system and institutions (though this term democratic would never be used by the Iranian establishment) and the massive grassroots support the regime enjoyed among the population. The final act in the return of Iran as a major player was to be in the regime showing the world the robustness of its political institutions and the effectiveness of its participatory processes. Ahmadinejad and his allies expected that on 13 June the world would wake up to a celebration of its political openness and people power as prescribed in Iran's Islamic system. Indeed: 'Just one day before the June 12 presidential election, the Islamic republic had never been so powerful. Tehran had not only survived three decades of diplomatic isolation and economic sanctions but had emerged a regional superpower, rivalled only by Israel. Its influence shaped conflicts and politics from Afghanistan to Lebanon.'[5]

To be sure, Ahmadinejad's first term had not been free of problems and was, in fact, one of the most turbulent of administrations in the Islamic Republic's history.

The economy had been severely damaged by his administration's populist policies. The unprecedented and massive oil income had been largely squandered, and inflation and unemployment had reached high levels while productivity had slumped. Also, UN-imposed sanctions due to Iran's unwillingness to suspend uranium enrichment had begun to hurt the economy, deterring foreign investors and raising the premium on doing business with Iran. Politically too there had been much instability. There had been a dozen high-level resignations and dismissals between 2006 and 2009, and the president had managed to alienate all strata of core elite members because of his management style and ill-advised utterances. More fundamentally, his first term in office had also marked extensive securitization of society and state, with the paramilitary personnel increasingly present in the ministerial, economic and political corridors of power. Universities, intellectuals, the media and public space more generally were severely constrained during his presidency and, in sharp contrast to the administration of his predecessor, pressures on civil society and democratic discourse were increased.

But overall, the president, the Supreme Leader (Ayatollah Khamenei) and their allies were confident going into the election that *their* Islamic Republic was secure and its future as a beacon of Islamic resistance assured; moreover, Iran itself was all powerful too and acting on the world stage on its own terms. Iran was a humiliated country no more and thanks to the revolution and the 'principalist' (fundamentalist) policies of President Ahmadinejad, Iranians could hold their head high knowing that their country was a player of influence. Furthermore, thanks to President Bush's two wars in the Middle East, Iran was secure in the knowledge that its voice in the region was significant and also that its Arab neighbours were in no position to effectively challenge its role. The regional setting in which Ahmadinejad had operated since 2005 had facilitated his hard-line stance on so many regional issues, and the spectacular success of pro-Iran Hezbollah militias in 2006 in the Lebanon war between the Hezbollah Movement and Israel sealed Iran's place as the most important Muslim state standing in front of Israel. But, the regional environment in which Ahmadinejad had operated between 2005 and 2009, and the one in which he was to start his second term in office would prove to be entirely different. While in the first period the region was still in the throes of the Bush doctrine (on which more to follow), whose policy outcomes seemed to facilitate Tehran's radicalism and its support for the so-called 'resistance front' in the Arab world, the post-Bush era was to give birth to a whole new American outlook.

The regional and international environment under President Bush

In looking at the regional setting, it is worth noting that the region's international relations are complex and unpredictable, and in this context it is useful to remember the region's strategic setting in the period following the tragedy of 9/11. Later, 11 September 2001 brought into even sharper focus the security dilemmas of the Middle East and North Africa (MENA) region, at the same time also altering some features of interstate norms by the inclusion of the war on terrorism as a mandatory aspect of the West's relations with the Muslim world in general, and the United States' contacts with the Middle East in particular. The war on terror demanded the adoption of a new grand American strategy, which would seek to eradicate the three key sources of threat to America and its interests worldwide, these being: terrorism, weapons of mass destruction in the hands of rogue actors (states or groups), and regional states pursuing policies deemed hostile to the United States. As Steve Wright notes, for the neoconservative-led Bush adminis-tration, 9/11 provided the logic for pre-emption, 'anticipatory self-defence', as the country's first line of defence.[6] Indeed, the Middle East became the testing ground of the new America project. The Arab world within it was identified as the source of what the US administration insisted was the new danger, and one even greater than that of the old Soviet threat. The new task of American foreign policy was not just to use force proactively but also to reshape the domestic environment of several 'failed states' in the Middle East, whose incompetent governments and stagnant economies had nurtured anti-American terrorism. On another front, the impression of intervention as part of a grand strategy was further reinforced by the democra-tization component of the Bush doctrine. President Bush brought this issue to the forefront of his national security strategy in November 2003, in the course of two major speeches, delivered in Washington (6 November) and London (19 November), respectively. In speaking of a 'forward strategy of freedom in the Middle East', he spoke of the need to change America's relations with the region. In Washington, the president put the emphasis on the need for reform, there was a 'freedom deficit', he emphasized. In London on 19 November 2003 President Bush was even more candid, saying that 'we must shake off decades of failed policy in the Middle East … in the past [we] have been willing to make a bargain, to tolerate oppression for the sake of stability. Longstanding ties often led us to overlook the faults of local elites. Yet this bargain did not bring stability or make us safe. It merely bought time, while problems festered and ideologies of violence took hold.'[7]

Thus, post-9/11, the United States launched a 'root and branch' reform strategy, finally ditching one of the main planks of the West's Cold War policies in the Middle East, namely extending full support for all those rulers deemed to be friendly to the West and its interests, irrespective of their policies at home.

In general terms, there is considerable evidence to suggest that after 9/11 the regional balance of power did begin moving away from the great Arab powers and shifting towards such countries as Iran and Israel. But the policies of the Arab states have remained vital to the overall strategic make-up of the region, and their role cannot and should not be underestimated. Within the Arab region itself too, power has been shifting – the role of Saudi Arabia has grown among the big three, and some smaller players, with their considerable financial muscle and also US support, have grown in significance. The Gulf Arab countries of Qatar, the United Arab Emirates (UAE) and, to a lesser extent, Kuwait, fall into this category. These countries are said to be emerging as new influential actors in their own right in the Middle East arena, affecting regional politics in ways that does not always meet with the interests of the major regional actors.

Bush's war on terror benefited Iran quite directly, for regime change in Afghanistan (2001) and Iraq (2003) removed Iran's two enemies from its doorstep and also facilitated the extension of Iran's influence across the region. Regime change in Iraq also gave Iran another Shia-ruling regime in the region, the first one of its kind in the Arab world for the best part of a millennium. Once Iran was assured of its own security after the fall of Baghdad in April 2003 it began to plot for the extension of its role and influence, and once Ahmadinejad took the reins in September 2005 Tehran hardened its position on many regional issues, directly challenging the Bush doctrine in the Middle East. Until 2009, therefore, Tehran under Ahmadinejad was content to build on the failures of the Bush presidency in the region and flaunt its intransigence, assured in the knowledge that American's unpopularity in the Middle East would give Iran's open anti-Americanism a real boost on the so-called 'Arab street'. In November 2008, several months before Iran's own presidential race, the assumptions about American policies in the region had to be reviewed however. That is, against Iran's expectation, once Barack Obama had been elected to occupy the White House from January 2009 there was going to be a new game to play and one that was likely to be very different from that of President Bush.

The regional and international environment under President Obama

Thus, 2009 gave us a new start, for the one critically important new element in the region's strategic equation was the election of the new American president who had displayed a wholly new outlook and had new agendas to pursue. From global nuclear disarmament to combating climate change, to peace in the Middle East, his administration has attempted to change the rules of the game through multilateralism and engagement. President Obama, therefore, entered the White House professing a new policy of engagement with the Middle East. He expressed the interest and the intention to reach out to Iran and Syria, to work towards peace in Palestine, to reduce America's military presence in Iraq, and to generally mend bridges with the Muslim world. This is how he put it: 'I've come here to Cairo to seek a new beginning between the United States and Muslims around the world, one based on mutual interest and mutual respect, and one based upon the truth that America and Islam are not exclusive and need not be in competition. Instead, they overlap, and share common principles – principles of justice and progress; tolerance and the dignity of all human beings. I do so recognizing that change cannot happen over-night. I know there's been a lot of publicity about this speech, but no single speech can eradicate years of mistrust, nor can I answer in the time that I have this afternoon all the complex questions that brought us to this point. But I am convinced that in order to move forward, we must say openly to each other the things we hold in our hearts and that too often are said only behind closed doors. There must be a sustained effort to listen to each other; to learn from each other; to respect one another; and to seek common ground. As the Holy Koran tells us, "Be conscious of God and speak always the truth" (Applause). That is what I will try to do today – to speak the truth as best I can, humbled by the task before us, and firm in my belief that the interests we share as human beings are far more powerful than the forces that drive us apart.'[8]

This message of hope and diplomatic engagement is very significant for it signals a different body language to that of the Bush era. It also provides the new administration with breathing space as it sets about embedding America's new policies and priorities. An America at peace with the region will mean an Iran at odds with it, given that Ahmadinejad built his presidency on that of 'resistance' to 'World Zionism', Israel and the United States. What they will do with Obama's stretched hand, which has been there since his inauguration in January 2009, remains a mystery. Of equal interest is how Tehran might respond to Obama's qualitatively different 'carrot and stick' strategy towards Iran if the parties do not reach a negotiated agreement over Iran's nuclear programme. Threats of 'crippling economic sanctions' emerged alongside the political crisis caused in Tehran by the election result, reinforcing the siege mentality to which Ahmadinejad and Ayatollah Khamenei have both been prone. In this they both openly and vociferously have accused the West of plotting a 'velvet revolution' in their country, and were arguably therefore less inclined to grasp Obama's hand in friendship. That was, until the 1 October meeting in Geneva with the 5+1 in which Iran made some concessions to the international community – agreeing to seek further enrichment of fuel cells for its power reactors in Russia and China, and also allowing IAEA inspectors to undertake an inspection of its recently discovered secret facility near Qom.

It would appear that the absolute security of Israel is also being linked to the containment of Iran, evidently directly affecting the Obama administration's agendas with such global actors as China and Russia.[9] Clearly, containment has been the driver, even in the efforts to establish direct contact with Tehran. Iran's isolation, through a new American bridge-building exercise with Syria and a reshaping of the Levant's politics, has been viewed through the same prism, one can argue. Ironically, even the new White House's effort to reignite the peace process has cynics interpreting it as an effort to curtail Iran's influence in the region. So, while President Obama is seen as a breath of fresh air, regional friend (Israel and Egypt, say) and foe alike remain suspicious and weary of some of his proposed policies, and uncertain of the direction in which his professed priorities will take the region. For Tehran, therefore, in strategic terms a change of president in the US does not necessarily lead to fundamentally different policies in the Middle East. And so long as this is their mindset it should not be totally surprising to find that the pro-establishment factions in Iran would go out of their way to ensure the return to the presidency of Ahmadinejad – the hard-line and uncompromising president equipped to strengthen the line of regional 'resistance' and by extension the power base of the neoconservatives in Tehran. Domestic and external are organically linked!

Iran post-election

On 13 June a different set of issues were prevailing. How secure was the regime? How can it recover from its crisis of legitimacy? What will be its foreign policy priorities when so many at home question the legitimacy of its president and also the judgement of the Supreme Leader (the final policy arbiter in the country)? It is of course impossible to say with any certainty where the post-election crisis will lead and what kind of Iran will emerge from the other side. Political change can be rapid, or can require months of gestation before manifesting itself. Even then we will not be sure of the make-up of a 'new' Iran. But we can be confident of two things: first, that the relationship between state and society has been changed in ways beyond the regime's expectations. Society is fighting to throw the state off its back, and the more the state pressures the people the more likely that the people will become more daring in challenging the state and its symbols.

Secondly, the relationship between the forces that make up the Iranian power elite will never be the same again. The zero-sum game in play has made compromise supremely difficult and as both camps now fight their battles purportedly for the soul of the revolution and its ideals, we are probably witnessing the disaggregation of the republican state as a single ideological monolith. Failure of the Iranian Islamist Republic, therefore, could mean the following, in the absence of a huge power change or another revolution: 'Iran is at a crossroads … One road is complete militarization and control of the people and being completely cut off from the rest of the world like North Korea, and another road is being the dictatorship it is but opening up to the rest of the world and moving forward with the rest of the world in technology, in athletics and many other respects, which would in turn naturally provide a little bit more freedom for the youth each step of the way.'[10]

Concluding thoughts

Clearly securitization of the Iranian state has mirrored the rapid militarization of regional politics post-9/11. As the political arteries of the region hardened during the Bush era, so did the pro-security forces across the Middle East, including Iran. But it would be foolish to argue that the former was the catalyst, let alone the cause, of the latter. Iran's neoconservatives had been planning their bid for power at the height of President Khatami's presidency, well before events of autumn 2001. Furthermore, Iran's neoconservatives represent a coalition of political, military and clerical forces whose roots are to be found in the foundation stones of the Islamic Republic, but who are also representatives of the post-revolution generation. This group certainly reacted to 9/11 by accelerating the drive for power, but the group itself was not forged in response to 9/11.

Furthermore, despite President Obama's conciliatory tone one is left in no doubt that the three areas of concern originally highlighted by President Bush – terrorism, weapons of mass destruction (WMDs), anti-Americanism – continue to exercise his successor as well. In fact, some of the issues underlined then have acquired an even greater degree of importance and policy urgency since 2008, most notably of course the challenge of Iran's nuclear programme.

This being the case, it is again likely that Iran's fortunes will be shaped through its policies in the region and its perceptions of the outside world's policies towards the ruling regime. In this context, what transpires over Iran's nuclear programme is likely to prove decisive. For a paranoid regime whose whole worldview is shaped by conspiracy theories and fear of regime change, to have its very foundations shaken by its own citizens is not good news. But for a weakened regime, accommodation with the US for the sake of survival at home would be a price worth paying.

But, on the other hand, as the siege mentality gets reinforced there will be those in the establishment who could in all probability encourage the acceleration of the nuclear programme's weaponization dimension. For them, survival can only be assured through a strong deterrence: to deter outsiders from interfering in its suppression of the opposition movement at home. None of this is good news – not for the sake of non-proliferation, nor for the sake of a more stable Iran or hope of improved relations between Iran and the West. Post-June 2009, therefore, we entered a new period of uncertainty for the region, and given Iran's significant weight and influence in the broader Middle East, developments in the Islamic Republic will cast a long shadow over everything else in the region. Ironically, while Washington seems ready for a qualitative leap forward and a comprehensive deal for better relations with Iran, Tehran is nurturing a typical bunker mentality in which Western enemies are sought behind every street lamp and imagined conspiracies are uncovered in the most innocent of relationships. Tehran today seems less ready to chart a new path for the country in the world than at any time since the 1979 revolution. More than 30 years on from the revolution, Iran's place in the world remains ill-defined, as indeed does its role conception. As we have seen, the very nature of the political regime that grew out of the revolutionary coalition is now being openly contested and as this drama unfolds, things for Iran and also for the Middle East are unlikely to ever be the same again.

Notes

1 See my 'Iran's International Posture in the Wake of the Iraq War', *Middle East Journal*, vol. 58, no. 2, Spring 2004, 179–194.
2 Kasra Naji, *Ahmadinejad: The Secret History of Iran's Radical Leader* (London: I. B. Tauris, 2008).
3 See Anoushiravan Ehteshami and Mahjoob Zweiri, *Iran and the Rise of its Neoconservatives: The Politics of Tehran's Silent Revolution* (London: I. B. Tauris, 2007).
4 See Anoushiravan Ehteshami, 'Iran's Regional Policies Since the End of the Cold War', in Ali Gheisari (ed.) *Contemporary Iran: Economy, Society, Politics* (Oxford: Oxford University Press, 2009): 324–348.
5 Robin Wright, 'Tipping Point in Tehran', *Washington Post*, 14 July 2009.
6 Steve Wright, *The United States and Persian Gulf Security: The Foundations of the War on Terror* (Reading: Ithaca Press, 2007).
7 'President Bush Discusses Iraq Policy at Whitehall Palace in London', Office of the Press Secretary, The White House, 19 November 2003. Also see: http://www.foxnews.com/story/0,2933,103514,00.html (accessed 27 April 2011).
8 'Remarks by the President on a New Beginning', Office of the Press Secretary, The White House, 4 June 2009. Also see: http://www.pbs.org/newshour/updates/politics/jan-june09/obamaspeech_06-04.html (accessed 27 April 2011).
9 Jay Solomon, 'U.S. Engages Russia, Syria to Isolate Iran', *Wall Street Journal*, 4 March 2009.
10 Paneta Beigi, quoted in Samira Simone, 'Opposition Movement in Iran not Over, Experts Say', CNN, 1 July 2009.

9   Foreign policy as social construction

Hossein Salimi

Introduction

Beyond the rapid flow of progress and development of science and technology, international relations affect all aspects of human life, and remain one of the most important fields of human knowledge. This is the main reason behind the importance of understanding foreign policy in the new turbulent world. Besides, a sentence or a statement by a policymaker may bring about a catastrophe or remove a hazardous condition in some countries, regions and even the world. However, some questions arise. How are the behaviours in the international arena formed? Why does a state identify and introduce itself as a cooperative or hostile actor among others? And, finally, how is a foreign policy formed? These enquiries are always significant and permanently new, not only because the condition of international relations is changing but also because the way of thinking and tools of investigations are being transformed.

At the end of the 20th century, new concepts and different styles of understanding in international relations theories were introduced by new schools of thought. Meanwhile, by the time of the collapse of the Soviet Union and the end of the Cold War, new problems appeared in the world arena. The Islamic Republic of Iran is one of these new phenomena. Recently, particularly after George W. Bush's presidency in the US, the foreign policy of Iran has been at the core of international arguments. Therefore, some theoreticians have tried to understand Iranian foreign policy and its special issues by using the new concepts in differing tendencies to comprehend international relations. For instance, Vivienne Jabri makes an effort to understand the issue of Iran by using Michel Foucault's Analytics of War. Jabri asserts that, 'Iran is in the news once again. Having categorized it as a member of the so-called "axis of evil", George Bush was in effect placing Iran on notice; having dealt with Iraq, Iran was next on the list. … That Iran was next on the list seemed to vindicate voices in Washington that had long perceived Iran, the seat of the Islamic Revolution, as the primary threat to the security of the United States and the West more widely conceived.'[1] Jabri makes a new framework for analysing this matter, through Foucault's concept of the war condition. She describes her article by saying, 'This article revisits the postcolonial critique of Michel Foucault and argues that this critique comes into force when explored through Foucault's interpretation of the Iranian Revolution. This critique is highly significant for our present considerations of how the global articulation of power is at one and the same time implicated in redrawing the sphere of the international and in generating particular forms of resistance to such power. ... it was precisely the absence of imperialism, its practices, and modes of resistance against it, in Foucault's analytics of power that drew much of the postcolonial critique of his work, even as this critique is largely sympathetic to Foucault's overall work.'[2] On the other hand, some writers like Arshin Adib-Moghaddam reveal that there are another ways for understanding hidden dimensions of Iranian foreign policy. He concludes, in his *Iran in World Politics* that 'when one explore Iran's state-society relations, foreign policy, relations with the United States, Persian art, literature and poetry, it is not in order to link them together on the basis of a single methodology or a set of a-historical truths ... The horizon of critical Iranian studies is not science *per se*. Rather, its purpose is to engender dialectical analysis that divides up the diversity of contemporary Iran. ... [the book] was designed to ask "how" rather than "what", to present alternatives rather than imperatives, to diversity rather than unify, to explore the making of politics, culture, norms, institutions rather than getting engaged in the grand project of reifying them.'[3] It could be so significant that we find a theoretical framework for explaining diversities and somehow, contradictions, rather than elucidating everything with a rigid rationality.

Jabri and Adib-Moghaddam, like many other analysts, argued that realist and liberalist frameworks are not the only ways to analyse current issues of the international relations, and thus I shall also try to apply a different theory for understanding Iranian foreign policy. This theory is a special interpretation of constructivism, although I do not apply it in exactly the same way as Adib-Moghaddam. Before explaining my approach to this theory, I would like to pose some questions. My main question, not only in this chapter but in my understanding of other current issues of the international relations, which I am going to discuss here, is the following:

> *What is the cause of the emergence of revolutionary-hostile foreign policy in the contemporary world?*

I will try to answer this question theoretically and make a conceptual ground for my enquiry about foreign policy of Iran. Hence my secondary question shall be:

> *Is there any ground for the formation of overwhelming revolutionary-coarseness-hostile foreign policy in the main body of Iranian society?*

In this chapter I will elaborate my core ideas and answer these questions by assuming two hypotheses. In the main hypothesis, I will state my main idea about the subjective grounds of a special kind of foreign policy. So, my main hypothesis is, 'Theoretically some ideas such as illegitimate approach to international order and legitimacy of use of violence, which are socially constructed are the main grounds for revolutionary-hostile foreign policy.' I shall try to apply this approach to the foreign policy of Iran; therefore, my secondary hypothesis is ''In the main body of Iranian society, there are criticisms about international order but there are no inclinations to coarseness-hostile foreign policy.'

In studying these subjects, I will use two different methods. In answering my first question, I will use some theoretical debates that will help me to provide basic concepts for a constructivist understanding of Iranian foreign policy. In spite of some criticisms on the use of quantitative study of foreign policy in constructivism, I take advantage of some quantitative information for achieving a better interpretation of Iranian foreign policy. Part of this enquiry is based upon original research that has taken place, with cooperation of my PhD students in Iran.

The bases of constructivist understanding of social phenomena

Constructivism helps us in finding the genesis of political behaviours and the international positions and identities in the depth of beliefs and cultural trends in a society. It takes us beyond the usual and ordinary political discussions and opens new windows to see new aspects of political life. Friedrich Kratochwil believes that 'constructivism is neither a theory, nor even an approach to politics, but as little as e.g. "empiricism" is. Rather, in both cases a meta-theoretical issue is raised, i.e. whether "things" are simply "given" and correctly perceived by our senses (empiricism), or whether the "things" we perceive are rather the product of our conceptualisations (constructivism). They answer questions like "how do you know" more than questions which issues, variables, institutions, or whatever, are the elements out of which we built our "theories" of a certain subject matter. Social phenomena are consequences of inter-subjective interactions & collective ideas rather than material conditions.'[4] According to this attitude, the classic boundaries between the politics and other disciplines of humanities have collapsed. The differentiation between contending methods of research also falls down, and so we can construct a particular understanding of a political and international affair as well as of other human knowledge. Meantime, some of the theoreticians of cultural studies present the same view on politics. Michael Thompson, Gunner Grendstad and Per Selle assert that, 'The boundary line between the political and the non-political, Cultural Theories pointed out, is not self-evidence; it is socially constructed. And, since some people are busily constructing that line in one way and others in different ways, its position is always in dispute ... Cultural Theory's focus is on the various ways in which we bind ourselves to one another – social solidarities – integral to each of which, it argues, is a patterning of beliefs and values: a distinctive cultural bias.'[5] For this reason, now, a new term, *geographies of knowledge* has been formed. From this point of view, knowledge of politics, other disciplines in humanities and social sciences depend on the meaning systems in different regions. As John Agnew points out, 'The main claim here is that knowledge about world politics (or anything else) from one place is not necessarily incommensurable or unintelligible relative to knowledge produced elsewhere. Cross-cultural communication goes on all the time without anything being lost in translation. Indeed, knowledge in some places gains in both the possibility of greater geographical scope and cultural sensitivity when it is informed by knowledge coming from other places.'[6]

These phrases indicate that there is a different way for understanding human behaviour, particularly political behaviours. Although some of these different schools differentiate between their theories and well-known constructivists, I think all of them can be regarded as taking a constructivist approach, because constructivism is based upon the ability of human beings to make and build up political phenomenon through intersubjective communications and mental interactions within and out of a society. The bases of the constructivism approach are revealed in Wendt's words, 'Constructivism is a structural theory of the international system that makes the following core claims: (1) states are the principal units of analysis for international political theory; (2) the key structures in the states system are intersubjective, rather than material; (3) state identities and interests are in important part constructed by these social structures, rather than given exogenously to the system by human nature or domestic politics.'[7] My main concern in this chapter is the mechanism of forming Iranian consciousness about themselves and their worldly life. As John Ruggie asserts, 'Social constructivism is about human consciousness and its role in international life. As such, constructivism rests on an irreducibly intersubjective dimension of human action: the capacity and will of people to take a deliberate attitude towards the world and to lend it *significance*. ... Constructivists contend that not only are identities and interests of actors socially constructed, but also that they must share the stage with a whole host of other ideational factors emanating from people as cultural beings.'[8] Although some scholars have criticized the constructivism approach as a limited and practically useless theory, I believe that this theory has provided a new theoretical atmosphere for comprehending the depth of international affairs. Maja Zehfuss is one of the main critiques of constructivism. Zehfuss critiques constructivist theories of international relations, arguing that they stop us from acting responsibly. She uses Germany's shift towards using its military abroad after the end of the Cold War, something the country had not done before, to illustrate why constructivism does not work and how it leads to particular analytical outcomes, while foreclosing others. Zehfuss argues that this limits our ability to act responsibly in international relations. Despite the fact that constructivist theories of international relations are currently considered to be at the cutting edge of the discipline, Zehfuss finds them wanting and even politically dangerous.[9] But I think that we can improve our abilities for understanding by constructivism, because special considerations of constructivism can help us to find the hidden factors behind the formation of a political or an international phenomenon, and aid us in understanding the social genesis of international behaviours. By the use of these different views, I summarize and express my idea and my interpretation of constructivism through the theoretical framework of this chapter, as set out below.

1. Social phenomena are consequences of intersubjective interactions and collective ideas rather than material conditions;
2. Collective ideas represent themselves in the framework of culture and general identities;
3. For understanding human phenomena, we have to comprehend how human beings interpret themselves and understand their role in the world-life.

Concept of foreign policy

Foreign policy is a buzzword, but its definition is not clear. For classical theorists as well as for ordinary people, the definition is obvious: it is the behaviours and decisions of sovereign states in the international relations arena. But, for the new generation of theories, this simple definition is problematic, because it cannot solve any problem. To answer the question of what foreign policy is, we need deeper concepts that help us find out how states behave in the international scene. For some analysts, foreign policy is just some practical measures and diplomacy. But, as Roy Jones states, 'The essential characteristics of foreign policy are, then, practice and style'.[10] It is most misleading to limit foreign politics studies to some practical considerations. This crucial area of man's life is not just the business of politicians and diplomats but is a sign and symbol of a society's identity in its world-life. For some writers, foreign policy is the field of our actions in the world, as Christopher Hill explains, 'Foreign policy is a concept that has been neglected academically in recent years. Politically it has been given more attention, but mostly as a vehicle for ethical projects. ... Foreign policy provides us with a focal point for the debate about political agency – that is, how we may act in the world, and with what effects – which we avoid at our peril.'[11] However, we cannot comprehend this area without finding its social roots.

To constructivism, foreign policy is socially constructed. Some systems of meanings, within society and at the international level, create states' identities and form their decisions and attitudes. Then, foreign policy with all the symbolic trappings of sovereignty and statehood plays a significant role in the socio-political imagination of a collective identity.[12] *Foreign policy speeches often reveal subjective we-feelings of a cultural group that are related to specific customs, institutions, territory, myths and rituals. These expressions of identity indicate how foreign policymakers view past history, the present, and the future political choices they face.*[13]

These cultural norms and values could be interpreted as a national 'ideology' or belief system in foreign policy, in the sense that ideas about who 'we' are serves as a guide to political action and basic worldview.[14] Thus, this conceptual lens through which foreign policymakers perceive international relations tends to set the norm for what is considered by them as 'rational' foreign policymaking. This is the favourite concept of foreign policy in this chapter. In this framework we can also offer a definition of terrorism as a sign of a coarseness-hostile tendency. According to this approach, terrorism is made by particular mentalities and intersubjectivities within a social group. I define terrorism as, 'illegal and informal use of organized violence for realizing political and ideological aims'. Nevertheless terrorism as a social construction is the result of interconnected ideas that flow through the body of a society or specific social group, ideas such as the legitimacy of violence to achieve global objectives.

Finally, we need to observe the interpretation of a society or the elite of a society on themselves and, through this observation, we can find some of the hidden factors that form society's foreign policy objectives, particularly in Iranian society.

Mental grounds and public opinion on religion and foreign policy in Iranian society

The most important point of my interpretation of constructivism in the study of foreign policy is that there is no contradiction between this theory and scientific methods. We can be constructivist and use statistics and scientific analysis at the same time. This information and data as well as methodic analysis help us to better interpretation of socio-political phenomenon. Here, I shall elaborate my idea on Iranian society through some statistics and quantitative information. First, the religious tendencies in the community will be surveyed and then the attitude of the people to foreign policy and its effect on the political camps in Iran will be studied.

Have the religious beliefs and trends in the whole of the Iranian community been increasing or not? We need to find the answer to this question before studying Iranian attitudes to foreign policy, because in recent studies on Iranian society some writers have tried to connect particular types of Iranian policies to religious beliefs. I argue that, generally, religious beliefs, in two different parts of society, have different conditions. In the following figure, I compare the results of two significant national studies, one done in 1975 (four years before the Islamic Revolution) and the other in 2001, supervised by the Supreme Council of Cultural Revolution in the Islamic Republic of Iran. This comparative study shows that, from the Iranian point of view, the religious tendencies in society will decrease in future. In 1975, Iranian people thought that their society was becoming more religious, but, in 2001, most people thought this inclination was reducing.

The comparison of Iranians' views and public opinion on the future of religious tendencies in Iran (Figure 9.1).

Of course, we cannot interpret this information as a non-religious trend in the Iranian society. Other statistics show that the religious political tendency is quite high and that belief in God and participation in religious rituals is increasing. Simultaneously, half of society took a political approach to religion while 40 per cent inclined to secular beliefs. This is a polarized situation in Iranian society. This polarization has been demonstrated in Iranian voting behaviours in a couple of elections. About 40 per cent of people (seculars) have not taken part in most elections since 2002, and about 20 per cent were unable to make a final decision until the last hours of the elections. This condition confirms the polarized situation in Iran. The following table indicates the views of Iranians in response to four indicators of secularism (Table 9.1).

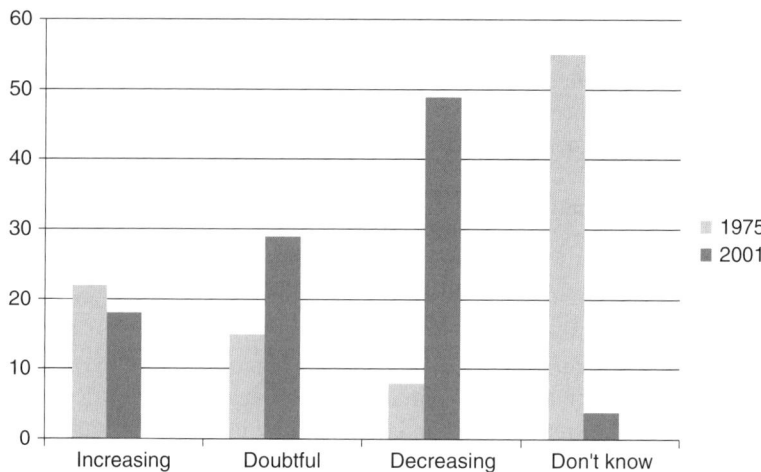

Figure 9.1 What is your opinion of the number of religious people in the future of Iranian society?

Source: Mohammad Reza Tajik, *Third Decade, Estimates and Managements* (Persian) (Tehran: Strategic Studies Department of Presidency, 2003), p. 79.

Table 9.1 Iranian views of secularism, 2000

Indicators of secular trends	Number of samples	Completely opposite (%)	Opposite (%)	Doubtful (%)	Agree (%)	Completely agree (%)
Religious beliefs are individual	16,669	12.6	35.6	12.6	31.5	7.7
The main criteria of religion are a clean heart and conscience, not religious behaviours and rituals	16,732	17.4	36.7	10.2	26.6	9
If we separate religion from politics, it will be cleaner	15,899	8.1	33.9	21.5	28.4	8.1
It should not be allowable for non-religious people to have political authority	15,899	8.1	33.9	21.5	28.4	8.1

Source: Mohammad Reza Tajik, *Third Decade, Estimates and Managements* (in Persian) (Tehran: Strategic Studies Department of Presidency, 2003), p. 79.

This sort of polarization in the Iranian society can be found in cyberspace and within Iranian blogs as well. The result of John Kelly's and Bruce Elting's research on Iranian weblogs reveals that, politically and religiously, Iranian weblogs cluster to two main poles: secular/reformist and religious/conservative. They state that, 'The secular/reformist pole features the significant participation of expatriate Iranians and women. It comprises a single structural group, though attentive cluster analysis reveals underlying tendencies and differences in focus among secular/ reformist bloggers. The other pole, conservative/religious, overwhelmingly contains bloggers living inside Iran, and who are, with a few exceptions, male. The conservative/religious pole features three structurally distinct sub-clusters, each of which largely comprises is its own distinctive attentive cluster.'[15] This research shows that the polarization of the political scene in Iran is rooted in the polarization of society as well as its cyberspace: part of society is becoming more religious and the second part is inclining to more secular beliefs. At the same time, a third part of society is becoming more depoliticized and neutralized on public affairs.

In spite of this polarization, some of criticisms on the political situation in the world have been formed in all areas of society. According to some official polls, there is a sort of critical orientation on the current rules of international relations. The monopolized state broadcasting and media with a permanent bombardment of anti-American and anti-Israel slogans as well as an anti-imperialism view in all textbooks at all educational periods, from primary school to university, and a vast number of religious missionaries, have contributed to a fundamental criticism of the world order in Iranian society; such opinions are held not only in pro-revolutionary groups but also in the reformist groups and opposition camps. The table below clarifies the principles of criticism in Iranian public opinion on the international order (Table 9.2).

I think that the idea and wish to constitute the Islamic state throughout the world is not a desire in the current world, but is a sign and result of Shi'ite beliefs

Table 9.2 Iranian views of world affairs

Views	Should support oppressed people throughout the world	Releasing of occupation of Ghods (Jerusalem) in favour of Muslims	Wish to constitute Islamic state in the world	Opposing the United States
Opposite (%)	12.1	7.5	9	22.5
Doubtful (%)	7.9	8.7	10	13.5
Agree (%)	80	83.8	81	64
Samples (%)	4,503	4,399	4,375	4,321

Source: National Plans Department, *Views and Values of Iranians: The Second Wave* (in Persian) (Tehran: NPD, 2003), p. 201.

in a saviour/hidden spiritual leader (Imam Mahdi) who shall cause a worldwide revolution at the end of history and build a just and ideal society for the whole world.

Some other polls on public opinion bring the negative view of Iranians on the world order and the United States' government, as well as the negative view of Americans on Iran's state and even people, into light of diagnosis. Both peoples, particularly the Iranians, would like to solve the problems by negotiation, conciliation and cooperation. That is to say, the negative view does not require a hostile foreign policy and confrontation. The World Public Opinion Organization in partnership with the Search for Common Ground designed the parallel studies. Both polls used probability-based national samples of 1000 respondents or more. The US poll was fielded by the Knowledge Networks during late November and early December 2006. The Iranian poll, which included 134 questions, was executed by an independent Iranian agency that interviewed respondents face to face from late October through to December. Most Iranians have negative attitudes towards the United States. Some 76 per cent say their opinion of the United States is unfavourable (65 per cent very) and only 22 per cent say it is favourable (5 per cent very). Views of the current US government are even worse: 93 per cent unfavourable (84 per cent very). This is about equal to the 92 per cent of Iranians who hold an unfavourable opinion of President Bush (86 per cent very) (Figure 9.2).

Despite their mutually negative views on each other, Iranians and Americans tend to look positively on a series of measures aimed at strengthening US–Iranian relations. Strong majorities of Americans support nearly all of the proposed steps

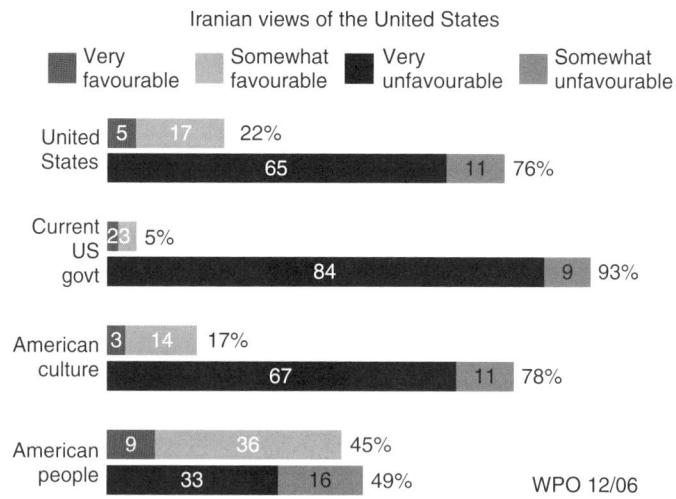

Figure 9.2 World public opinion, 'Iranians and Americans Believe Islam and West Can Find Common Ground'.
Source: www.worldpublicopinion.org, published 30 January 2007 (accessed 4 April 2008).

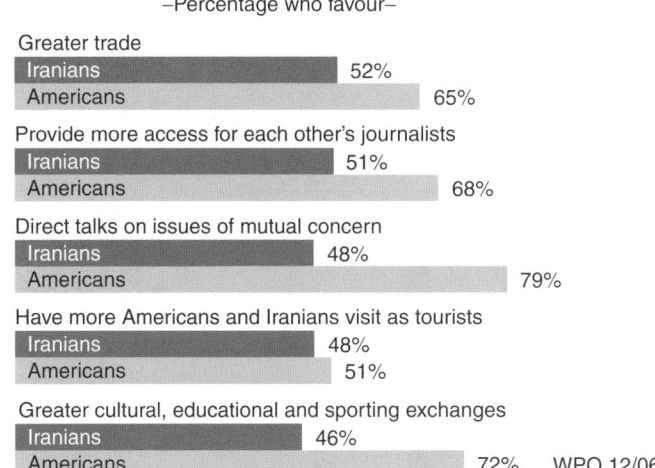

Figure 9.3 Steps for improving US–Iran relations.

while more modest majorities or pluralities of Iranians do. Presented with a list of possible steps for strengthening relations, Iranians tend to be most supportive (and least opposed) to improving trade relations. Fifty-two per cent favour greater trade with the United States and only 26 per cent are opposed. Nearly as many (51 per cent) favour granting more access to journalists from both countries, though a large minority (39 per cent) is opposed. Other measures elicit more divided responses. While 48 per cent of Iranians support direct talks between the two governments on issues of mutual concern, 42 per cent do not. Having greater cultural, educational and sporting exchanges between the two countries garners good support (46 per cent) and relatively little opposition (31 per cent) (Figure 9.3).[16]

The results of our original research on Iranian society also reveal that the main tendency of the people is towards positive relations with the rest of the world. In that research, we assume that university students are a proper sample for most of the Iranian population, especially the middle class. In society, the most part of the middle class is shaped by university graduates. The rapid rate of growth of academies will increase the role of the university graduates in social and political flows. Every year about 1,500,000 new young graduates enter into Iranian society, with their need for jobs and welfare, and with new attitude and desires.[17] In our new research, we selected 150 samples of four main universities in Tehran and offered a questionnaire about foreign policy. The result of the analysis of two questions of the questionnaire shows that more than 75 per cent of respondents believe that negotiation is the best way for carrying out foreign policy goals. About 65 per cent of them believe that cooperation is the best way forward for promoting national interest. The following chart is driven from the analysis of the responses to those questions (Figures 9.4, 9.5 and 9.6):

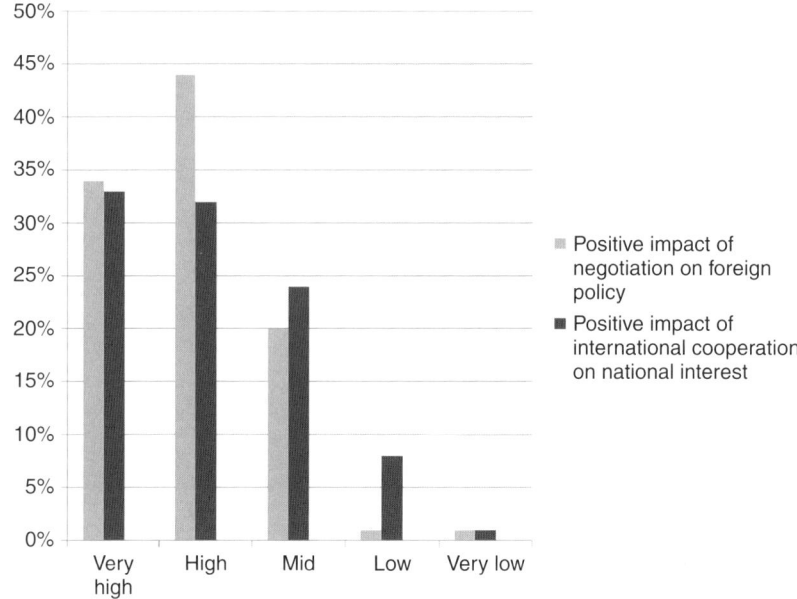

Figure 9.4 Cooperation or confrontation?

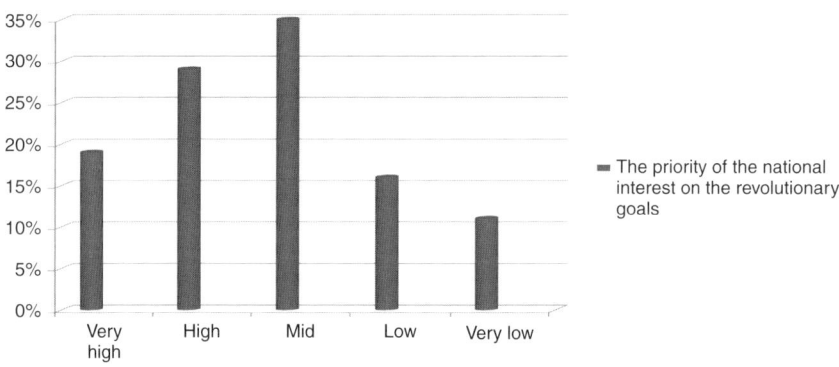

Figure 9.5 The priority of national interest in revolutionary goals.

Views of Iranian university students on foreign policy, original research.

Analysis of responses to another question revealed that in spite of some revolutionary ideas in the society, Iranian university students would go for national interests rather than revolutionary goals. This will cause the political trends to change in the main body of society. This analysis is showed in figure 9.6:

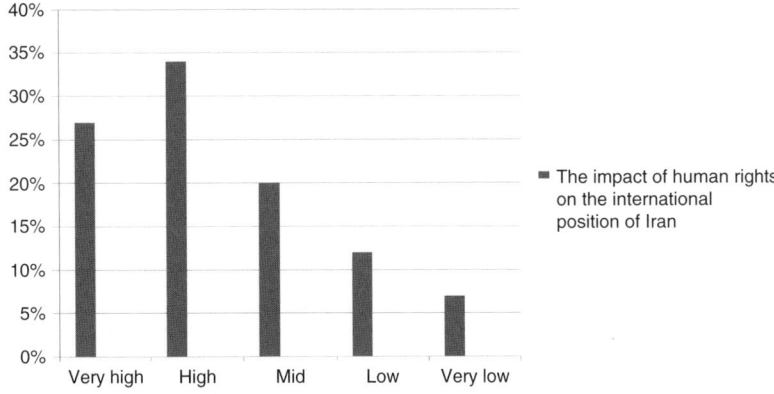

Figure 9.6 The impact of human rights on the international position of Iran.

This process can also be found in the social view on human rights. One of the main lines in some media propaganda is the negative role of the discourse of human rights in the current world. However, the poll indicates that the students' view on human rights and its function in foreign policy is positive.

In the research, some questions about foreign policy were asked of 100 staff and diplomats of the Ministry of Foreign Affairs. The result of the analysis of two questions of that questionnaire revealed that most of them do not incline towards the hostile policies and positions, they rather agree with negotiation and positive cooperation with the rest of the world (Figure 9.7).

These statistics testify the lack of hostile-coarse tendency in Iranian society as well as in the agents of foreign policy, despite their critical approach. Although, in

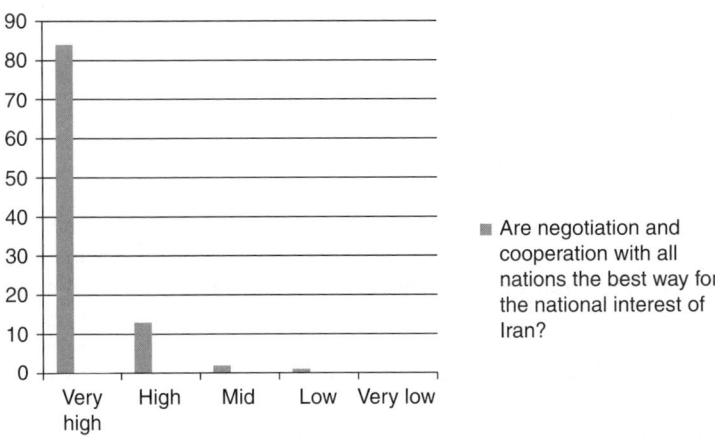

Figure 9.7 Views of Iranian diplomats and Ministry of Foreign Affairs' staff on foreign policy, 2007.

the international system and its system of meaning, which is created by the media, academicians and politicians, there is a quite different interpretation of the positions of political camps in Iran. A glance at the main political tendencies shall reveal that there are some common opinions and stands among them that could correspond with the public trends. Before studying the positions of political camps, we need to recognize the outstanding tendencies.

Main political trends in Iran

There is no doubt that the perception and attitude of the political camps in Iran differ, either in their mentalities and beliefs or in their actions. There are some huge differences and gaps between the political camps in Iran, which can be explained by the constructivist view. However, there are some common positions among them, which are the reflection of Iranian ideas and demands, and here I just want to survey these common stands. Although, of course, the process of creating ideas between the main body of society and the elite is reciprocal, I would here like to elaborate the correspondence between public opinion and the elite perceptions.

In this chapter I study just those political tendencies that intend to play a key role within the current political system, not the opposition trends that are excluded from the system. Anoushiravan Ehteshami has a very interesting classification for understanding the current political camps in Iran. He elucidates, 'Iran is a country in which factional politics continue to reign, and its complex elite structure is divided among three distinct political camps: conservative, reformist, and neoconservative. The conservatives enjoy the support of the clergy and Ayatollah Khamenei's political circle, and this group believes in a mixed economy (state intervention alongside market forces), and an economy and society that are not closely associated with the West. The neoconservatives, in contrast, are closely associated with Iran's security apparatus and the radical factions of the clerical establishment. This movement represents a new breed of conservatism that is politically and economically populist and that is driven by the basic instincts of the revolutionary period. … Between these two factions stand Iran's reformists, who believe in the reform of Iran's power structures, the necessity of opening them up to public scrutiny and accountability, and the reform of Iran's economy and its foreign relations. This latter goal includes a desire for better diplomatic and political relations with the rest of the world, including the United States, and for open economic links.'[18] This classification can include all Iranian activists, although we may classify Iranian political camps in another way. For instance, we can divide them into four different camps: reformists, technocrat pragmatists, moderate conservatives and neoconservatives.

Reformists include the following:

- IIPF: Islamic Iran Participation Front Party (*Jebhe Mosharekate Irane Eslami*), democrat intellectual reformists, proponents of Hojatolislam Khatami.

- NTP: National Trust Party (*Etemade Melli*), democrat revolutionary reformists, led by Hojatolislam Karobi (former speaker of parliament).
- IRM: Islamic Revolutionary Mojahedin (*Mojahedine enqelabe Islami*), leftist intellectual reformists, led by Behzad Nabavi (former deputy prime minister and former deputy speaker of parliament) (Figure 9.8).

Technocrat pragmatists include the following:

- ARII: Agents of Reconstruction of Islamic Iran Party (*Kargozarane Sazandegi*), the technocrat pragmatist supporters of Hojatolislam Hashemi Rafsanjani and the former members of his cabinet.
- JDP: Justice and Development Party (*Edalat va Toseae*), the former MPs and supporters of Hojatolislam Hashemi Rafsanjani.
- The vast number of former officials (Figure 9.9).

Moderate conservatives include the following:

- MOP: Motalefe Party, traditional Islamist principalists, including Islamist capitalists.
- CCA: Combatant Clergy Association (*Jame'e Rohaniate Mobarez*), led by Ayatollah Mahdavi Kani.
- New generation of Islamic-educated principalist technocrats, including former members and commanders of the Revolutionary Guards. Led by Dr Larijani (new speaker of parliament), Dr Qalibaf (mayor of Tehran) and Dr Rezai (secretary of the Expediency Council) (Figure 9.10).

Neoconservatives include the following:

- Supporters and proponents of President Ahmadinejad.

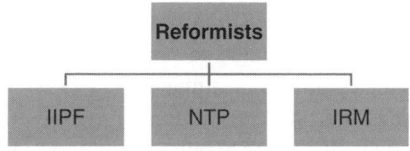

Figure 9.8 Reformist camp.

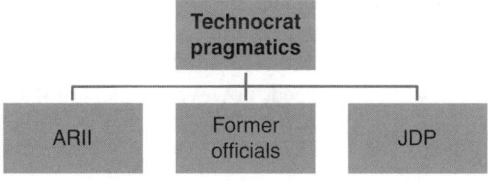

Figure 9.9 Technocrat pragmatist camp.

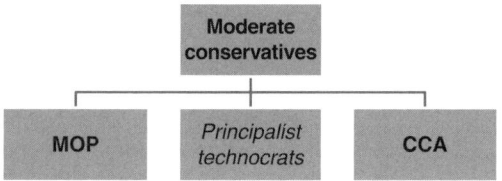

Figure 9.10 Moderate conservative camp.

This classification can help us to understand new changes in the Iranian political scene, as well. I think that two main camps, technocrat pragmatists and moderate conservatives, have cooperated in electing Dr Larijani as a new speaker of parliament (he did not receive any negative votes), and this type of political flexibility, therefore, could be a new way for political changes in Iran. It is a sign of innovative political interrelations. Here, I am going to show some common ground among the political camps in Iran.

Inevitably, all Iranian trends must align their positions and acts with the Supreme Leader Ayatollah Khamenei, if they are going to carry on and work within Islamic Republic framework. The Leader is not only the main decision-maker of the political arena but also the final arbiter in disputes between political trends and contending institutions that step forward in the policymaking process in foreign affairs. Alex Vatanca argues that, 'Still, while Ayatollah Khamenei is the final arbiter in Iran's foreign policy deliberations, he is not only exposed to but is primarily led by internal pressures and external demands. The pressures that Ayatollah Khamenei faces are to a significant extent related to his political rise and present status and authority within the regime. … In the realm of foreign policy, Ayatollah Khamenei's appointments and interventions are in the main neither hawkish nor ideologically-driven but intended to preserve the equilibrium that exists among Iran's major political groupings.' He also addresses that a sort of change in Khamenei's stands against the West and the United States can be observed: 'In the context of the US-Iran standoff … His January 3 remarks about relations with the US were intended to convey the message to his Iranian and foreign detractors that they not underestimate him and his political sway at a time of growing calls in both Tehran and Washington for a resumption of diplomatic ties.'[19] If any changes or new directions would be realized, they will inevitably get permission from the Leader, not only because of his legal position as the final decision-maker of the political system but also because of his religious position as the main author for legitimating any political behaviours. Indeed, the Supreme Leader's opinion as well as the population's view towards foreign policy might be changing, and gradually some signs legitimating positive relations with the West and the United States have surfaced; however, criticism of US policies and international order is still one of the main bases of the discourse of Iranian foreign policy.

The most important common political trends in Iranian foreign policy are criticism of the world order, US policies and the conditions of Muslim people in the

Middle East, and an evident inclination towards cooperation with the Western countries, even America, at the same time. If we see this phenomenon from a semiotics point of view, we find that all foreign policy speeches are neutral signs, to which signifiers in the international scene give different meanings. Sometimes, two politicians from two different camps state similar positions, but these are interpreted as having different meanings by dissimilar observers.

All political trends in Iran have included some criticism on the current situation of international relations, of course using different language and rhetoric. For instance, Mohammad Khatmi, as a symbol of reformism, criticizes the current world condition. He asserts, 'What needs to be denounced in our world is the existence and practice of double standards. We cannot and should not justify a state's total war against a defenseless population on the basis of its sovereignty and international recognition while condemning the violence perpetrated by that population as barbaric and inhuman. The converse holds true as well. A single standard must be accepted: rejection of violence. There ought to be the goal of a stable and lasting peace in the world. Peace, in its turn, cannot be achieved on bases other than justice, equality, and rejection of double standards.'[20] He invites Americans to revise their policies and stands, if they would protect and support peace and human rights. He states that, 'Today, we should heed not only the requirements of democracy on the national level but on an international scale. We are in a dire need of a global democracy and civil society ... Can the American nation and particularly its well meaning elites cast a new glance at international affairs; informed by their own history and free from the delusional atmosphere created by the powerful? Can they go even further and take a positive step toward persuading, politicians and the international organizations that are meant to protect human rights and peace, to inaugurate a new world system in which true international democracy can prosper?'[21] This idea, inspired by the Islamic Revolution ideology is simultaneously found in President Mahmood Ahmadinejad's stand, as a sample of neoconservatives in Iran. Ahmadinejad says that, 'current international system, particularly the system governing the United Nations and the UN Security Council, is inherited from the World War II and has been designed by the victors in the said War for dominating the world and for exerting power over global wealth, culture and economy'.[22] He also notes, 'In Iraq and Afghanistan too we are witnessing bitter events and disrespect for the main owners of the lands.'

Although, Khatami speaks philosophically and within the theoretical mainstream of social science, and Ahmadinejad speaks like a simple practical policy man, a common ground in their stands is observable. Both of them desire to have better relations with the West, although Khatami has never spoken about this matter directly, even during his presidency. He explains this aim by theoretical expressions, as his position in the centre of power in Iran is not strong, whereas Ahmadinejad addresses this policy directly. However, their positions in the international level have had different interpretations and reactions. Khatami states this inclination in the name of dialogue. He argues that, 'Realization of drastic changes in the international system as well as the models effective in improving peace and security in the world contributed to the presentation of the theory of dialog of civilizations. In order for this project to be realized, those models of power that rely on a militaristic realization of peace and security should be brushed aside in the world. This is a project that takes into consideration the mental satisfaction at an environment which is free from being influenced by software and hardware powers. This is a project that seeks to reduce the power of institutions engaged in structuring the society, as it encourages them to increase their contribution to dialog and participation in the world.'[23] Khatami explains his views and ideas about the world as, 'a new world that wants to fill the void in the current order, which is the lack of God, spirituality and morality, by submitting before the Ultimate Beauty. A new world that wants to understand and utilize religion in a way that it is not incompatible with freedom and progress, rather it sets us on a clearer path towards the future. Not only in the world of Islam, but in the entire global arena, we must condemn self-centeredness, discrimination, avarice, arrogance and violence anywhere and in any form, so we can have a calm and secure world for all. This is a task that can be pursued by the unprejudiced and informed section of the Islamic world and other non-Western worlds with the understanding of and alongside the unprejudiced section of the Western world.'[24]

At the same time, Ahmadinejad, at the peak of the pressures of Western countries against his administration, asserts, 'We firmly believe that durable peace and security are only possible through justice, honouring human dignity, respecting human beings and love and kindness. ... This is the main slogan of the Islamic Republic of Iran.' 'The Islamic Republic of Iran welcomes all countries that are willing to contribute to investment in Iran's projects in the economic, commercial, cultural, financial and banking sectors, said the president, adding that the Islamic Republic of Iran welcomes and supports all efforts for the defence of the rights of the oppressed, administration of justice and promotion of friendship, love and peace worldwide. ... *Iran wants expansion of relations with all nations and countries, except the illegitimate Zionist Regime.*'[25] Of course, sometimes he speaks from the top of a tower with the Western countries. He stresses that 'ground has been paved for European states and France, in particular, to revise their past approach towards the Islamic Republic of Iran',[26] and 'Tehran welcomes a democratic government in Washington which would be elected freely and would move on the basis of justice.'[27] 'The Iranian nation makes progress each day and the enemies would be obliged to cooperate with the Iranians in the future, however, the condition of the Iranian people would be different in the future from what is today, the president said, adding if the bullying powers do not accept Tehran's conditions today, they will face several problems in the future.'[28]

The critical approach towards the West and US policies, as well as the inclination to normalize the relationship with the international system and the United States can be found in the most reformist camp, as well as among new moderate con-servatives in the country. For instance, the Islamic Iran Participation Front, as a core of the reformist elite who are barred in the qualification process of the eighth parliamentary elections, has a critical position towards US policies. At the same time, they think that the best way to face the conspiracies of America is the through the promotion of pacifism and democracy. In the statement of the 10th

Congress of the party, they announced that, 'After the collapse of the Soviet Union, the world has been an area of unilateralism and adventurousness of the United States. In this world our foreign policy should use of the global competitions with US against its policy. America tries to make Iran a threat to the world as a priority, for covering its frustration in Iraq. We must offset the US conspiracy. Our special geopolitics in the region can be implemented as an opportunity in this regard. Promotion of peace-loving, pacifism and democracy-seeking and carrying out these in the internal system is a main solution in this concern and will grow the security level and will offset the American's propaganda.'[29] Therefore, it is misleading to suppose that reformist thought in Iran includes no criticism of the United States and the West. It goes without saying that their weak position within the power cycle is one of the main reasons for this kind of statement, but it should not be forgotten that this is one of their principles. On the other side, conservatives try to show Western politicians that they are rational thinkers. They have enough legitimacy in the core of power and can announce their positions directly and obviously. For example, Mohammad- Baqer Qalibaf, the mayor of Tehran and one of the main candidates for the presidential election, thinks that positive competition and cooperation between Iran and the West, particularly the US, can solve many regional and international problems. This idea differs from the ideological belief of the satanic essence of the United States. He asserts that, 'Right now, the U.S. is supporting powers in this region who don't even value the 50% of their populations who are women, where there is no democracy, no election. ... Our country holds a lot of potential and its role in the Middle East is paralleled by few others ... I think in fact that Iran and the U.S. have many common interests in the region; our position in the region should not be one of opposition, but friendly competition with other powers. As the Supreme Leader Ayatollah Khamenei pointed out as well, no one said that there will be conflict between us forever.'[30]

There is no doubt that the attitude and beliefs of political camps in Iran are very different, but this study reveals that they have some significant common views on foreign policy. Of course, the meaning of these positions will depend on signifiers in the international system and how they would interpret the position and way of thinking of these political camps.

Finally, I summarize a number of the common positions and stances of political tendencies in Iran on foreign policy as follows:

1. Criticism of the current world order
2. Cooperation with the international economic system
3. Opposing and criticizing the arrogance of US government and negotiating with them at the same time
4. Illegitimacy of Israel
5. Extension of relations with Europe
6. Extension of relations with China and Russia
7. Spiritually supporting Islamic and Shi'ite movements
8. Cooperation and good relations with neighbouring Countries and the Gulf Cooperation Council.

Conclusion

By using the constructivist approach to understand Iranian foreign policy, we found that there has been a change in the mentality and perception of the Iranian elite that is related to the new socially constructed public ideas. A critical view on the current world order has spilled over into different parts of society, but, at the same time, an obvious inclination towards having positive relations with the West as well as the United States is growing. Iranian society, with regard to religious beliefs, as well as in the political arena, has been polarized, but some signs of more tendencies towards democracy and human rights can be found in the main body of the community. These ideas are reflected in Iranian foreign policy positions. Despite crucial differences among political camps in Iran, we can observe their common stances on foreign policy. These positions lead them to more positive, adaptive, moderate and accommodative foreign policy.

Finally, it could be said that in this society, in spite of criticizing the international order, there is no coarse-hostile tendency, either in the system of ideas in the main body of Iranian society or in the contending political elites. Criticism does not mean a revolutionary act, that is, a desire for emancipation, but it could be realized through pacifist and constructive foreign policy.

Notes

1 Vivienne Jabri, 'Michel Foucault's Analytics of War: The Social, the International, and the Racial', *International Political Sociology*, 2007, 1, p. 67.
2 Ibid., p. 69.
3 Arshin Adib-Moghaddam, *Iran in World Politics: The Question of the Islamic Republic*, London: Hurst, 2007, p. 194.
4 Friedrich Kratochwil, 'Constructivism: What It is (Not) and How It Matters', *EUI Florence*, Spring 2007, p. 3.
5 M. Thomson, G. Grendstad and P. Selle, *Cultural Theory as Political Science*, New York: Routledge, 1999, p. 1.
6 John Agnew, 'Know-Where: Geographies of Knowledge of World Politics', *International Political Economy*, 2007, 1, p. 139.
7 Alexander Wendt, 'Collective Identity Formation and the International State', *American Political Science Review*, June 1994, 88, p. 385.
8 John Ruggie, 'What Makes the World Hang Together? Neo-utilitarianism and the Social Constructivist Challenge', *International Organization*, Autumn 1998, 4, p. 54.
9 See Maja Zehfuss, *Constructivism in International Relations*, *The Politics of Reality*, Cambridge: Cambridge University Press, 2002.
10 Roy E. Jones, *Analysing Foreign Policy: An Introduction to Some Conceptual Problems*, New York: Routledge, 1970, p. 14.
11 Christopher Hill, 'What is to be Done? Foreign Policy as a Site for Political Action', *International Affairs*, March 2003, 79(2), p. 233.
12 B. Anderson, *Imagined Communities*, London: Verso Books, 1991.
13 Lisbeth Aggestam, 'Role Conceptions and the Politics of Identity in Foreign Policy', ARENA working paper.1998/99.
14 C. Jönsson, *Super Power: Comparing American and Soviet Foreign Policy*, London: Frances Pinter, 1994, pp. 42–43.

15 John Kelly and Bruce Etling, *Mapping Iran's Online Public: Politics and Culture in the Persian Blogosphere*, The Berkman Center for Internet and Society, at Harvard Law School, Research Publication No. 2008-01, 6 April 2008, p. 18, http://cyber.law.harvard.edu/publications (accessed 8 April 2008).
16 World Public Opinion, 'Iranians and Americans Believe Islam and West Can Find Common Ground', 30 January 2007, www.WorldPubilicOpinion.org (accessed 4 April 2008).
17 See Hossein Salimi, 'The Role of Growth of Universities in Political Graduates on Changes in Iran', (Persian), *Law and Politics Research*, Allame Tabatabai'e University, 2004.
18 Anoush Ehteshami, 'The Rise and Impact of Iran's Neocons', Policy analysis brief, Stanley Foundation, www.stanfoundation.org/publications/pab/RiseandImpact Ehteshami08PAB.pdf (accessed 7 April 2008).
19 Alex Vatanka, *Ali Khamene'i: Iran's Most Powerful Man*, Middle East Institute Policy Briefs, March 2008, no. 10, p. 1.
20 Seyed Mohammad Khatami, *Address of H.E Seyed Mohammad Khatami in the Harvard University*, 11 September 2006, http://www.khatami.ir/lecture.php?uid=20&lang=fa&lang2=en (accessed 10 April 2008).
21 Ibid.
22 Mahmood Ahmadinejad, 'Lecture: Iran Wants Expanded Ties with All States Except Israel', January, 2008, http://www.president.ir/en/ (accessed 10 April 2008).
23 Seyed Mohammad Khatami, *Dialog of Civilizations and Regeneration of Security and Peace in the World*, 14 November 2006, http://www.khatami.ir/lecture.php?uid=26&lang=fa&lang2=en (accessed 10 August 2008).
24 Seyed Mohammad Khatami, Lecture, 11 February 2006, http://www.khatami.ir/lecture.php?uid=6&lang=fa&lang2=en (accessed 10 April 2008).
25 Ibid.
26 Mahmood Ahmadinejad, Interview with *Le Monde*, January 2008, http://www.president.ir/en/ (accessed 10 April 2008).
27 Ibid.
28 Mahmmod Ahmadinejad, Interview with *El Pais*, February 2008, http://www.president.ir/en/ (accessed 10 April 2008).
29 The Statement of Tenth Congress of Islamic Iran Participation Front, Persian, 2007, http://norooznews.ir/news/4576.php (accessed 10 April 2008).
30 Mohammad-Baqer Qalibaf, *Interview with Time; A Rival for Iran's Ahmadinejad*, 18 March 2008, http://www.Time.com/time/world/article/0,8599,1723250,00.html (accessed 11 April 2008).

10 Discourse and violence

The friend–enemy conjunction in contemporary Iranian–American relations

Arshin Adib-Moghaddam

The supreme art of war is to subdue the enemy without fighting.

– Sun Tzu

The one mind may err with regard to the same thing, especially if this mind does not reflect frequently on the opinion to which it adheres and does not consider it with an examining and critical eye.

– Abu Nasr Farabi

Iranian–American relations have been beset by mistrust and occasional outbreaks of vitriol and violence for the past three decades. In this narrative I attempt to map, theoretically and empirically, the 'discursive field' in which relations between Iran and the United States reveal themselves. I am interested in representations of Iran and the United States, and how the fundamental friend–enemy distinction, setting the two countries politically apart, has come about. I take as a starting point, together with critical theorists of international relations (see, among others, Campbell 1992, 1993; Jackson 2005), that discourse has a real and present impact on policy and that a lot that is happening in world politics can be adequately contextualized with an appreciation of the linkages between 'utterance' and 'action'.

What do I mean by the term 'discursive field'? I have explained in detail elsewhere how politico-cultural inventions affect and condition the way in which we perceive our surrounding social worlds (Adib-Moghaddam 2003, 2008a). Perceptions in world politics are particularly compromised and manipulated because the ontological fabric of the international system is professionally constructed. Discourse and, at a more basic level, language, are central to this process of wilful interference. The articulation of words represents the most sophisticated form of self-externalization in society; it is the first step to defining ourselves and others and to understanding our status within a world that has been pre-created and whose historical fabric is beyond our control. This is what Karl Marx (1973, p. 146) meant when he observed that 'Men [and women] make their own history … not under circumstances they themselves have chosen but under the given and inherited circumstances with which they are directly confronted.' Structure, expressed and embedded in history, is everywhere for Marx and penetrates our consciousness. Discourse narrates history; it is a fundamental building block – always also political (and thus violent) – in our efforts to invent cultural realities. 'The facts which our senses present to us are socially preformed in two ways', writes the German critical theorist Max Horkheimer (1997, p. 200), 'through the historical character of the object perceived and through the historical character of the perceiving organ.' He (1997, pp. 200–201) adds the important caveat that '[b]oth are not simply natural; they are shaped by human activity. ... The perceived fact is therefore co-determined by human ideas and concepts, even before its conscious theoretical elaboration by the knowing individual.' It should follow from this that any interaction in the social world, including Iranian–American relations, is not revealing itself within a detached or neutral habitat. Rather the contrary. International relations, including Iranian–American relations, are entirely constituted and conditioned by norms, institutions and other cultural artefacts that are socially engineered and thus subject to human manipulation.

We can derive an important methodological premise from the short discussion above. Whenever we encounter what Michel Foucault (2002, p. 41) terms a 'discursive formation'; whenever 'between objects, types of statement, concepts, or thematic choices, one can define a regularity (an order, correlations, positions and functionings, transformations)', we are compelled to delve into the dynamics of this field, into the rapturous and tumultuous forces that are actively preoccupied with the production and transformation of reality and the subjectivication of knowledge. So, for instance, the 'reality' that Iran is a 'terrorist' state is one subject that has emerged out of the discursive field of Iranian–American relations. The 'fact' that the United States is a 'neo-imperial' force, indeed that its government represents the very reincarnation of satanic evil, is yet another.

On the linkages between discourse and the construction of cultural realities, of which world politics in general and foreign policies in particular would be a part, there are more lessons to be learned from an essay by Walter Benjamin published originally in 1921 and entitled 'Critique of Violence'. In this essay, Benjamin (1986, p. 289) asks if the non-violent resolution of conflict is possible. His response is yes: 'Nonviolent agreement is possible wherever a civilised outlook allows the use of unalloyed means of agreement. ... Courtesy, sympathy, peacableness, trust ... are their subjective preconditions.' Benjamin puts primary importance on language as a mediating and ameliorating force, central to the build up of these subjective preconditions. According to him (1986, p. 289), there exists 'a sphere of human agreement that is nonviolent to the extent that it is wholly inaccessible to violence: the proper sphere of "understanding", language'.

That language can be a source of mediation, empathy and intercultural dialogue has become central to communicative theories of politics, most famously expressed by Jürgen Habermas (1984). On the level of the functions of language for not only 'achieving understanding' (*Verständigung*) but also 'empathetic understanding' (*Verstehen*), Habermas recaptures Benjamin's point that language is central to processes of reconciliation. In this regard Habermas remains within a tradition that takes understanding of the 'other' as one of its main goals. This ambition has been rightly termed the 'rationalising' core of Habermas's communicative action theory, which is said (Calhoun 1995, p. 51) to 'inform a view in which establishing consensus is the program both for living within that social world and for building bridges to other social worlds'. Benhabib (1986, p. 241) adds that in Habermas's conceptualization of communicative action, reaching out to such other social worlds requires taking 'a stance in relation to the reasons which agents in those cultures would consider "good" or "appropriate" to justify certain claims'. From this perspective, in language, instead of setting boundaries between ourselves and others, we are urged to engage in rational discourse, which by itself presupposes recognition of the other while leading to an unprincipled exchange, the aim of which would be to find a mutually acceptable, smallest denominator that would mitigate conflict. According to Thomas Risse (2000, p. 7, emphasis added):

> Arguing implies that actors try to challenge the validity claims inherent in any causal or normative statement and to seek a communicative consensus about their understanding of a situation as well as justifications for the principles and norms guiding their action. Argumentative rationality also implies that the participants in a discourse are open to being persuaded by the better argument and that relationships of power and social hierarchies recede in the background. *Argumentative and deliberative behaviour is as goal oriented as strategic interaction, but the goal is not to attain one's fixed preferences, but to seek a reasoned consensus.* Actors' interests, preferences, and the perceptions of the situation are no longer fixed, but subject to discursive challenges. Where argumentative rationality prevails, actors do not to seek to maximize or to satisfy their given interests and preferences, but to challenge and to justify the validity claims inherent in them – and they are prepared to change their views of the world or even their interests in light of the better argument.

But what about interfering factors that do not allow for an exchange that yields a 'reasoned consensus' as Risse foresees? What if discourse reveals itself within a field of violence and suspicion such as in international politics? What if language itself is inscribed with pain and terror? What if it prescribes murder? What if our words are untrustworthy?

Michel Foucault points to such epistemic violence, which he finds inscribed in language and expressed through the disciplinary powers of institutions and larger constellations he calls 'regimes of truth'. According to Foucault (2002, p. 131) each society is endowed with such a regime, which defines not only 'the types of discourse it accepts and makes function as true', but also the very 'mechanisms and instances that enable one to distinguish true and false statements'. Foucault suggests that violence is inscribed in discourse and that it may not yield understanding of the other, but his or her condemnation. The discursive field enveloping Iranian–American relations serves as an example here. What US and Iranian political elites are reacting to is not the immediate reality of the other side, but representations of that reality, which are filtered through thick layers of normative and institutional structures. What makes the relationship between Iranians and

Americans conflict-ridden is not some innate antagonism between the two peoples due to the hostage crisis in 1980 or the CIA (and MI6) engineered coup d'état, which deposed Iran's first democratically elected prime minister, Mohammad Mossadegh, in 1953. What have hampered relations between the two countries – the true impediments of reconciliation – are invented myths about the other side that have not been entirely dispelled either politically or even intellectually.

Within such a discursive field, which is pierced by violent narratives reified by those powerful stakeholders who have a particular interest in keeping the two countries apart, communicating rationally in a Habermasian sense has resembled a Sisyphus act. Former President Mohammad Khatami (1997–2005), who reached out to the United States via his 'dialogue amongst civilisation' initiative, and US President Barack Obama today had/have it so difficult not because they are not genuinely interested in facilitating trust-building measures between the two countries, but because they are operating within a discursive field that is permeated by memories of violence and populated by powerful social agents who are entirely antagonistic to the other side. Hence, repeatedly, the 'rational majority' have managed to roll the rock up halfway to the top of the mountain, only to see it roll back down again (in the case of Khatami, crushing him and his reformist movement along the way). Consequently, in order to address why there has not been a major rapprochement between the two states yet, some understanding about those sources of mistrust is necessary. Of course, the signposts presented cannot be fully explained within the confines of this chapter. I will not be able to dissect the institutional sites that give stakeholders in Iranian–American relations the status of 'authorities'. Neither do I claim to delve into the wider politico-cultural system that accommodates the politics of enmity between the two countries. All I can do is to point to a few narratives that are indicative of the signs and symbols that populate what I have called, rather sketchily, the *discursive field* enveloping Iranian–American relations, to give some understanding of the syntactical settings of that field. What I am bringing into focus, ultimately, is the movement 'within' the dash that seems to set Iranian–American relations politically apart.

Pahlavi Iran, Aryan myths and the Indo-European bond

It was Edward Said (1997, p. 6) who argued most forcefully that after the Islamic Revolution in 1979 and the subsequent occupation of the US Embassy in Tehran on the 22 October, Iran and Iranians became a major source of anxiety and anger within the United States. 'An important ally, it lost its imperial regime, its army, its value in American global calculations during a year of tumultuous revolutionary upheaval virtually unprecedented on so huge a scale since October 1917.' The international focus on Iran intensified further after the end of the Cold War. From the perspective of Said (1997, p. 7), Iran 'and along with it "Islam", has come to represent America's major foreign devil. It is considered to be a terrorist state because it backs groups like Hizbollah in South Lebanon.' Said is maybe too obsequious to his 'Orientalist' paradigm (1995) here, but he is right to point out that reactions to events such as the occupation of the US embassy cannot be divorced from a larger discursive constellation that represents post-revolutionary Iran as an entirely fanatical, irrational and evil entity.

This emerging narrative of the 'mad Mullahs' that Bill Beeman (2005) ponders, lodged its fulminate force into a discursive field, the ideational attributes of which were radically transformed after the revolution in 1979. Before the revolution, political elites in the United States dealt with an image of Iran that was rather amenable to 'Orientalist' notions of the country as historically friendly and generally closer to the Western canon than the 'Semitic Arabs'. Iran was Persian, Aryan, whiter than the Arabs surrounding them and seemed to be, on the ideological surface, more like Western nations. The shah himself was mystified as an occasionally autocratic but enlightened leader, who was on the path of transforming Iran into a modern (viz. 'Western') country. Correspondence from the US Embassy in Tehran from 1951, that is, two years before the shah was ousted by Mossadegh and subsequently reinstated by the CIA/MI6, is indicative of official attitudes towards the shah during that period. In this memo (cited CIA 1972, p. 7) the shah is described as 'confused, frustrated suspicious, proud and stubborn, a young man who lives in the shadow of his father'. At the same time he was deemed to have 'great personal courage, many Western ideals, and a sincere, though often wavering, desire to raise and preserve the country'. Nine years before the revolution in 1979, the shah was described (cited CIA 1972, p. 7) as 'completely self-assured' and 'confident that he is leading the country in the right direction'. US officials also found him to be 'well-informed' and they were convinced by his 'ability to keep abreast of developments around the world' and by his 'agile mind'. Richard Nixon, in a private conversation with Alexander Haig and Douglas MacArthur II on 8 April 1971 (Conversation Among President Nixon, Ambassador Douglas MacArthur II, and General Alexander Haig, 1971) was equally impressed. 'Iran's the only thing there', he said. 'By God, if we can go with them, if we can have them strong, and they're in the centre of it, and a friend of the United States.' Nixon also seemed to be impressed by the ability of the shah 'to run, basically, let's face it, a virtual dictatorship in a benign way. … Because, look, when you talk about having a democracy of our type in that part of the world, good God, it wouldn't work, would it?' 'No Sir', MacArthur replied. 'They don't even know – they don't know what it is. You know what happened in the Congo? … Belgium gave them a constitution, wonderful buildings, all the nice trappings, but these people had never practiced it at all.' Those endorsements of the Iranian monarch were topped by the by now famous proclamation of former President Jimmy Carter on New Year's Eve in 1977. Raising his champagne glass Carter toasted the shah at a lavish state dinner in Tehran calling him 'an island of stability in one of the more troubled areas of the world.' A year later the shah was in exile.

This representation of the shah as an enlightened and visionary, if periodically indecisive, yet pleasingly pro-Western leader was reified in the mainstream scholarly discourse about his rule. Roger M. Savory (1972, p. 286), for instance, writing in 1972 in the *International Journal of Middle East Studies*, the flagship journal of the field in North America, accentuated the 'warmth and spontaneity of the Shah's welcome by the people when he returned to Iran on 22 August 1953'. Whereas the shah is complemented for his progressive social reforms, the nationalists, the Left and their intellectual avant-garde were considered naive, blind, unrealistic and utopian. Moreover, their opposition was inexcusable 'since it should have been obvious to them that Mohammad Riza Shah was not, and could not become, the same type of despot as his father' (Savory 1972, p. 293). 'Much has been written recently about the politics of cynicism and pessimism in Iran', Savory observes further, 'and, in my opinion, much of the political unrealism of the Persian intellectual from 1907 onwards stems from a cynical and pessimistic outlook. ... Is it too far-fetched to suggest', he (p. 294) adds in typical Orientalist parlour, 'that this attitude has its roots deep in two traditional channels of Persian thought: first, Persian mysticism, and, second, Shi'ite martyrology?'

Here we find why and to what purpose Said (1995, p. 3) defined Orientalism 'as a discourse ... by which European culture was able to manage – and even produce – the Orient ... politically, sociologically, militarily, ideologically, scientifically, and imaginatively during the post-Enlightenment period'. Although Orientalism asserts factual validity, even a scientific status, Said points out that it is the product of ideological fiction, with no real linkage to the cultures and peoples it claims to explain. It follows for Said that Orientalism has muted the Orient. The subject (the Orient) is not represented in the discourse of Orientalism, it does not speak; it is entirely *spoken for*, constituted all the way down to its personality by the 'Orientalist brotherhood' of scholars whose modern lineage Said (1995, p. 122) traces back to the writings of Silvestre de Sacy, Ernest Renan, Edward William Lane and the Napoleonic expedition to Egypt between 1798 and 1801 more generally.

Other than proving that the ideologues of the Pahlavi state in Iran, and the Pahlavi monarchs themselves were somehow products of European Orientalism, Said's argument that representations of the other can be entirely constituted by a discipline such as 'Orientalism' is difficult to maintain. In other words, Orientalisms of any kind are dialectical formations (Adib-Moghaddam, 2008b). There is both an outflow of representations of self and other and an inflow; subject and object may be entirely reversible, they interpenetrate each other, they are hybrid. Let me give an example. When in 1971 Nixon (Conversation Among President Nixon, Ambassador Douglas MacArthur II, and General Alexander Haig, 1971) says that Iran 'at least has got some degree of civilisation' in contrast to 'those Africans' who, according to him, 'are only about 50 to 75 years from out of the trees'. When he considers Iran to be not 'of either world, really', that is, neither Arab (Muslim) or 'western' (Christian), when he considers Iran a bit whiter, a bit more civilized, he is not only articulating an Orientalist bias with particularly racist connotations, he is also reacting to the self-designation of the shah himself, who was adamant in legitimizing his alliance with the 'West' via processes of discursive engineering. To be more precise, it was a particular function and goal of the discourse of the Pahlavi monarchs to represent themselves as 'Aryan', different to the Arab-Semitic other and thus closer to the 'Indo-European' family of Western nations. This strategy was deemed to be functional in order to solidify Iran's relationship with the 'West' ideationally. At the same time, it served to legitimate this alliance to suspicious domestic constituencies who protested against Iran's dependence on foreign countries, and here especially on successive US governments.

The Aryan and Indo-European narrative was institutionalized by Reza Shah, the founder of the short-lived Pahlavi dynasty who was ousted by the British in 1941 in favour of his son Mohammed Reza, who was only 21 years old when he ascended to the throne in the same year. Ervand Abrahamian (2008, p. 86) notes how during the reign of the first Pahlavi monarch organizations such as *Farhangestan* (Cultural Academy), the Department of Public Guidance, the National Heritage Society, the Geography Commission, the journal *Iran-e Bastan* (Ancient Iran) and the government media via newspapers such as *Ettela'at* (Information) and *Journal de Teheran* 'all waged a concerted campaign both to glorify ancient Iran and to purify the language of foreign words … especially Arab ones, [which] were replaced with either brand new or old Persian vocabulary'. The most consequential step towards institutionalizing the Aryan myth came in 1934 when Reza Shah decreed that the country's name should be changed from Persia to Iran in all international correspondence and cartographic designations. Abrahamian (2008, p. 87) notes that in order to 'invoke the glories and birthplace of the ancient Aryans', the National Heritage Society went even as far as to build a rival 'Aryan' mausoleum next to the religious pilgrimage site in Mashhad which is dedicated to Imam Reza, the seventh descendant of the Prophet Muhammad and the eighth Imam of the Ithna Asharia (12er Shia) branch of Shi'ism, which is followed by the vast majority of Iranians. Adopting methods developed in the science of phrenology, members of the Society dug up 'bodies to inter in these mausoleums [and] meticulously measured skulls to "prove" to the whole world that these national figures had been "true Aryans"'.

When, during the Pahlavi dynasty, Iranian scholars and the state itself adopted a scientific discourse that was meant to 'prove' the purity of the Aryan race, they were not only reacting to the Orientalist theses expressed, among others, by Count de Gobineau and Ernest Renan, who argued that Persians are racially superior to the Arabs and other 'Semitic races' because of their 'Indo-European' heritage. True, forerunners of the Aryan myth in Iran, cultural luminaries such as Mirza Fath Ali Akhunzadeh and Mirza Agha Khan Kermani, did internalize Orientalist notions of racial purity and introduced these ideas to the intellectual life of late 19th-century Persia (Adib-Moghaddam 2006, pp. 16ff.; Kashani-Sabet 2002, pp. 166ff.). But there was also an 'Occidentalist' breeding ground for such narratives to gain currency among the intelligentsia of the country, a whole range of nationalist myths that have survived throughout the centuries and that have been repeatedly tapped into in order to define, somewhat metaphysically, the national narrative in Iran. The Pahlavi monarchs were fascinated by the imperial history of pre-Islamic Persia, and found its historical vigour conducive to legitimate their rule. To that end, they invoked the myth that their dynasty was somehow related to Xerxes, Cyrus and Darius, the legendary Kings of the Achaemenid Empire. Thus, Mohammed Reza Shah adopted the official title 'Aryamehr' or light of the Aryans, celebrated 2500 years of Iranian monarchy in a lavish festival in Persepolis in 1971 and subsequently abandoned the Islamic solar hegra calendar in favour of an imperial one, suddenly catapulting Iran into the year 2535 (based on the presumed date of the foundation of the Achaemenid dynasty), traversing both the confines of Muslim history and Western modernity. In the imagination of the shah this was the beginning of a new era for Iran, an era that was meant to set the country apart from its Islamic heritage, fast forwarding it to the gates of a 'great civilisation' (*tamadon-e bozorg*).

The subject that emerges out of the shah's official discourse in Iran is the Aryan Persian, Indo-European, heir to a lost civilization but willing to catch up under Western tutelage. This subject has a tolerated presence in mainstream Western high culture via the discourse of Orientalism. It reminds us of Zarathustra, Scheherazade, Sindbad, Ali Baba, the tales of *One Thousand and One Nights*: the shah ↔ the West ↔ Aryanism ↔ Indo-Europeanness ↔ Orientalist blowback. A new subject now emerges out of the turmoil of the Islamic Revolution in 1979. Now we are confronted with the revolutionary Iranian, somewhat Arab, certainly more Muslim and third worldly, darker and more radical in the unsettling sense of the term. Suddenly, the discursive field signifying Iranian–American relations is populated by different representations of the 'other:' Ayatollah Khomeini ↔ the Orient ↔ Islam ↔ the Third World ↔ revolution ↔ terrorism. The reading of Iran changes. Consider Henry Kissinger (1982, p. 671) in this regard: 'The rootless, the newly powerful, the orthodox, and the spiritually dispossessed came together with disparate, often conflicting motives and swept away the Shah's rule in an orgy of retribution and vengefulness', he writes in his memoirs. 'But retribution for what?' he asks incredulously. ... [N]othing that happened can compare with the witch trials, executions, terrorism, and lunacy that followed, reminiscent in bloodiness and judicial hypocrisy of the worst excesses of Robespierre.' For bestselling author Mark Bowden (2006, pp. 4–5) what was happening in Iran during those days of 'rage and trepidation' was even more momentous. 'The capture of the U.S. Embassy in Tehran', he writes, 'was a glimpse of something new and bewildering. It was the first battle in America's war against militant Islam, a conflict that would eventually engage much of the world.' These lines were published in 2006, that is, in the middle of the 'war on terror', which was adopted as the main strategic plank of the George W. Bush administration after the terrorist attacks on the country in September 2001. Bowden is clearly echoing the pronounced view of US neoconservatives that Iran, Iraq, al-Qaeda, Hesbollah, Hamas and so on are all part of the same problem: the global Islamic threat. 'Iran's revolution wasn't just a localised power struggle; it had tapped a subterranean ocean of Islamist outrage' (Bowden 2006, p. 5). How archaic and alien does it seem to us today that Pahlavi Iran was considered to be of 'either world' and a courted member of the international, viz. 'Western', community of nations, despite the dictatorship of the shah, despite his human rights abominations, despite his nuclear energy programme, despite his support to bombing/insurgent/guerrilla campaigns conducted by Kurdish factions in Iraq in the 1970s.

Revolutionary Iran and the terrorist subject

I have argued that in 1979 a massive rupture occurred within the discursive field enveloping Iranian–American relations. This space, where representations of Iran and the United States reveal themselves and interact with each other in an ungracious simulation of reality, is created dialectically. In other words, there is both an inflow and outflow of signs and symbols, defined in terms of social constructions of self and other, subject and object, which are entirely interpenetrated and thus interdependent phenomena, but claim, nonetheless, 'factual' validity as something distinct. The authorship of the signs and symbols that penetrated this field so vigorously, the idea of Iran as revolutionary, anti-imperial, Islamic, the vanguard in the fight of the 'oppressed' multitudes against the 'arrogant' forces, lay with Iranians themselves. My point is that the revolution equipped Iranians with the irresistible power to express their own narrative, which was enunciated, nonetheless, primarily in relation to and in vigorous cross-fertilization with the concept of the 'West'.

The social engineering of Iran's post-revolutionary identity discourse was precipitated and seriously affected by the writings of activist intellectuals whose ideas were widely disseminated among the anti-shah intelligentsia, especially in the late 1960s and 1970s. Two narratives, *gharbzadegi* (or Westtoxification) and *bazgasht be khishtan* (return to the self), were particularly hegemonic. The former was the title of a highly influential book authored by Jalal al-e Ahmad. In this book al-e Ahmad likens the increasing dependence of Iran on Western notions of modernity to a disease he terms *gharbzadegi*. If left untreated *gharbzadegi* would lead to the demise of Iran's cultural, political and economic independence, because society was made susceptible to penetration by the 'West'. 'Today', writes al-Ahmad (1982, p. 19), 'the fate of those two old rivals is, as you see, this: one has become a lowly groundskeeper and the other the owner of the ballpark.' In order to escape this fate, al-e Ahmad argued, Iran had to be turned into the vanguard in the fight of the oppressed 'East' against the imperialist 'West', if necessary through revolutionary action.

Ali Shariati was equally adamant about challenging the policies of the shah and his real and perceived dependence on the politics of the United States. The narrative of *bazgasht be khishtan* picked up al-e Ahmad's theme accentuating cultural authenticity, and the wider anti-colonial struggle at the head of which Iran should position itself, not least in order to find a way back to the country's 'true' self, which Shariati defined in socialist and Islamic terms. In an intellectual tour de force, Shariati turned Jesus, Abraham, Mohammad and, above all, Imam Hussein (grandson of the Prophet Mohammad) and his mother Fatimah into revolutionary heroes who were positioned at the helm of a new movement for global justice and equality. In his many speeches and written tracts, Shariati emphasized that Islam in general and Shia Islam in particular, demands that the people revolt against unjust rulers. At the centre of Shariati's oeuvre we find Imam Hussein, who is represented as the ultimate *homo Islamicus*, a martyr in the cause of justice who fought the 'tyranny' of the Ummayad caliph Yazid and who sacrificed his life and that of his family at the

Battle of Karbala in AD 680. 'Look at Husayn!' Shariati (Donohue and Esposito 2007, p. 364) demands in 1970:

> He is an unarmed, powerless and lonely man. But he is still responsible for the *jihad*. … He who has no arms and no means has come with all of his existence, his family, his dearest companions so that his *shahadat* [bearing witness to God, martyrdom] and that of his whole family will bear witness to the fact that he carried out his responsibility at a time when truth was defenceless and unarmed. … It is in this way that the dying of a human being guarantees the life of a nation. His *shahadat* is a means whereby faith can remain. It bears witness to the fact that great crimes, deception, oppression and tyranny rule. It proves that truth is being denied. It reveals the existence of values which are destroyed and forgotten. It is a red protest against a black sovereignty. It is a shout of anger in the silence which has cut off tongues.

The narratives of *gharbzadegi* and *bazgasht be khishtan* simulate a bifurcated syntactical order: justice ↔ oppressed (*mostazafan*) ↔ Muslim ↔ Islam ↔ revolution *versus* imperialism ↔ oppressors (*mostakbaran*) ↔ superpowers ↔ the West ↔ the United States. In the writings and speeches of Ayatollah Khomeini, the dichotomies prescribed by this syntactical order find their explicit political articulation. The great utopia of universal justice, central to the former side of the dichotomy, could be turned into 'reality' by the *vali-e faqih*, the supreme jurisprudent who would position himself at the helm of a global movement carried by the 'oppressed' masses of the world. With Ayatollah Khomeini, Islam not only becomes a desirable object of history, it is turned into a revolutionary, anti-imperial ideology with a universal claim. During the same period that the shah proclaimed Iran's new civilization based on the country's pre-Islamic heritage, and at the same time as mainstream scholars in the United States were explaining to us the benevolence of his rule, a different meaning of Iran was being *formula*ted; a discourse that produced 'revolutionary Islam' and its 'Muslim' subject. On the necessity to establish the ideal Islamic polity in order to ward off imperial intrusions, Ayatollah Khomeini (1981, pp. 48–49) was explicit: '[T]he imperialists and the tyrannical self-seeking rulers have divided the Islamic homeland', he lectured in exile in Najaf (Iraq) in 1970.

'They have separated the various segments of the Islamic umma from each other and artificially created separate nations. There once existed the great Ottoman State, and that, too, the imperialists divided. … In order to assure the unity of the Islamic *umma*, in order to liberate the Islamic homeland from occupation and penetration by the imperialists and their puppet governments, it is imperative that we establish a government. In order to attain the unity and freedom of the Muslim peoples, we must overthrow the oppressive governments installed by the imperialists and bring into existence an Islamic government of justice that will be in the service of the people. The formation of such a government will serve to preserve the disciplined unity of the Muslims; just as Fatima az-Zahra (upon whom be peace) said in her address: "The Imamate exists for the sake of preserving order among the Muslims and replacing their disunity with unity."'

I have provided a mere microcosmic look at what was happening below the surface of the official discourse sponsored by the shah's state apparatus in the 1960s and 1970s. The identity discourse of Iran was being populated by new symbols and signs. Suddenly, the same people who were represented as heirs to the pre-Islamic Persian empires, as Aryan, Indo-European and largely non-Muslim by the Pahlavis, appeared as primarily Islamic, anti-imperialistic, revolutionary and supportive of the struggles of the 'third worlds'. The occupation of the US embassy in 1979 was the practical epitome of this discourse. It was not merely planned in response to the admittance of the shah to the United States for medical treatment, which was interpreted as the beginning of yet another plot to reinstate his rule in Iran. The self-proclaimed 'students following the line of Imam Khomeini' were driven by ideas; coded by the powerful revolutionary narratives, some of which I have sketched above. As Massoumeh Ebtekar (2000, p. 80), one of the female students who was involved in the occupation of the US Embassy writes in her account of the events: 'My sense of women's rights and responsibilities derived much from the Iranian context, from Dr. Shariati's book *Fatima is Fatima*, in which he describes the Muslim woman and her role in the world of today with a mixture of eloquence and penetrating insight.' Note that Fatima, conceptualized as the ultimate female vanguard of the new order, reappears here. She travelled from 7th century Arabia to claim a presence in the writings of Shariati and Khomeini (see above) and in the very consciousness of the revolution. More strategically, the students deemed the occupation of the US embassy a necessary step towards achieving Iran's full independence from the international system, even if that meant that Iran would be labelled a pariah or rogue state by its most potent guardians. In other words, the choice to detach Iran from the system that was deemed corrupt and geared towards the imperial interests of the superpowers was self-consciously made by the more radical forces that gathered around Ayatollah Khomeini. As Ebtekar (2000, p. 241) writes: '[T]he Islamic Revolution in Iran transformed a once devoted ally of the West into a "rogue state" that insisted on taking orders from none other than God.'

The message of an author and the reception of her oeuvre are different matters. The subject that emerged out of the revolutionary narratives weaved into Iran before and after the revolution was not welcomed as the new vanguard who would rescue humanity from its fallen present of course. The 'revolutionary Muslim' subject that confronts us now, came to us full of residues of the past, carrying the heavy baggage of Orientalism with all its historical suspicion towards the Muslim other. The occupation of the US Embassy and other signposts of escalation of violence, such as Ayatollah Khomeini's fatwa against Salman Rushdie in 1989, in effect reified that pre-existing image of Muslims as violent, archaic and fanatical in the imagination of many stakeholders dealing with the region. A revolution (during the Cold War) – a concept associated with communism, Fidel Castro, un-American 'leftists' and the Soviet other – in the name of Islam – a concept associated with the Arabs and Turks, the fiercest competitors with the idea of the 'West' and its Christian residue – has made it very difficult indeed to move beyond the canonized archives of Western Orientalism, even after the Iranian revolutionaries re-evaluated the project to export their Islamic republican model after the end of the Iran–Iraq War and the death of Ayatollah Khomeini in 1989. So the 'terror' label stuck, not because its point of origin lay in the abominations of Iran's radical politics, not because of the violence unleashed by the revolution per se, but because it confronted US foreign policies and their beneficiaries, primarily the Israeli state, through a radically alternative discourse that threatened to alter the political composition of a region that has been considered vital to US national interests because of its oil resources. In other words, Iran and its allies were not a military threat to the status quo as they did not purport to change the political composition of the region through military conquest. But they were a discursive one, which made it necessary to fight them with a potent counter-discourse: hence the terror narrative emerges.

To those who would immediately interject by saying that Iran was associated with terror because the country supported a range of movements, Palestinians, Lebanese, Iraqi, Afghan and so on, organizations, such as Fatah, Hamas and Hezbollah, which use political violence in order to further their political aims, allow me to respond that 'terrorism' as a noun, and 'terroristic' as an adjective, are the terminological surface effect of discursive representations: they are concepts that emerge out of a particular politico-cultural configuration that commands its own signifying powers, out of which the terror label and its derivatives are distilled. I am not saying that killing civilians is not immoral and taboo, of course; it is and it should be. I am saying that in the reality invented for us, it is not that moral taboo that represents a country or movement as terroristic, but the discourse that signifies the fundamental categories of friend and foe, terrorist and freedom fighter. The normative difference between these categories cannot be measured and defined in terms of the type of political violence unleashed, but by its representation in the political and media discourse of a particular period.

Let me give you a few empirical examples with regard to the discursive field under scrutiny here. In the early 1970s the shah, via his intelligence organization SAVAK, the CIA and the Israeli MOSSAD, sponsored a sustained 'covert war' of Iraqi-Kurdish factions under the leadership of Mustafa Barzani against the Ba'thist leadership in Iraq, which led to bombings of oil installations in Kirkuk and other infrastructural facilities of civilian use, and subsequently to a fully fledged insurgency. Among us, we may deem the methods employed by the Kurdish movement 'terroristic'. But this was certainly not the official view in Washington (or Britain, Iran and Israel). A White House memorandum authored by Henry Kissinger and dated 5 October 1972 (White House Memorandum 1972, p. 1) refers to 'Mustafa Barzani's Kurdish resistance movement'. In the same memo (p. 1) it is indicated that CIA director Richard Helms reports the delivery of 'money and arms … to Barzani via the Iranians without a hitch. More money and arms are in the pipeline', it is stated. 'Barzani received the first two monthly cash payments of each for July and August … By the end of October, the Iranians will have received for onward shipment to the Kurds 222,000 pounds of arms and ammunitions from Agency stocks and 142,000 pound from [Retracted].' Note also that since its inception in 1979, the Iraqi government was put on the US State Department's list of state sponsors of terrorism. The country was taken off that list in 1982 in the middle of the Iran–Iraq War and at a time when the Reagan administration was aware of Saddam Hussein's directives to use chemical weapons against advancing Iranian army units and Iraqi civilians who resisted his regime (Adib-Moghaddam 2006, 2008). Iraq was put on that list again after its invasion of Kuwait in 1990. Ultimately then, the allocation of the terror label shifted with the particular political context in which it was employed.

Moreover, other declassified documents from the 1970s show that the label 'terrorist' was readily applied to student activists protesting the dictatorship of the shah. A US State Department telegram of August 1972 (US Department of State 1972, p. 1), for instance, observes that 'Terrorist activities in Iran seem to be increasing instead of usual summer subsidence due to vacation for students, perhaps indicating better organisation and broadening of appeal to non-student groups.' In the same memo (p. 1) it is indicated that there 'have been 28 confirmed explosions (11 of which directed against US presence), ten shootouts and several other incidents including unsuccessful attempt to kidnap daughter of Court Minister Alam, and plot to sabotage Isfahan steel mill.' The fact that these 'terrorists' seemed to use similar measures as the Kurdish movement that the Nixon administration supported during the very same period was not the measure according to which the terror label was allocated here. Rather, it was the fact that the students were acting against a leader who was considered to be an ally of the United States that turned them into 'terrorists'. So in the discursive field I am dissecting here, the term terror and all its derivatives do not have any normative or analytical value beyond their signification within a particular politico-cultural constellation. Not because it is I who am blurring their meaning for the sake of my argument, but because politicians have twisted and turned them for their own purposes since the 'birth' of the term during the 'reign of terror' in the aftermath of the French Revolution.

Dialectical conjunctions and the Iranian–American syntax

Let me return to the beginning of this chapter and recapture the issue of trust within such an untrustworthy discursive field. The subject that emerges out of the turmoil of the revolution and the subsequent devastating war between Iran and Iraq (1980–1988) does not speak to the American side in order to mitigate conflict, but to accentuate difference. Revolutionary Iran was adamant that it would define the Islamic Republic in strict juxtaposition to the West in general and the United States in particular. This discourse has suggested, as I mentioned, a bifurcated syntactical order within which the fundamental boundary between subject and object, self and other has been cemented with layers and layers of narrated inventions, all of which were meant to solidify the fundamental difference between the two states. In other words, the political independence of Iran has been achieved via a discursive dependency. By defining Iran's new 'self' in relation to the American 'other', the discourse of the Islamic Republic has become entirely dependent on invented images of the United States in particular and the concept of the 'West' more generally. Thus an oppressive syntactical dependency has been created which demands that Iran takes the US and the West permanently into account at each and every twist and turn of the country's official political discourse: *marg bar Amrika* (death to America), *marg bar engelis* (death to England), *marg bar Israel* (death to Israel); calling for the 'death' of America, England and Israel guarantees their syntactical existence in the here and now. So the 'West' has a rather pronounced presence in Islamic Iran indeed, particularly among the right wing, the supporters of Ahmadinejad who utter those slogans and whose iron fist is crushing Iranian pro-democracy activists at the very moment I am writing these lines. It should not come as a surprise that these young people are accused of colluding with the 'West': within contemporary Iran it is inevitable that 'you' reappears as a major focal point of the political discourse.

I am emphasizing that a discursive field is always social, but that that sociality could be violent, neutral, intimate or friendly; it could be charged with negative or positive energy, but it always remains the loci within which shifts from enemy to friend or ally to foe can be signified. Note that I am accentuating the effects of discourse, our language towards the other, as the main source of trust-building measures. I am re-emphasizing this because Iran and the United States did occasionally reach out to each other out of expediency without changing their language towards the other side. When the 'great satan' and the 'mad mullahs' colluded via Israel in what became to be known as the Iran–Contra Affair in 1986, they remained just that: staunch antagonists who made a deal not in order to engender trust, but as a means to achieve divergent strategic interests. In the case of the Iranian leadership, the deal was necessary in order to secure a supply of arms and weaponry during a period when the chemical weapons attacks by Saddam Hussein's troops were beginning to demoralize the Iranian army. The Israeli government of Shimon Peres, on the other side, acted on the premise 'that moderate elements in Iran can come to power if these factions demonstrate their credibility in defending Iran against Iraq and in deterring Soviet intervention. To achieve the strategic goal of a more moderate Iranian government', it is stated in a White House memorandum (1986, p. 1), authored by then US national security advisor, John Poindexter, 'the Israelis are prepared to unilaterally commence selling military material to Western-oriented Iranian factions. … It is their belief that by so doing they can achieve a heretofore unobtainable penetration of the Iranian governing hierarchy.' In response to this memo, President Reagan (White House Memorandum 1986, p. 4) authorized assisting individuals and groups 'sympathetic to U.S. Governments interests … for the purpose of: 1) establishing a more moderate government in Iran, 2) obtaining from them significant intelligence … and 3) furthering the release of the American hostages held in Beirut'. It should become clear that in this clandestine transaction none of the stakeholders were interested in pursuing strategic trust-building measures, which would have involved, at a minimum, the acknowledgement of the 'trustworthiness' of the other side (Booth and Wheeler 2008, pp. 229ff.). The first major step towards that direction after the revolution in Iran was made by former president Mohammad Khatami (1997–2005) via the 'dialogue amongst civilisation' initiative, which did not yield, however, the results that he and his supporters envisaged. On the contrary, Iran was named a part of the 'axis of evil' and a major target in the global 'war on terror', as pronounced by the administration of George W. Bush in the aftermath of the terror attacks on the country in September 2001 (Adib-Moghaddam, 2008, part 3). Thus far, this narrative–counternarrative dialectic has not delivered a pacified discursive field in which a strategic leap towards trust could be signified.

Discursive fields are never immutable or unchangeable; they are impure, creolized phenomena, porous and polluted spaces that are open for interpretive penetration. Their relative ontological salience does not emanate from the ahistorical codification of the objects that engage each other therein, but from the fact that none of them can be explained solely by their own properties. In this sense discursive fields are violently social phenomena; representations of self and other are entirely interdependent. Iranians and Americans may have parodied seemingly divergent identities aimed at setting each other apart, but their performative acts achieved the opposite. By allocating to the other side a prominent discursive presence, the interdependence between the two countries increased. Before the revolution, Iran and the United States were entangled in a social relationship that was beset by trust; after the revolution they were immersed in a social relationship beset by active distrust.[1] The latter state required far more laborious political construction efforts, because a) the intentions of the other side were largely obscured and not immediately visible (there was no easily accessible 'intelligence' in CIA parlance) and b) the enemy image (mad mullah, great satan) had to be constructed within a discursive field that was suddenly ruptured by the Islamic Revolution.

Premise a) can be immediately linked to Sun Tzu's (1963, p. 84) ancient note of caution: 'Know the enemy and know yourself; in a hundred battles you will never be in peril' or to the popular proverb that you should 'keep your friends close, but your enemies closer', which reappears in Francis Ford Coppola's movie adaptation of Mario Puzo's novel *The Godfather*. In other words, after the revolution Iran and the United States had to take each other permanently into account; they had to open up spaces for the other side in their official discourse because, in the absence of diplomatic relations, both sides suffered from a pronounced sense of insecurity about each other's intentions. Indeed, a quick perusal of the main strategic speeches of successive US presidents indicates that the presence of Iran in the syntax of US foreign policy proclamations has progressively increased to the extent that today President Obama mentions the country whenever he addresses three central international issues (the first and third of which are global): the topic of nuclear disarmament and the NPT, international relations in western Asia and US relations with the 'Muslim world'.

Premise b) refers to the process via which the unknown enemy has to become the socially engineered invention par excellence because he has to be made visible. Turning him into a 'real and tangible enemy' requires ongoing performative processes, the ultimate aim of which would be to reveal his hidden face. An incredible amount of Kantian *Einbildungskrtaft* (power of imagination) is needed here in order to turn him into something easily recognizable. If the enemy image is conducive to the politics of the day, the expressions of his face have to be drawn threateningly enough to mobilize the libidinous anger of the nation that would, ideally, stare at him with outrage. Of course, once this image is created it is difficult to be re-manipulated; indeed it threatens to become a self-fulfilling prophecy.

Political elites deceive themselves whenever they believe that they can monopolize the signification of a particular discursive field without taking the other side into account. No hegemony is all encompassing, no discourse can be co-opted fully by a particular agent, no discursive field is indifferent to temporal change. In a situation that is intensely social, where the bonds between country A and country B are not easily dissoluble, violence towards the other will always involve some blowback. The psychological (that is, strategic) impact of violence between family members is more intimate than a pub brawl, the violence between Iran and the United States causes more strategic and cognitive scars (on both sides) than the violence between, say, the United States and Brazil or Iran and Austria. It is in this sense that the United States and Iran share a 'common fate' in western Asia; not because their strategic goals are compatible, not because of expedient foreign policy reasons, not because Iran could act, once again, as a junior partner to the United States, not because the country is needed in order to pacify Afghanistan and Iraq, but because Iran and the United States inhabit the same discursive universe; their grammatical existence is inextricably linked.

At the beginning of this chapter we presumed that the dash setting the two terms 'Iranian–American' apart is a sign of unbridgeable difference. Certainly, after the Iranian Revolution in 1979 there have been immense efforts on both sides to convince us that Iran and the United States are essentially different entities, that there is an inherent epistemological difference between these two ideas. But upon closer inspection the dash reveals itself as a conjunction, a grammatical particle, a via media that indicates that in the word formation 'Iranian–American' nothing is detachable, autonomous, at liberty. We are confronted with a particular form of what Gilles Deleuze (2004, p. 55) termed 'disjunctive synthesis', the interdependence of radically exclusive concepts: Iran (Iranian, mad mullahs and so on) on the one side, America (American, great satan and so on) on the other. Ultimately, within the discursive field we are looking at, each of these terms is intensely interdependent; they do not only signify a common discursive field, but also a conjoined cognitive region. It is time that we catch up with this political paradox – with the violently interdependent, latently empathetic potentialities of word formations. Uttering trust towards the other, after all, calls for the triumph of the conjunction 'and' over the predicate 'is'.

Note

1 I would like to thank Nick Wheeler for suggesting this term.

References

Abrahamian, E., 2008. *A History of Modern Iran*. Cambridge: Cambridge University Press.
Adib-Moghaddam, A., 2006. *The International Politics of the Persian Gulf: A Cultural Genealogy*. London: Routledge.

Adib-Moghaddam, A., 2008a. *Iran in World Politics: The Question of the Islamic Republic*. New York: Columbia University Press.

Adib-Moghaddam, A., 2008b. 'A (short) history of the clash of civilisations'. *Cambridge Review of International Affairs* 21:2, pp. 217–234.

Beeman, W., 2005. *The Great Satan vs. the Mad Mullahs: How the United States and Iran Demonize Each Other*. London: Greenwood.

Benhabib, S., 1986. *Critique, Norm and Utopia: A Study of the Foundations of Critical Theory*. New York: Columbia University Press.

Benjamin, W., 1986. *Reflections: Essays, Aphorism, Autobiographical Writings*. Ed. P. Demetz. New York: Schocken Books.

Booth, K. and N.J. Wheeler, 2008. *The Security Dilemma: Fear, Cooperation and Trust in World Politics*. London: Palgrave.

Bowden, M., 2006. *Guests of the Ayatollah: The First Battle in the West's War with Militant Islam*. London: Atlantic.

Calhoun, C., 1995. *Critical Social Theory: Culture, History, and the Challenge of Difference*. Oxford: Blackwell.

Campbell, D., 1992. *Politics Without Principle: Sovereignty, Ethics, and the Narratives of the Gulf War*. London: Lynne Rienner.

Campbell, D., 1993. *Writing Security: United States Foreign Policy and the Politics of Identity*. Manchester: Manchester University Press.

CIA, Directorate of Intelligence, 1972. *Intelligence Report: Centres of Power in Iran*. Available from: http://www.state.gov/documents/organization/70712.pdf (accessed 21 July 2009).

'Conversation Among President Nixon, Ambassador Douglas MacArthur II, and General Alexander Haig'. *Washington*, 8 April 1971, 3:56–4:21 p.m. Available from: http://www.state.gov/r/pa/ho/frus/nixon/e4/71804.htm (accessed 12 June 2009).

Deleuze, G., 2004. *The Logic of Sense*. London: Continuum.

Al-e Ahmad, J., 1982. *Plagued by the West (Gharbzadegi)*. Trans. from the Persian by Paul Sprachman. New York: Caravan.

Ebtekar, M., 2000. *Takeover in Tehran: The Inside Story of the 1979 U.S. Embassy Capture*. Vancouver: Talon.

Foucault, M., 2002a. *Power: Essential Works of Foucault*, vol. 3. Ed. J.D. Faubion, trans. R. Hurley *et al*. London: Penguin.

Foucault, M., 2002b. *The Archaeology of Knowledge*. London: Routledge.

Habermas, J., 1984. *Theory of Communicative Action, vol. 1: Reason and the Rationalisation of Society*. Boston: Beacon Press.

Horkheimer, M., 1997. *Critical Theory: Selected Essays*. London: Continuum.

Jackson, R., 2005. *Writing the War on Terrorism: Language, Politics and Counterterrorism*. Manchester: Manchester University Press.

Kashani-Sabet, F., 2002, 'Cultures of Iranianness: The evolving polemic of Iranian nationalism'. In: N.R. Keddie and R. Matthee, eds *Iran and the Surrounding World: Interactions in Culture and Cultural Politics*. Seattle: University of Washington Press, pp. 162–181.

Kissinger, H., 1982. *Years of Upheaval*. London: Weidenfeld and Nicolson.

Khomeini, R., 1981. *Islam and Revolution: Writings and Declarations of Imam Khomeini*. Trans. and annotated by H. Algar. Berkeley: Mizan Press.

Marx, K., 1973. *Survey from Exile*. Ed. D. Fernbach. Harmondsworth: Penguin, 1973.

Risse, T., 2000. ' "Let's Argue!" Communicative Action in World Politics'. *International Organization* 54:1, pp. 1–39.

Said, E.W., 1997. *Covering Islam: How the Media and the Experts Determine How We See the Rest of the World*. London: Vintage.

Said, E.W., 1995. *Orientalism: Western Conceptions of the Orient*. London: Penguin.

Savory, R.M., 1972. 'The Principle of Homeostasis Considered in Relation to Political Events in Iran in the 1960's'. *International Journal of Middle East Studies (IJMES)* 3:3, pp. 282–302.

Shariati, A., 2007. 'On Martyrdom (*Shahadat*)'. In: J.J. Donohue and J.L. Esposito, eds. *Islam in Transition: Muslim Perspectives*. 2nd Edition. Oxford: Oxford University Press, pp. 361–365.

Sun Tzu, 1963. *The Art of War*. Trans. Samuel B. Griffith. Oxford: Oxford University Press.

US Department of State, August 1972. 'Continuing Terrorist Activities in Iran'. Available from: http://www.state.gov/documents/organization/70763.pdf (accessed 20 May 2009).

White House Memorandum, 17 January 1986. 'Covert Action Finding Regarding Iran (with attached Presidential finding).' Available from: http://www.gwu.edu/~nsarchiv/NSAEBB/NSAEBB210/15-Reagan%20Finding%201–17–86%20(IC%2002181).pdf (accessed 20 July 2009).

White House Memorandum, 5 October 1972. 'Progress Report on the Kurdish Support Operations'. Available from: http://www.state.gov/documents/organization/72019.pdf (accessed 20 July 2009).

11   Energy security and Iran's role in international relations

Paul Rogers

Introduction

The Gulf region is, by a substantial measure, the richest source of oil and natural gas resources in the world. Iran is unique in having both oil and natural gas reserves that are among the largest, with oil reserves second only to Saudi Arabia and natural gas reserves second only to Russia. These form part of the region's importance to the world's most powerful countries and are significant determinants of Iran's role in international relations, especially in the matter of regional security. In the short and medium term this may be advantageous to Iran, but the impact of climate change over the next 20 years means that most countries will have to move rapidly to low-carbon economies, with demand for oil and gas falling drastically over that time-scale. Developing the Iranian economy will therefore involve difficult decisions and a willingness to engage in profound technical and economic transformations.

Oil and gas reserves

The world's oil industry developed primarily in the United States, utilising deposits in Ohio and Pennsylvania in the 1890s. It expanded into the Caucasus and what was then the Dutch East Indies and later into South America and the Middle East.[1] The United States remained one of the world's largest producers for much of the 20th century, and was largely self-sufficient in oil production until the 1970s. North Africa and the Gulf countries became significant in the second half of the century and five countries around the Gulf now dominate world reserves. (Table 11.1.)

The concentration of oil reserves in the region is remarkable. In approximate terms Saudi Arabia has 25 per cent of the world's total, Iran has 12 per cent, Iraq 10 per cent and the Emirates and Kuwait each have 9 per cent. In total, nearly 65 per cent of the world's oil is found in these five countries, with over 80 per cent of the entire world's oil found there together with Russia, Venezuela and Kazakhstan.

Natural gas reserves are even more concentrated (Table 11.2). Again, five countries have well over 60 per cent of the world total, but just three countries, Russia, Iran and Qatar, account for over 55 per cent (see Table 11.3).

There are two important further points that need to be appreciated. In the case of oil, the countries that have the largest reserves are not necessarily the world's largest

Table 11.1 World oil reserves (billion barrels)

	1985	1995	2005
Saudi Arabia	171.5	261.5	264.2
Iran	59	93.7	137.5
Iraq	65	100	115
Kuwait	92.5	96.5	101.5
United Arab Emirates	33	98.1	97.8
Venezuela	55.4	66.3	79.7
Russia	n/a	n/a	74.7
Kazakhstan	n/a	n/a	39.6
Libya	21.3	29.5	39.1
Nigeria	16.6	20.8	39.1
United States	36.4	29.8	29.3
Canada	9.6	10.5	16.5
China	17.1	16.3	16
Qatar	4.5	3.7	15.2
Mexico	55.6	48.8	13.7

Source: BP Statistical Review of World Energy, June 2006.

Table 11.2 World natural gas reserves, 2008 (trillion cubic metres)

Russia	44.7
Iran	26.9
Qatar	25.6
Saudi Arabia	7.2
United Arab Emirates	6.1
United States	6.0
Nigeria	5.2
Venezuela	4.7
Algeria	4.5
World total	175.4

Source: CIA World Factbook, May 2009.

Table 11.3 World natural gas reserves, 2008 (percentage of total)

Russia	25.5
Iran	15.4
Qatar	14.6
Saudi Arabia	4.1
United Arab Emirates	3.5

Source: Based on Table 11.2.

producers. The United States, for example, is a major producer but is running down its own reserves in the process. Iran has more than four times the oil reserves of the entire United States including Alaska, but the rate at which the United States is consuming its reserves means that this ratio is changing year by year in Iran's favour. This is part of an overall 'resource shift', which also applies to some strategic ferroalloy metals, in which countries of the South are becoming steadily more significant as providers of key non-renewable resources to the industrialised world.

The second point is that all of the world's major industrialised countries (except Russia) and the key newly emerging economies of China and India are heavily dependent on imported oil. This has long been true of Japan, South Korea and Western European states (apart from the UK) but the really important trend is the change in oil import dependency for the United States and China. These two giant economies have increased their import dependency at a remarkable rate. The United States moved from near self-sufficiency to around a 55 per cent dependence on oil imports in the 35-year period from 1970 to 2005. In the case of China, the change has been dramatically faster. Because of the sustained high levels of economic growth of recent years – on occasions around 10 per cent per year – and the exhaustion of many of the domestic reserves, China has moved from self-sufficiency in 1993 to a 50 per cent import dependency by 2009.

This does not mean that the United States and China are critically dependent on Gulf oil at present since they have diversified sources of supply from Latin America, sub-Saharan Africa and elsewhere, but it does mean that these other sources are relatively small compared with the Gulf States. It follows that as these become depleted over the next two decades, the reserves of the Gulf States will grow in strategic significance. This will be at a time when natural gas becomes increasingly attractive as an energy source, with just two Gulf States, Iran and Qatar, being leading sources.

To repeat – what is significant is the combination of the sheer size of the region's reserves combined with steadily greater reliance of major industrialised and industrialising states on oil and gas imports as their own resources are depleted.

Oil security

While natural gas is an increasingly significant energy resource, oil remains the overwhelmingly imported traded resource and its availability has long been related to perceptions of security. Many conflicts during the 20th century had elements within them related to the securing of oil supplies, including aspects of the war plans of Germany and Japan. More recently, Iraq's motivation in the 1980–1988 war with Iran, and coalition responses to the Iraqi occupation of Kuwait in 1990 were both oil related, as was the US action to terminate the Saddam Hussein regime.[2]

US concern over the security of supply dates back to the Roosevelt administration in the early 1940s[3] but developed rapidly in the wake of the 400+ per cent increase in oil prices following action by the Organization of Arab Petroleum Exporting Countries (OAPEC) during the 1973 Yom Kippur/Ramadan War. In the wake of that conflict, studies were undertaken concerning the risk of major interruptions to oil supplies, the overall conclusion being that the United States did not have the military capacity to intervene in the Middle East in order to secure supplies.[4]

Much of the concern at that time was with the risk of Soviet intervention in the Middle East, and President Jimmy Carter issued Presidential Directive 18 in 1977, requiring the armed forces to plan for interventions in areas outside the main spheres of US military operations.[5] In spite of inter-service rivalry, the Joint Rapid Deployment Task Force (JRDTF), more commonly known as the Rapid Deployment Force, was established three years later. Under the Reagan adminis- tration, issues of resource security were of much greater concern, especially after the Iranian Revolution, and the 1982 *Military Posture Statement* from the US Joint Chiefs of Staff placed considerable emphasis on oil security.[6] The main result of this was the expansion of the Rapid Deployment Force into a new comprehensive military command, Central Command (CENTCOM), responsible for US security interests across an arc of 19 countries stretching from North-East Africa through the Middle East to West Asia.

In the past 20 years, US military forces have established or expanded numerous bases across the region, especially in Kuwait, Qatar and Bahrain, as well as a major pre-positioning site at Diego Garcia in the Indian Ocean. In addition there are currently two major bases in Afghanistan at Bagram and Kandahar, and four large bases in Iraq. While a withdrawal of the majority of US forces in Iraq is intended by 2011, it is certainly possible that 35–50,000 will remain in some form, if largely confined to bases outside the cities. Even if most of these are withdrawn, some forces will remain given the size of the US diplomatic presence in Iraq, not least at the world's largest embassy, the recently completed complex in Baghdad.

Furthermore, the United States maintains substantial forces in Kuwait, has a major air base in Qatar and the headquarters of the US Navy's Fifth Fleet in Bahrain. Meanwhile there is a considerable surge in US forces in Afghanistan currently under way, leading to a total NATO contingent of around 100,000 troops by the end of 2009, the majority of them American, with many more US troops likely to be deployed by mid-2010.

Iran, energy and international relations

While US deployments in Afghanistan and Pakistan are less related to oil security, the military presence in the Gulf region is far more connected and is likely to remain so over the next two decades whatever administration is in power in Washington. China, on the other hand, chooses mainly to exercise influence through long-term energy development and supply agreements, with significant recent negotiations with Iran, Saudi Arabia and Iraq.[7] China does maintain a military relationship with countries in the region, but primarily through the medium of arms sales – its supply of a range of equipment, especially anti-ship missiles, to Iran being a case in point. These missiles, both shore-based and deployed on warships, are particularly significant in relation to the security of the crowded waters of the Persian Gulf, especially in the vicinity of the Straits of Hormuz.

The overall implications to be drawn from this brief overview are that the Gulf region in general and Iran in particular, will be the sustained focus of US, Chinese and other interests over the next two decades. Furthermore, the resource shift will tend to result in the region increasing in significance. Although the current global economic recession may result in temporary decreases in oil and gas prices, these are unlikely to persist beyond five years. The prognosis, other things being equal, is for sustained high oil and gas prices.

The immediate implications for Iran are twofold. One is the tendency to rely on oil and gas revenues to prop up a relatively inefficient economy – a form of 'short termism' that carries considerable political and social risks. In effect, the ready availability of oil and gas means that Iran risks neglecting its wider economic development in terms of agriculture and manufacturing industries. This is particularly dangerous in view of the demographic environment, with Iran having a high proportion of educated young people who, in such circumstances, will have limited employment prospects.

The second implication is that Iran is in a strong position in its relationship with countries such as China and the United States, but also exists in a region with high levels of military spending combined with substantial rivalries and uncertainties. At the same time, more effective economic planning and management, combined with a willingness to engage more fully with neighbouring states and more distant external powers would ensure good prospects for internal development and regional influence.

Climate change

Although what has been outlined above is a broadly positive prognosis, it can be argued that it is actually a dangerously short-sighted outlook which ignores the rapidly rising significance of climate change and its probable impact on world oil and gas markets.

Climate change is caused primarily by the release of carbon dioxide into the atmosphere as a result of the burning of fossil fuels, principally coal and oil, but also natural gas. The phenomenon has been recognised for some decades but the seriousness of the impact is only now appreciated.[8] In the worst case scenario there could be irreversible climate change leading to such damage to the global ecosystem over several decades that the great majority of the world's population will not survive. Even the more limited impacts include sea level rises inundating coastal cities and some of the world's richest low-lying croplands, and far more intense tropical storms. More serious still is the risk of a drying out of tropical and sub-tropical land masses, including the Gulf region. Such impacts are well-nigh certain unless drastic action is taken to reduce carbon emissions.[9]

The risks from climate change are recognised primarily in Northern states and currently attract far less attention in the South. This may be understandable in view of the many development problems that are seen as far more pressing, but the impacts of climate change are going to be massive for Southern states. Moreover, because of their relatively weak economies, they will have far greater difficulty in responding to the potentially devastating consequences of climate change.

Reductions of around 80 per cent in carbon emissions compared with current activity are now believed to be necessary across the world, with the initial changes being undertaken by the major carbon emitters of the industrialised world. While many politicians see this in terms of a 40-year timescale, climate change analysts believe that a 15–20-year timescale is more appropriate.

Positive feedback systems are now in operation, which are speeding up the rate of climate change, two of the most significant of which are operating in the Arctic and near-Arctic. The more immediate of these is that Arctic sea ice is melting more each summer, leaving open water, which absorbs solar radiation more than ice. These means the sea warms faster, melting more ice, which further speeds up the melting. The longer-term and more serious feedback is that the warming of the Arctic and near-Arctic is starting to melt the permafrost, releasing large quantities of methane from the decaying vegetation. Methane is a far more dangerous climate change gas than carbon dioxide and its large-scale release will accelerate the process of warming, speed up the melting of the permafrost and release further methane.

What needs to be emphasised here is the transformation of the scientific understanding of climate change that has taken place over the past 15 years. Partly because of the ideological opposition of the Bush Administration to recognising the significance of climate change, the seriousness of the issue was minimised over the eight-year period from 2001 to 2009, even though scientific evidence of the accelerating nature of climate change was accumulating. With the change in administrations in Washington following the election of Barack Obama, that blockage has been removed and it is therefore wise to assume that the entire issue will rise rapidly up the international political agenda, providing the motivation needed to make the changes.

As the necessary moves towards low carbon economies start to have their impact, there will be a substantial decrease in demand for coal, oil and natural gas, with consequent decreases in price. The impact on the economy of any country that continues to rely primarily on energy exports will be considerable, especially if that country has a large and youthful population. Iran is precisely such a country and there is a very strong argument for developing an economic strategy that meets this challenge effectively.

At present, the major option being pursued is the development of civil nuclear power, but there are serious questions over the long-term advisability of this path, given the exceptional problem of nuclear waste. The United Kingdom was the first country to invest heavily in civil nuclear power in the 1950s and 1960s and most of the first generation of reactors are now shut down and have to be decommissioned and cleaned up. The costs are turning out to be prohibitive, so much so that if they were borne by the UK nuclear industry it would be economically defunct. Instead, the UK government has removed the costs and given the responsibility to the Nuclear Decommissioning Authority, which is funded principally by taxation. The clean-up costs of just the first of the three generations of nuclear power plants that have been built in the UK are currently estimated at about US$100 billion. Nuclear power may seem like a good option, not least because it is seen as an indicator of modernity. In reality it is a relatively primitive technology that needs to undergo far more development before it can be considered either safe or mature.

It is significant that there is little interest in developing a new generation of nuclear power plants in the United States and Western Europe because private companies are not convinced that they will be economically viable.

Iran has considerable potential for using renewable energy resources, including an expansion of existing hydroelectric power and the development of solar power. It also has considerable potential for energy conservation. These would appear to be advisable options for assisting the country in meeting the climate change challenge that will increasingly affect all the countries of the world but will have a particularly significant impact on countries that are economically dependent on energy exports.

Notes

1 For an account of the early development of the oil industry, see: Daniel Yergin, *The Prize* (New York: Simon and Schuster, 1993).
2 One of the very few analyses of the role of oil in US policy towards Iraq is Atif Kubursi, 'Oil and the Global Economy', in: Rick Fawn and Raymond Hinnebusch (eds) *The Iraq War: Causes and Consequences* (Boulder and London: Lynne Rienner, 2006).
3 Michael Klare, *Blood and Oil* (London and New York: Hamish Hamilton, 2004). See also: Toby Shelley, *Oil, Politics, Poverty and the Planet* (London: Zed Books, 2005). Political aspects of the world oil industry are discussed in: Bulent Gokay (ed.), *The Politics of Oil: A Survey* (London and New York: Routledge, 2006).
4 One of the few open access studies published was: *Oil Fields as Military Objectives: A Feasibility Study*, Report to the Special Subcommittee on Investigations of the House Committee on International Relations (Washington DC: Congressional Research Service August 1975).
5 For a more detailed account see: 'Oil and the War on Terror', in: Paul Rogers, *Why We're Losing the War on Terror* (Cambridge: Polity Press, 2008).
6 The Organization of the Joint Chiefs of Staff, *US Military Posture for FY 1982* (Washington DC: US Government Printing Office, 1981).
7 Gina Chon, 'China Reaches $3 Billion Deal to Develop Oil Field in Iraq', *Wall Street Journal*, 29 August 2008.
8 As a global environmental constraint, the phenomenon of climate change is in line with the seminal 'limits to growth' analysis of 40 years ago: Donella H. Meadows, Dennis L. Meadows, Jorgen Randers and William W. Behrens III, *Limits to Growth*, (London: Earth Island, 1972).
9 A thoughtful and wide-ranging discussion of climate security is. Nick Mabey, 'Delivering Climate Security: International Security Responses to a Climate Changed World', *Whitehall Papers 69* (London: Royal United Services Institute, 2008).

12 The impact of Iran's tenth presidential elections on its relations with the EU and Mediterranean states

Mahboubeh Sadeghinia

The Islamic Republic of Iran's (IRI) foreign policy, political orientation and its ability to achieve its objectives have been largely dependent on its security environment. The security environment is undeniably influenced by the international system, and hence security is an important element in the IRI's foreign policy. This element has grown in influence since the disputed presidential election of 12 June 2009, which was interpreted by opposition groups as a palace coup. Iran's current unstable socio-political situation has been heightened by the disputed re-election of Iranian President Mahmoud Ahmadinejad, protests against which led to the brutal crackdown and suppression of dissenting voices. This, together with a faltering economy, has threatened the regime's potential for survival. In order to establish foreign relations under such conditions, Iranian leadership has to fight to increase its legitimacy at home.

Consequently, Iran's evolution in the post-election turmoil led Tehran to focus on its domestic politics rather than on any of its bilateral or multilateral relationships, including those with the European Union (EU) and Mediterranean states. Due to the importance of beginning and the outcome of US negotiations with Iran on Tehran's foreign policy towards the EU and Mediterranean states, IRI's relationship with these countries is expected to be affected by both US–Iran relations as well as Iran's domestic socio-political development.

Because of the country's economic woes and international posture its foreign policy became central to the Iranian electoral debate for all candidates, including Ahmadinejad. Moreover, while all candidates linked the economy to Iranian–Western relations and there were debates on how to begin negotiations to overcome economic issues, the tension in Iran's foreign relations with the West, and the EU in particular, regarding the post-election turmoil caused any improvement in their bilateral and/or multilateral relationship to be delayed even further and more complicated. This was due to:

a)   Tehran's efforts to link the domestic unrest to foreign powers. Tehran's leadership accused the West of having provoked the mass protests against the government, and condemned Western support for the dissidents and for the public criticism of its mass trial of moderates charged with spying and trying to topple the regime after the disputed presidential vote. Tehran's allegations extended even to the arrest and trial of some of the employees in the British and French embassies in Tehran, along with some 4,000 Iranians who were arrested. In the months after the election about 100 of those arrested were put on trial. As Ahmadinejad announced his new cabinet on 30 September he condemned policies adopted by the EU and the US following the disputed election, 'You have clearly interfered in Iran's internal affairs and were naïve enough to think that you can damage the system but with God's help you failed.'[1] Moreover, there were calls in the Iranian parliament to revise relations with some European states, specifically Britain, France, Germany and Sweden, although, according to Hassan Qashqavi, the Speaker of Iran's Ministry of Foreign Affairs, at that time Tehran did not have any plan to decrease its relations with the EU members.

b)   The EU supported the popular unrest against alleged fraud in the June presidential election and did not acknowledge the re-election of President Ahmadinejad. The 27 EU member states also summoned the Iranian ambassadors in their countries and expressed their disapproval of what they called 'show trials' against more than 100 detained demonstrators, local embassy employees and former reformist officials.[2]

Therefore, the continuance of social unrest and the legitimacy problem of Tehran's leadership made it difficult for the international bodies (states and organisations) to decide how to adjust their relations with IRI. This was especially true since the West, and more specifically the US, needed to sustain political interaction in order to convince Iran to adopt cooperative and transparent policies with the International Atomic Energy Agency (IAEA) in regard to its nuclear activities, and also to secure its cooperation regarding regional crises in Iraq, Afghanistan and the ME peace process.

The post-election turmoil and its potential to continue also entangled Tehran in a very complex situation, especially as the regime's two major red lines had been crossed: the Iranian hard-liners are fearful for the regime's security as well as of threats to the absolute rule of the Vali-e Faqih, while Ayatollah Khamenei's justness and legitimacy has been under constant questioning and attack – from a variety of different groups and individuals, reformists and some conservatives. Furthermore, the empowerment of the Islamic Revolutionary Guard Corps (IRGC) and its growing influence in all affairs of the country may be problematic and might eventually leave the country in the hands of the IRGC. Additionally, the violent, illegal and suppressive policy of the rulers against its own people has caused widespread international embarrassment for the leadership and has left IRI in a difficult dilemma. If Tehran continues a policy of repression, social unrest will increase and further damage its international position. However, if it leaves the political atmosphere more open, it may pave the way for a critical social turn.

Therefore, it seems that, besides its impact on domestic methods of crisis management (e.g. judicial and parliamentary efforts to rebuild public trust by appointing independent committees to investigate current disputed issues), the people's democratic movement is acting as the most significant and determining element with direct impact on the IRI's foreign policy too.

Another complexity in dealing with Tehran is the necessity of understanding recent significant changes in Iran's socio-political landscape. It is important to realise that, regardless of any future progress by the Green Movement, the general socio-political situation in Iran has changed and that the country will never return to the situation of 12 June 2009. For this reason, international bodies need to design and execute foreign policy according to the current situation. Despite the Iranian regime's ignorance about the profound changes that have taken place in the country and its pretence of a normal atmosphere in which Ahmadinejad's authority is being smoothly re-established, it is obvious that the components and criteria of legitimacy and authority in Iran have been deeply shaken. This is why people have been so sensitive about political leaders and countries that swiftly welcomed the re-election of Ahmadinejad regardless of the regime's repressive attitude in the post-election era (even though this was a rare occurrence). While the regime tended to blame post-election unrest on foreign enemies, in particular the West, the Green Movement has targeted its anger towards some of the regime's allies, such as Russia, or Tehran's Middle East (ME) policy.

If the rulers of the IRI do not take the massive post-election democratic movement's enquiries seriously and continue to justify their violent and illegal behaviour by blaming others for the post-election events, the social gap will increase and they will lose the opportunity to end Iran's international isolation. This is especially true regarding Iran's dispute with the West about its nuclear activities and how to develop confidence-building measures to overcome its economic problems. Moreover, if the regime continues its current policies, Tehran will have fewer opportunities to use its ME bargaining cards with the West to solve its problems, especially when the West is still trying to exclude Iran by opening dialogue with its allies in the ME and disconnecting them from Tehran as much as possible. Washington's traditional policy of Iran-phobia has assisted such an approach and has been successful in turning Iran into the domestic ME enemy in an effort to solve the problem of Israel's regional recognition as well as preventing Tehran's influence in the region. Another disadvantage for Tehran would be the lack of active diplomacy – whereas active diplomacy could enable Iran to use its trade and economic relationship as strong leverage for improving its political relations and so decreasing its international isolation. In addition, the EU is considering the imposition of further political and economic pressures, legitmiating its action by claiming to support the Iranian people's human rights. Hence, if the West's previous policy against Iran had a military and security emphasis in the post-presidential election, it has now changed its emphasis to a stance supposedly protective of civil rights, which has a wider impact and provides Tehran with fewer possibilities to defend its foreign policy stances.

The West's and especially the US's recent détente policy towards Syria in particular, as well as their efforts to subdue resistance groups in the region – Hezbollah and Hamas – through agreement or defeat, could be interpreted as an opportunity for the West to find solutions without Tehran's interference, given that Iran is focusing on its domestic unrest. However, excluding Iran and leaving this major ME player behind could have its own disadvantages for the West, a fact that may encourage the West to include Tehran in the security of the ME.

First, every time the West endeavours to reach out to Syria in an effort to further isolate Iran and develop the peace process, Tehran, given its security concerns, retaliates with a more confrontational policy towards the West. Moreover, the West should not count on a major disentanglement of the strategic partnership of Iran–Syria. The reason is that Damascus does not trust the West–US, and its strategic partnership with Tehran is not based only on the ME peace process, although it this is a major factor. Geopolitics also plays an important role in Syria's involvement in ME issues and its efforts to shift in the political balance within the region to its own interest. For instance, as Trita Parsi states 'Damascus may want to use the Syria-Iran-Hezbollah axis to put pressure on the Obama administration.'[3] Also, apart from Tehran's considerable financial and military support of Syria and Tehran's and Damascus's very similar regional and international concerns and challenges, Iran's regional influence has been significant in boosting Syria's status in the ME. Moreover, it is more likely that Syria will take advantage of, rather than lessen, its chance to improve relations with the US and to mediate Iranian relations with Washington to increase its options in the region. Hence, by involving Syria in the ME security system the possibility of building a new Syria and West–US axis against Iran seems unlikely.

Regarding Lebanon, given the warm relationship between Tehran and Beirut since the Islamic Revolution of Iran in 1979, and despite the Hezbollah losing some of its seats and thus its power of veto in the 2009 parliament elections, Tehran is unlikely to confront serious challenges from Lebanon. In June 2009, Lebanese President Michel Suleiman was amongst the few world leaders who quickly congratulated Ahmadinejad following his disputed re-election as Iranian President. In his phone call, Suleiman indicated his desire that Iran and Lebanon continue to strengthen their mutual relations.[4]

Turkey, as a major ally of the US in the region and a NATO member, was among those countries that followed a similar policy. In June 2009, Turkish President Abdullah Gul called his Iranian counterpart to congratulate him on his re-election and wished Iran continued success. Due to Ankara's and Tehran's mutual national security concerns with regard to the Kurds, and also their bilateral and regional interests, especially regarding their energy policies, their continued cooperation is a necessity regardless of their domestic issues. Given Turkey's post-bipolar policies, which indicate Ankara's maintaining the security umbrella provided by the US and NATO while pursuing independent and self-interested policies, it is unlikely that the Iran–Turkey relationship will be influenced by the US–West ME policy to disconnect the allies and neighbours of Tehran or to contest the disputed re-election of Ahmadinejad.

Further, it is assumed that the result of the re-election of Ahmadinejad, which was closely monitored in the Arab world, and especially in countries exhibiting the most hostility towards Iran, namely Egypt, Saudi Arabia, Bahrain, Morocco and Jordan, has relieved those nations' rulers and will not have any specific impact on their further relationships with Iran. The standing of many Arab rulers has been based more than ever on the politics of polarisation. As many observers understand, there is little doubt that exploiting this polarisation – upon which these rulers are so dependent – could be facilitated by the re-election of Ahmadinejad as Iran's president.[5] The greatest fear of these countries was that the elected president would be a less controversial and more pragmatic, diplomatic and soft-spoken leader such as Khatami (were he still in the race), Mousavi or Karroubi. As Rannie Amiri states:

> [During Ahmadinejad's presidency they] found comfort in laying blame for their domestic and regional woes on Iran and their (perceived) allies. The fiery rhetoric of Ahmadinejad, whether pertinent or not, has undoubtedly helped bolster their case. This has taken shape in many forms, including accusing Iran of 'cultural infiltration' as Morocco has recently done, importing the 'Shiite ideology' into Egypt, and 'interfering' in the internal affairs of Bahrain and Saudi Arabia. These leaders also fear an Iranian president more amenable to overtures from the United States. A thawing of relations between the US and Iran will render needless the monetary, military and diplomatic benefits that being guardians against 'Iranian expansionism' bring. The latter is meant to redirect attention from a purely domestic issue – the fallout from longstanding discrimination against Bahraini and Saudi Shia Muslim citizens – abroad. Meanwhile, Egyptian president Hosni Mubarak seeks to ever legitimize his own rule by continuing to foment sectarianism.[6]

Secondly, with its strategic depth and growing regional influence in the ME, Iran desires to be recognised as a regional power and is sensitive to public opinion in the Arab world, particularly when it comes to the Israeli-Palestinian issue. As a result of this Iran might take a more radical stance if it perceives the continuation of the US–Western security policy of Iranian exclusion. A radical foreign policy is likely, especially when Tehran is under domestic and international pressure due to the post-election turmoil. Domestically, the regime in Iran could highlight the threat and the continuation of the hegemonic and aggressive foreign policy of the foreign enemy, the West–US, and, internationally, it could play a leadership role in the Arab and Islamic world of supporting the Palestinian issue.

This is despite the fact that: a) Iranians were hoping that the result of the election would be to enable them to solve their economic and diplomatic problems by adopting a more pragmatic and moderate foreign policy. It was generally believed that Ahmadinejad's tough anti-US and anti-Israel rhetoric had worsened Iran's isolation in the world, hence it was hoped that the election would lead to a change in the 'extremist' image that Iran had earned abroad during his presidency; b) the Iranian people's new resentment of the swift and strong endorsement of Ahmadinejad by the leaders of the resistance movements in the ME, namely Hezbollah and Hamas, despite the regime's brutal treatment of protestors against the disputed election, added to the rumours about the presence of members of these movements crushing street demonstrations in that period. As Hossein Ziai states, 'it is very unlikely that the same sort of sympathy for the Arab cause would be ever the same among the Iranian people'.[7] However, the conservative hard-liners in IRI have proven that they place their own ideological interests in the region, as well as their geopolitical interests, above their own people's appeasement, welfare and civil rights. Hence, as long as Iran is excluded from regional diplomacy, it retaliates by using issues in various areas in order to undermine major US foreign policy goals in the ME. It is hard to believe that, especially given the contested re-election of Ahmadinejad, an eventual shift in Tehran's stance towards ME issues will take place.

However, the IRI has shown that it is a pragmatic system, which adjusts its foreign policy according to its role in the security system in the region. Furthermore, the regional importance of Iran makes it vital for there to be proper relations between Iran and those extra-regional powers with interests in the region. Tehran perceives Iran's value in this respect, as well as the West's–US's need to cooperate with it in order to solve its crises in Iraq and Afghanistan. While being a significant player in the Arab-Israeli peace settlement, Iran's foreign policy could be potentially modified if there was an Arab-Israeli agreement; this process could be mirrored in other areas of conflict in this region and thereby promote successful resolution of the crises.[8]

Nevertheless, as long as the region remains far from approaching an Arab-Israeli agreement, the West's policy should be centred on active diplomacy that includes Iran and which is based on the complexities of the ME political landscape, where each factor and event affects each other; hence the necessity of pursuing a comprehensive solution involving Islamic movements such as Hezbollah and Hamas as another major issue to ensure security in this region. These groups participate in the political processes of their respective countries, and, despite receiving support from Iran, are increasingly independent of Tehran. They should therefore be counted as independent variables in the ME peace process.

The complex relationship between Iran and the West in the post-election period

In general, the peaceful street demonstrations of large numbers of Iranians who believed that the presidential election was rigged in Ahmadinejad's favour, the brutal suppression of dissent – an attempt to intimidate and silence individuals who were calling for change – together with the trials of some of the leading reformers and hard-liner rivals as a political purge, have caused serious problems for the Iranian leadership in establishing its legitimacy.

Domestically, these incidents have caused paranoia, which, as Gary Sick observes, feeds on itself and systematically destroys trust and relationships.[9] Internationally, these events have met with widespread diapproval, especially from the West, which interpreted them as a very strong signal that this is a regime not to be trusted. Moreover, as Kayhan Barzegar affirms, Ahmadinejad's radical foreign policy seems more like a voice of complaint without any further action in it. The reason is that, besides his lack of understanding of world politics, he lacks sufficient power and is afraid of the world around him.[10] These factors suggest two major options for Ahmadinejad's future foreign policy. To deal with serious mistrust and lack of legitimacy as well as economic problems at home, his government might consider major concessions in its foreign relations, especially with major Western or emerging powers such as Russia and China. However, the result of Ahmadinejad's bargaining with the West would determine his stance towards either the West or the emerging powers. Given Tehran's long-standing fear of a foreign-inspired upheaval, especially from the West, and its perception of its regional importance for the West–US, Ahmadinejad is likely to take a more radical foreign policy if his bargaining with the West fails, and thus accelerate Tehran's strategy of looking towards the East.

Nevertheless, in the post-election period the conditions in which the West, and specifically the US, could negotiate with Iran became more complicated. This was due to general factors in Iran's foreign policy together with the public speeches and comments between Iran and the West that were influenced by the outcome of Iran's presidential election and its aftermath. Under these circumstances, domestic issues in Iran and the West's concerns about Tehran's foreign policy caused delay in the Obama's Administration's adoption of practical policy changes towards the IRI, so that they could only pursue a public diplomacy. Coupled with this, the EU's cooperation with Iran was well below potential and both economic and political talks were put on hold.[11] In addition, with the West's various announcements of possible further sanctions against Tehran, it was very likely that, despite efforts to pursue dialogue with Iran on regional security, which would also upgrade Tehran's geostrategic position in the ME, the US–West was facing problems. These are discussed in what follows.

Time limits in diplomacy

At a time when the US Administration was announcing its intention to adopt a new course in its relations with Iran, discourses about more international pressure such as sanctions or suggesting time limits in diplomacy with Tehran over its nuclear programme were unlikely to be successful. This was an alternative form of 'stick and carrot' policy, which has proved to be very ineffective in dealing with Iran. Despite the West's concerns that Iran uses long-term negotiation as a strategy, the failure of the confrontational policy through sanctions and isolation over the last three decades confirms the necessity of giving diplomacy a better chance. A time limit policy could stimulate the region's current confrontational and militarised atmosphere, which has been caused by the hegemonic strategy and the containment policy of the US.

Tougher economic sanctions

The consequences of strengthening economic sanctions in spite of efforts to target only the Iranian leadership and specific industries are likely to be counter-effective. There are some major risks to applying further sanctions on Iran. This is despite assumptions that with Iran's current unstable socio-political situation the new Ahmadinejad government might be anxious to stay away from further economic distress. In this context, sanctions might be an influential leverage and might thrust the regime into serious negotiation. But further sanctions may have several impacts.

First, the may affect people's daily lives as well as the country's long-term development plans. Secondly, they may serve to consolidate the Iranian public's support for the current leadership where Iranian nationalist and radical anti-foreigner sentiments are likely to increase. Behzad Nabavi, the prominent reformist who was arrested soon after the presidential election in 2006 said: 'Those who threaten and pressure from the outside forget that we still think in traditional ways about national sovereignty. If we have to choose between individual freedom and national sovereignty, we will choose the latter. We hope we don't have to choose.'[12] This could be especially true with regard to Iran's nuclear policy, as there is a strong consensus on the nuclear issue and on how the West's offers should be responded to. Moreover, Ahmadinejad, who used Iran's nuclear technological advancements despite Western sanctions as a trump card in his tours of provincial Iran and also in his recent presidential campaign as a platform to build popular support, can take advantage of Iranian nationalism once again. Thirdly, further sanctions would ensure the IRGC's economic domination, including in the energy sector, while it lacks any accountability and has a monopoly on contracts. The recent incidents before and after the tenth presidential election confirmed speculation that, due to international sanctions in recent years, and the government's vast generosity in handing out contracts to the IRGC and its paramilitary adjunct, the Basij paramilitary volunteer militia was fuelled by its increasing dependence on these two military institutions and the need to pay back its dues incurred by their support during Ahmadinejad's first election.[13] The IRGC, who seem to have been the prime movers in post-election events, along with Basij, have become major players in the Iranian economy. Under the Ahmadinejad Administration, the increasing economic role of these two military institutions has, in turn, enhanced their political and social profile. In addition, IRGC's domestic allies, such as the right wing and the *bonyads* (trust funds), have a long practice of using illegal import networks during previous sanctions.[14] Furthermore, a sanction on petrol, for instance, would also be considered to be a confrontational policy by the government and could lead to retaliation. While being aware of their vulnerability, Tehran's leaders are seriously pursuing efforts to deal with further possible sanctions. As John Bolton states, 'Iran, with extensive Chinese involvement, has already begun building new refineries and expanding existing facilities with the aim of approximately doubling domestic capacity by 2012.'[15] Additionally, building on Ahmadinejad's slogan in the second round of his presidential campaign, in the post-election era the Iranian Oil Ministry announced its agreement with Iran's Central Bank to issue $1 billion bonds that for the first time would give ordinary people a share in Iran's oil income, providing an opportunity to compensate for the lack of foreign investment in Iran's hydrocarbon's industry.[16]

The Supreme Leader's beliefs/ideas

Ayatollah Khamenei's security focus and his belief in the satanic character of the democratic and liberal West, specifically the US, has kept his opponents within the regime, whether reformists or more pragmatic conservatives, off centre. He operates on the assumption that anyone who asks for reforms and alternative policies must be an outsider who is trying to sabotage the revolution, probably in association with foreign states. This is why the political, social and economic roles of the IRGC as the Supreme Leader's main arm and the protector of the revolution's values have been growing since Ahmadinejad's first government in 2005. There are also assumptions that Ayatollah Khamenei's confrontational policy with the West– US might be based on 'tactical advantages in stringing out some process of engagement with the United States, ultimately key elements of his constituency would probably fear the impact of a less isolated Iran. An international opening could, for example, make it more difficult for hard-liners to maintain social and religious restrictions. It would also introduce foreign competition to the IRGC in its increasingly important role in the economy.'[17]

The role of the Iranian president

The role of the president in the foreign policy decision-making process is relatively weak. The president is not the key figure in this regard and needs the Supreme Leader's approval to take any decision of strategic significance. Despite the lack of change in the functionality of a consensus process in decision-making, which stems from the multiple power centres in the IRI, it seems that in the post-election era the power struggle between some elements has intensified. The Supreme Leader also needs the support of the regime establishment on foreign policy, and especially of the president, as head of the executive and Chairman of the Supreme Council for National Security, though it seems that the extent of the president and the Supreme Leader's rivalry has exceeded the extent of their cooperation. The tension in their relations has been revealed more clearly, especially since the Supreme Leader opposed Ahmadinejad's attempt in the final months of his first term as president to wrest control of the Hajj Pilgrimage revenues from the clerical establishment (*Sazmaneh Haj Va Oghaf*). In the immediate post-election period the president's decision to appoint Esfandiar Rahim-Mashaii as the first vice-president was criti- cised by the Supreme Leader because of his remarks about Israel. After the Supreme Leader ordered Ahmadinejad to dismiss Rahim-Mashaii, the president refused to remove his top deputy for a week, and despite harsh public criticism, even from Ahmadinejad supporters, he granted him another high profile post and immediately appointed Rahim-Mashaii as his Office Secretary.

Confrontation between Ahmadinejad and the Supreme Leader seems to be motivated by several factors. First, to improve who has the final say on state matters, the Supreme Leader with contributions from its power pillars, especially IRGC and Basij forces, the state-run media, particularly the Iranian only broad- casting and the Friday prayer leaders in city mosques, has been determined to stop anything that would prevent him from seizing absolute power. Hence Ayatollah Khamenei, who is considered by hard-liners to stand above the law and to be answerable only to God, is willing to remain the single most critical actor in foreign policy as well as domestic issues. On the other hand, Ahmadinejad, against whom even some conservatives have turned, believing the crackdowns on reformists to have gone too far and complaining that he is trying to steamroll any competing political voices, seems to be enjoying an increased loyalty from the Revolutionary Guard. In paying back the dues incurred by their support during his second election about half of the 21 members of the Ahmadinejad's new cabinet have been members of the IRGC or Basij force. Also, for the first time in the IRI a military figure, the former Defence Minister in Ahmadinejad's first Cabinte, has been appointed to the Interior Ministry. Mostafa Mohammad Najjar is a top commander in the elite Revolutionary Guards Corps, who has a strong relationship with Ahmadinejad. A manoeuvre made by Ahmadinejad and IRGC's solidarity was the same attack made by Ahmadinejad and later Mohammad Ali Jafari, the Commander of IRGC, against the former President Khatami and other major reformist figures as potential foes of the ruling system. This occurred only days after Ayatollah Khamenei's declining claims on their links to foreign powers. Such issues raise questions about the size of the gap between Ahmadinejad and Khamenei and how this could actually affect the state.

Secondly, besides the similarity between Ahmadinejad and Ayatollah Khamenei's self-centeredness, the parallel departments/organisations under the control and/or management of the Supreme Leader's Office have resulted not only in competition but also increased complexity and the loss of a smooth and coordinated process of decision-making in the country.

Thirdly, Ahmadinejad, who came from a poor political, cultural and economic background, didn't have the personal strength to adapt himself to his new high-profile position. As a result he misinterpreted the support of the Supreme Leader and of the public during his last two presidential elections. Hence, he is specifically criticised because it is thought that his policies are based on delusion and superstition.

Fourthly, due to Ayatollah Khamenei's strong support of Ahmadinejad and his post-election stance, the Supreme Leader has lost legitimacy, become the main target of criticism and been held up as the major player responsible for the post-election incidents. This illegitimacy has been seen in the slogans of the protestors and in the critical statements of the reformists' leaders and even high-ranking clergy in the holy cities of Shiites, Qom and Najaf. Under such circumstances, the decision to launch dialogue and establish new relations with the US in particular, which requires coordination and cooperation as well as legitimacy, might be difficult and challenging for Tehran's leadership.

Providing an IT facility for the Iranian people

Any IT provision for the Iranian people from the outside world, intended to counter government censorship, would also be considered to be as an aggressive policy and could lead to retaliation. The Internet emerged as a vital channel for news and information from Iran when the Iranian authorities continued their crackdown on opposition rallies, foreign journalists, and Internet facilities after the disputed presidential election. Hence, the Iranian government would consider such a technological facility as a threat to national security, and for this reason the government is likely to endeavour to further control and restrict people's access to such facilities.

Iran's policy of stimulation irrationality

Stimulation irrationality is a policy instrument that the IRI takes advantage of to confuse its enemies; 'the calculation being that enemies will be more reluctant to attack Iran if Iran's response cannot be predicted and won't follow a straight cost-benefit analysis'.[18] However, this is a policy that in the long run causes public mistrust and confusion in the foreign policy decision-making process of other countries towards Iran and so might lead to more international isolation.

Russia's strategic ties with Iran's hard-liner leadership

Washington's other problem in dealing with Iran is Moscow's strategic ties to Tehran's hard-liners, in particular Ayatollah Khamenei and Ahmadinejad, which negates the US's power and influence in the region. Four days after his contentious re-election on 12 June, Ahmadinejad was warmly hosted by the Russian government in Yekaterinburg, the Shanghai Cooperation Organization (SCO) summit venue, making Moscow the first foreign government to host the beleaguered hard-liner.

Speculation regarding Russia's support of the controversial president soon after his re-election suggests that Moscow knew that an isolated Iran would, politically and economically, be a very valuable card to play, and would help prevent Russia from being accused by the Iranian leadership of external meddling in the country's domestic upheaval – as they had accused the West of doing. Politically, Russia has taken advantage of Iran as a regional power, using it as a victory card in its relations with the West. Economically, as long as Iran remains a rogue state, Moscow can use the country as a market for its old-fashioned jets and aircrafts as well as used products and industrial equipment. This is due to Russia's growing trade with Iran, where soviet-manufactured arms have taken the place of US and other embargoed Western arms. Nuclear technology boycotted by Washington and its allies has also been partly supplied by Russia. As Byman *et al.* note, 'the relationship [of Iran and Russia] is businesslike rather than based on shared interests or warm intergovernmental relations. The technology transfers and training that Moscow supplies remain strictly tied to Iran's capacity to pay.'[19] Given the lack of transparency in Iran's military expenses, various sources offer different estimates; however, all indicate a significant increase in Russian exports to Iran. For instance, according to the Council on Foreign Relations, while in 1992 Russia's exports to Iran constituted $249 million, in 2005, they totalled roughly $2 billion.[20] A major deal in 2005 was an agreement to supply up to 30 surface-to-air missiles to Iran worth $700 million;[21] a controversial deal that has not yet been concluded.

Russia's influence in Iran, as effective as it has been, presents Moscow with a multidimensional dilemma. In Iranian public opinion, the slogan of 'Death to Russia' seen in anti-Ahmadinejad's government street demonstrations indicates that if Moscow does not adjust its policy, taking into account Iran's new reality, its policy towards Iran will be counterproductive in the long term. Moscow's defence of Ahmadinejad's government could also damage Russia's position in the ME, where countries such as Egypt and Saudi Arabia worry about the further empowerment and influence of Iran in the ME. Moreover, pursuing its policy of supporting Iranian hard-liners could disturb Moscow's tense relations with some European capitals which, particularly since its war against Georgia, are trying to reduce their dependence on Russian gas due to the associated political risk. This stance holds despite the EU's predicted energy deficiency, and is also based on Moscow's efforts to ensure its position as a major energy importer to Europe and its wish to dominate Europe's markets as well as to support its domestic and foreign policy objectives. This is one of the reasons that some countries, such as Britain, alongside efforts to rely increasingly on renewable energies, would rather maintain a balanced approach to Iran, which holds about 50.1 trillion cubic metres or 15.5 per cent of the world's gas reserves.[22]

Consequently, there have been two principal assumptions about the impact of Moscow's strategic ties with Tehran's hard-liners:

1. While Moscow is missing various opportunities, Iran is taking advantage of its ties with Russia to polarise the Group of 5+1, the five permanent members of the United Nations Security Council plus Germany, over Iran's nuclear programme. Iran's later agreement with the IAEA to allow its inspectors to have access to the Arak heavy water reactor, after a year of refusing any such visits, and to upgrade its monitoring equipment at the Natanz enrichment plant were interpreted as an attempt to cancel or delay the possibility of an overall agreement on tougher sanctions. In this respect, as Borzou Daragahi mentions, in August 2009 an influential Russian newspaper published an article urging Moscow to 'adjust' its policy toward Iran so as not to catch too much flak if President Ahmadinejad goes down. The editorial of the privately owned *Nezavisimaya Gazeta* pointed out that while it is believed that Ahmadinejad will not shift his policy in order to bolster his domestic or international standing and therefore will be pushed aside by more moderate forces in Iran, Moscow was urged by Russian analysts to develop contacts with other political players in Iran. According to this article, published on 6 August, 'Russians are being singled out by the West and Iranians themselves as the primary backers of Ahmadinejad, possibly to Moscow's disadvantage.'[23]

2. In its uneven strategic ties with Iran, Moscow gains through its close ties with Tehran's hard-liners. Besides keeping Iran away from the Western camp, the possible failure of US negotiations with Iran, or Tehran's refusal to enter into negotiations with the US could strengthen Washington's stance in the European Union and lead to tougher sanction on Iran. Strengthened relations with Russia over the Iranian question could also make it easier for the US to convince the Security Council to impose tougher sanctions. This is a possibility that Iran would like to avoid, but Russia would benefit from it either way, politically and economically.

Israel

Fearful of Iran's ambition to play a dominant role in the ME and to challenge Israel's strategic manoeuvrability, Israel has sought to encourage Washington and the EU to exert pressure on Tehran and continue the policy of containment in Iran. The successful diplomacy of the Obama Administration with Tehran, a diplomacy supported by the EU, can assist Washington with many issues and problems, especially at a time when the US needs more than ever to remove its forces from Iraq and to stabilise Afghanistan. Nevertheless, the dominant belief in Israel is that such diplomacy does not necessarily put enough pressure on Tehran's hard-liner leadership to make it change its position regarding Israel. This is the reason for Israel's rhetoric and propaganda about its possible military offensive against Iranian nuclear sites, its seeking tougher sanctions against Tehran and its asking for deadlines for negotiations with Iran. Israel knows that even under the current social turmoil Iran is not an easy target, unlike Iraq in 1981, and that Israel will not be able to tolerate the backlash from an attack. Hence, Israel has been trying hard to internationalise Iran's nuclear dossier to prevent a nuclear-capable Iran or any US agreement without the consideration of Israel's strategic interests in the region. Hence, some analysts, such as Trita Parsi, believe that the major reason for Israel's manoeuvres is not necessarily the fear of a nuclear clash, but that 'The real danger a nuclear-capable Iran brings with it for Israel is twofold. First, an Iran with nuclear capability will significantly damage Israel's ability to deter militant Palestinian and Lebanese organisations. Gone would be the days when Israel's military supremacy would enable it to dictate the parameters of peace and pursue unilateral peace plans.'[24]

Given the consequences of this Israeli policy, another obstacle in the way of the US adopting a diplomatic solution has been Tehran's uncertainty about Washington's intentions regarding real negotiation. In addition to the past thirty years of aggressive US policy against the IRI, the tough stance and rhetoric from Israel as well as some EU members, in particular France and Germany, makes Tehran fearful of entering negotiations that could be engineered to fail and ultimately justify further sanctions or even strengthen the possibility of military action against Iran. Such a process and its expected result cannot persuade Tehran that it will be entering a just and constructive negotiation. Its concerns are also due to the fact that, since much of the regime's legitimacy at home and influence in the region rests on its opposition to the US, only the assurance of engaging in a positive negotiation with the US can pay back its price of dealing with the 'Great Satan'.

Hence, with increasing instability at home, Iran has had two major possibilities for a positive and beneficial dialogue with Washington that will help to overcome its economic problems and political isolation, or increase its influence in the region, particularly in Iraq, Afghanistan and Lebanon and pursue its nuclear programme as a level of deterrence against the perceived US (and in extension Israeli) threat. This is why Basiji Brigadier General Hassan Firouzabadi, chief of Iran's Joint Armed Forces, confirmed that the IRI's support for Palestinian groups and other freedom movements, besides its human aspects, ensures Iran's national security as well as regional dominance. Firouzabadi, who was speaking at the farewell ceremony of the former defence minister and the inauguration of the new minister on 9 September 2009, also referred to IRI's support of Palestinians and said such support has various political and financial costs for Tehran as well as impacts on the media.[25]

This statement was interpreted as Iran's using these freedom movements as political leverage to gain regional and international privileges – an influential card, particularly against Israel, in order to persuade Washington that successful diplomacy would be the US's only logical option.

Added to these factors, it is true that Washington can never ignore Israel's security and interests, especially in dealing with Iran. Therefore, Israel's interest in the region, particularly at a time when Iran could play a great role in decreasing US entanglement in the region's crises, may be to stop seeking obstacles against diplomacy.

Conclusion

Iran's evolution in the post-election turmoil has forced Tehran to focus on its domestic politics rather than on any of its bilateral or multilateral relationships, including those with the EU and Mediterranean states. Moreover, due to the importance of beginning and the outcome of US negotiation with Iran on Tehran's foreign policy towards the EU and Mediterranean states, the IRI's relationships with these countries are expected to be influenced both by US–Iran relations as well as Iran's domestic socio-political developments.

Hence, after three decades of tension, the factor of timing the start of negotiations with Washington is critical for the IRI. This is mainly because Iran sees the US's new president as a less controversial and more realistic character, who provides an opportunity to begin dialogue to overcome Iran's economic woes and international position. Consequently, while the IRI needs national unity and cohesion more than ever to strengthen its participation at the negotiating table with its old enemy, beside its serious problem of legitimacy at home, with no capacity for dissent's compensation, the hard-liners leadership seems to have chosen the worst and most brutal kind of crackdown and suppression of dissent since the revolution. The rulers in Iran are pursuing three major aims through this oppression; a widespread internal political purge to defeat their reformer rivals (opposition groups) for good; to show their sovereignty at home at the negotiation table; and given the US's need for Iran's help to overcome its regional problems, especially in Iraq and Afghanistan, to improve its international position so that domestic illegitimacy will be ignored and the country can therefore move towards solving its economic problems.

Nevertheless, such policy engineering among Iran's hard-liner leadership contains substantial contradictions: the brutality and undemocratic posture of radical conservatives over the Islamic Republic points to the militarisation of Iranian politics as well as the development of a fanatical/Talibanesque presence in the country; among the international community, it indicates that this is a regime not to be trusted. Therefore, such elements cannot give Iran a strong position at the negotiating table.

As mentioned above, in the post-election era the West–US has its own problems and concerns in designing its foreign policy towards Tehran, such as general factors in Iran's foreign policy or the role of the major actors in the Mediterranean states in complicating and slowing the process of US diplomatic advances.

However, one of the major complexities in dealing with Tehran is the necessity of understanding the recent significant changes in the socio-political landscape in Iran and designing foreign policy according to this undeniable reality. Being aware of this new socio-political landscape is significant both for Tehran itself and for foreign countries.

Since the Islamic Revolution in 1979 there have been two more major socio-political upheavals, each stronger than the previous, which compelled the regime to pay more attention to its domestic problems than its foreign policy. First was the second Khordad event, when the populace rejected the existing policy and emphasised the necessity for real social, economic and particularly political reforms. This event ended in 1997 with extraordinary support for Khatami's reforms. It was only after 1997 that discussions of civil society expanded beyond a small cautious circle of intellectuals and assumed its current importance at the level of national politics in Iran.[26] The second upheaval came with the new political atmosphere and the issues raised by the tenth presidential election, in which the Iranian people sought to improve their lives and solve their problems peacefully.

Despite all the foreign threats and antagonistic policies against the IRI since the revolution, especially from the West and in particular the US, the major challenges to the IRI's survival have been internal issues. The Iranian people have proven that they consider democracy a necessity not a luxury, and hence, if the hard-liner rulers do not take the agenda of the democratic movement seriously and continue in their ignorance and blaming of others for incidents in Iran, the societal gap will not only get wider but a third wave of upheaval may be expected, which this time will be much stronger and more destructive. This is despite the fact that at present the IRI would face losing the opportunity to end its international isolation too.

On the other hand, besides sending similar signals to countries in the West and the Mediterranean regarding their foreign policy towards the hard-line leadership, the message of the democratic movement in Iran to these countries is that those external pressures and antagonistic policies, namely, the threat of invasion and the imposition of tougher economic sanctions, risk further postponing the advent of a real democracy and the integration of Iran into the global economy. Moreover, through unsuccessful diplomacy the West would lose an opportunity of attracting the IRI's cooperation in decreasing regional crises. Hence, this is a very difficult time for all sides to choose, design and execute the right policy.

Notes

1 Iranian state media, including IRNA, ISNA.
2 *Deutsche Welle*. Retrieved 29 August 2009 from: http://www.dw-world.de/dw/article/ 0,,4575223,00.html?maca=en-aa-pol-863-rdf.

3 Trita Parsi, 'The United States and Iran: What are the Prospects for Engagement?', *Middle East Policy Council*/Forums. Retrieved 1 September 2009 from: http://www. mepc.org/forums_chcs/56.asp

4 IRNA, 'Lebanese President Congratulates Ahmadinejad On Re-election', 14 June 2009. From: http://www.irantracker.org/foreign-relations/lebanon-iran-foreign-relations.

5 For instance see, Rannie Amiri, 'The Politics of Polarization: Iran's Elections: Why Arab Leaders Want Ahmadinejad to Win', *Global Research*, 10 April 2009. From: http://www. globalresearch.ca/index.php?context=va&aid=13135

6 Ibid.

7 Hossein Ziai, 'Have Hezbollah and Hamas Turned Their Backs on Iran?'. Retrieved 7 September 2009 from: http://www.youtube.com/watch?v=bDR1PkBBn0o.

8 For similar discussion also see, Parsi, 'The United States and Iran'.

9 Gary Sick, 'Iran's chilling Show Trials', 15 August 2009. From: http://garysick.tumblr. com/search/iran+foreign+policy

10 Kayhan Barzegar, 'The list: Iran's Presidential Wannabes', June 2009, *Foreign Policy*. From: http://www.foreignpolicy.com/story/cms.php?story_id=4989.

11 EU negotiations with Iran since 2002 have covered political aspects (WMD, Human Rights, Terrorism, Middle East Peace Process), as well as a trade and cooperation agreements. They were followed by a nuclear agreement between UK/France and Germany with Tehran (the so called 'Paris Agreement') in November 2004, by which Iran agreed to suspend its enrichment related and reprocessing activities, to be verified by the IAEA. Retrieved 2 September 2009 from: http://ec.europa.eu/external_relations/iran/relations_en.htm.

12 International Crisis Group (ICG), p. 25, interview with Behzad Nabavi, former minister of industries and deputy speaker, Tehran, 1 August 2006.

13 Maziar Bahari, 'An Iranian Dissects U.S.-Iran Talks', 24 November 2006. *Post Global*. Retrieved 20 March, 2007 from: http://newsweek.washingtonpost.com/postglobal/ maziar_bahari/2006/11/an_iranian_dissects_usiran_tal.html.

14 For futher detail, see for example Abbas Milani, 'U.S. Foreign Policy and the Future of Democracy in Iran', *The Washington Quarterly*, vol. 28, no. 3 (2005), pp. 49–50.

15 John Bolton, 'Sanctions Won't Work against Iran', 31 August 2009. From: http://online. wsj.com/article/SB10001424052970204731804574383162213828906.html

16 ILNA, 1 September 2009. From: http://www.ilna.ir/newsText.aspx?ID=74667 (accessed 17 May 2011).

17 Mahmoud Alinejad, 'Between Defiance and Détente: Iran's 2009 Presidential Election and its Impact on Foreign Policy', June 2009, *The Lowy Institute for International Policy*, p. 14.

18 For further detail, see for instance, Parsi, 'The United States and Iran'.

19 Daniel Byman, Shahram Chubin, Anoushiravan Ehteshami and Jerrold Green, *Iran's Security Policy in the Post-Revolutionary Era* (Washington, D.C.: National Defense Research Institute (RAND), 2001), pp. 59–60.

20 Lionel Beehner, 'Russia's Nuclear Deal with Iran', 28 February 2006, *Council on Foreign Relations*. From: http://www.cfr.org/publication/9985/russias_nuclear_deal_ with_iran.html.

21 BBC News, 'Russia Condemns US arms Sanctions' (August 2006): http://news.bbc.co. uk/1/hi/world/europe/5252074.stm.

22 For more details about Russian support policy of Ahmadinejad's government also see, Borzou Dargahi, 'Iran: Russia Urged to Hedge Bet on Ahmadinejad', 10 August 2009. From: http://latimesblogs.latimes.com/babylonbeyond/2009/08/iran-russia-urged-to-hedge-bet-on-ahmadinejad.html; also Meir Javedanfar, 'Iran's Nuclear Dilemma', 24 August 2009. From: http://www.realclearworld.com/articles/2009/08/24/irans_ nuclear_dilemma__97091.html; and Meir Javedanfar, 'Russia Must Reassess its Iran Policy', 17 August 2009. From: http://www.realclearworld.com/articles/2009/08/17/russia_ must_reassess_its_iran_policy_97064.html (accessed 17 May 2011).

23 Borzou Daragahi, 'Iran: Russia Urged to Hedge Bet on Ahmadinejad', *Los Angeles Times*, 10 August 2009. From: http://latimesblogs.latimes.com/babylonbeyond/2009/08/iran-russia-urged-to-hedge-bet-on-ahmadinejad.html.

24 For further detail see Trita Parsi, 'Israel's Military Threat against Iran is a Bluff That Keeps Giving', 13 April 2009, *Monthly Review Press*. From: http://www.monthlyreview.org/mrzine/parsi130409.html.

25 BBC Persian quoted from Iranian state agency: http://www.bbc.co.uk/persian/iran/2009/09/090909_si_firoozabadi_palestine.shtml

26 Mahboubeh Sadeghinia, *Security Arrangements in the Persia Gulf, with Special Reference to Iran's Foreign Policy* (London: Ithaca Press, April 2010).

13 The 2009 Iranian presidential elections in comparative perspective

Luciano Zaccara

Introduction

The controversial presidential electoral process that took place in Iran on 12 June 2009 brought to attention the importance of the guarantees of transparency and integrity of its electoral procedures, mechanisms and publication of the results. The reliability of the final outcome of the polls serves as an instrument of legitimacy for every political system in the world, in particular for those which were established through revolutionary means. The Iranian electoral system and its history are a perfect study case to observe how elections work to legitimize or delegitimize the government, and how seriously the elite pays attention to the electoral procedures and final outcomes.

This chapter is the consequence of my direct observation and historical analysis of Iranian elections over the last five years, within the Election Watch project I direct at the Autonoma University in Madrid and in continuation of my research into the evolution of the Iranian political system since the Islamic Revolution of 1979.

In the following pages I will explain the main characteristics of the complex Iranian political, electoral and party systems. After that, I will summarize the mains aspects of the last three presidential elections – between 1997 and 2005 – focusing on the comparative data of the final results, previous opinion polls and the common irregularities observed throughout those elections.

Finally, I will dedicate the last part to analysing the events surrounding the last presidential elections of 2009. Special emphasis will be put on the unusual electoral campaign and the contested electoral results, with the aim of clarifying both the validity of the official results and the complaints put forward by the opposition.

The political and party system

The Iranian political system is composed of several elective and non-elective institutions that form a complex net of mutual controls that prevent the possibility that one of these institutions can exercise absolute power. The central position is occupied by the Spiritual Leader, with a large range of constitutional faculties and attributions. However, this central position was effectively exercised only by the designer of the system and first Leader, the ayatollah Ruhollah Khomeini. Before

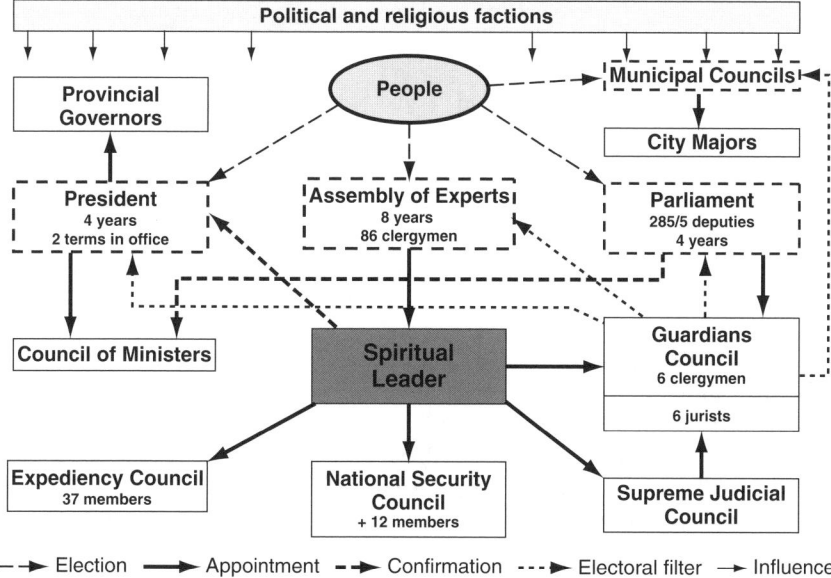

Figure 13.1 The Iranian political system.

his death in 1989, the constitution was reformed, giving the presidency more functions with the dissolution of the position of Prime Ministry, and reducing the relative capacity of the Leader's position. Moreover, the lack of charisma that his successor, Ali Khamenei, showed, contributed to diminishing the capacity to decide without consensus within the political elite and through consultation with the new collective institutions created under the new constitution. Figure 13.1 illustrates the centrality of the Leader's position in the political system, and the place of elective and non elective institutions regarding the Leader and the Iranian population.

The necessary intra-elite consensus to control and maintain the system is achieved inside the non-elective institutions: the Expediency Council for general political issues, the National Security Council for foreign and defence policy, and the Guardian Council for legislative and electoral issues. Of these three, the Guardian Council is the most relevant for the electoral system and process. This non-elective upper house is composed of 12 members, of whom six are clerics appointed by the Spiritual Leader, and acts as an electoral filter for nominations of all elective institution members, including the Assembly of Experts.

Among the elective institutions are the Presidency, the Assembly of Experts, the Local Councils and the Islamic Consultative Assembly. The president is elected every four years, and there is only one opportunity for re-election. It is not necessary to be a cleric to stand for election, and although women are not prohibited from standing for Presidency, no woman has been approved by the Guardian Council in the ten presidential elections.

The Assembly of Experts is composed of 86 clergymen elected every eight years. It has the authority to appoint, confirm and also dismiss the Leader, but the latter right has never been exercised.

The Islamic Consultative Assembly is elected every four years. It comprises 290 deputies, 285 on a provincial representation basis. The rest represent the religious minorities recognized in the constitution: one Zoroastrian, one Jewish, one Christian-Assyrian and two Christian-Armenian.

The local councils were elected for the first time in 1999, under Mohamed Khatami's presidency, and every four years since then. This has been the only move towards decentralizing the political system since the establishment of republican institutions.

Following the Islamic Revolution several parties of different ideological tendencies have participated in Iranian political life, but after a short period all the leftist and regionalist parties were banned. Finally, by 1983 all political parties were prohibited, with the party in power, the Islamic Republican Party, being dissolved in 1985, although parties are still recognized in Article 26 of the 1989 Constitution. Since then, the Iranian political elite has been organized into three different kinds of groups:

1. Semi-formal and permanent political-religious associations formed by several personalities, mainly clerics, without clear ideological definition or political programme. Currently there are around 300 registered associations in the Interior Ministry, including: Association of Combatant Clergy; Society of Combatant Clerics; Islamic Society of Engineers; National Trust Party; Society of Teachers at Qom's Seminars; Islamic Revolution Mujahedin Organization or Executives of Construction Party.

2. Parliamentary groups formed in every legislature relating to specific positions on issues mainly in the economic and political debates in Parliament. There are usually two or three different parliamentary groups, that do not always correspond with the electoral alliances which put them in the Majlis: Maktabi/Hojjatieh/ Fence sitters (1980s); Rohaniyun/ Rohaniyat (1990s); Fundamentalists/ Pragmatics/Reformists (late 1990s) or 'Principalists'/Reformists (since 2005).

3. Flexible and temporary electoral alliances created to support presidential or legislative candidates which exist only during the electoral processes. Many appear in every election, with two or three main ones. The main examples are: second Khordad Front; Front for Iran Islamic Consensus; Broad Fundamentalist Alliance; Reformist Alliance or United Fundamentalist Front.

These three kinds of groups are totally flexible and can change their support and composition in a short period of time. Moreover, the fact that a person belongs to one group does not mean that he or she cannot belong to another. In fact, many clergymen from part of several such groups concurrently. There is no party registration or discipline, as was evident during the last presidential elections. The executive board of the conservative Association of Combatant Clergy decided not to support either of the main candidates – Mir Hussein Mousavi or Mahmoud Ahmadinejad – giving leave for some provincial branches, like Tabriz, to declare themselves in favour of Mousavi. The same happened with the Hashemi Rafsanjani's Executives of Construction Party, which officially, supported Mousavi's candidacy, but the number two man in the party, the former mayor of Teheran and former collaborator of Khatami, Gholam Karbaschi, headed the campaign for the other pro-reform candidate, Mehdi Karroubi.

The electoral system

The resulting electoral system derived from this party system is very complex. The ballot structure is candidate-based. No closed or open lists exist, only individual candidates who register themselves at the Ministry of the Interior without any connection with other candidates or parties. As a result, all the candidates are theoretically independent. The only condition to be a candidate is to pass the Guardian Council's filter.

The existence of individual candidatures means that the lists provided for the voters, in legislative and local elections, are not actually organized by candidates who have decided to stand jointly. As was mentioned earlier, the electoral system operates with several lists of candidates drawn up by the permanent political groups or the electoral alliances created for each electoral process. Many candidates appear in several lists simultaneously and even in lists of opposite political tendencies. This also means that many of the disputing factions declare electoral victories which are very difficult to verify.

In all kinds of election, every citizen must choose the candidates in the constituency in which they vote, writing by hand their chosen candidate names and code numbers on the ballot paper. During legislative elections at the Tehran capital constituency every citizen must write 30 names out of hundreds of candidates, posted on several panels around the ballot box. Furthermore, no envelope is provided for the ballot paper, making it impossible to guarantee a secret vote.

The electoral system does not provide prior registration of voters or a census to determine the constituencies in which every citizen should vote, meaning that every man or woman over 18 years old can vote in any city of any province they wish.[1] This greatly hinders the identification of real rates of participation because there is no comparative element and also makes it difficult to detect errors and electoral fraud. Nevertheless, the stamp on the 'shenasnameh' (identification document) and the ink on the finger of voters act to prevent multiple voting. Figure 13.2 summarizes the main technical characteristics of the Iranian electoral system.

The complexity and lack of clarity of the system, even for Iranians themselves, is coupled with the lack of transparency of the Interior Ministry when publishing the final results. It is very common to observe incomplete or wrong data on the Ministry website, when it is not completely erased after several months. In some cases it is very difficult to determine if the information is totally wrong or simply impossible to accept statistically.[2] Moreover, the overlapping competences of the Interior Ministry and Guardian Council regarding publication of final results and dealing with electoral complaints has been a regular feature in every election, with a fierce struggle in the first decade of the republic and during Kathami's presidencies.

Active vote (voters)	>18 years old, men and women No voter's registration – No census
Passive vote (candidates)	Iranian citizenship >30 years old Master's degree or similar Clean record and good health
Electoral campaign	8 days, 20 days for presidential elections
Type of candidatures	Uninominal
Vote expression	Plurinominal (except presidential)
Electoral formula	Two round system TRS/majority (Threshold 25% in parl., exp. & loc. – 51% in pres.)
Term in office	President: 4 years – renewable once Members of Parliament: 4 years – renewable indefinitely Assembly of Experts: 8 years – renewable indefinitely
Candidatures acceptation	Guardian Council
Electoral supervision	Guardian Council

Figure 13.2 Main characteristics of the Iranian electoral system.

Between 1979 and 2009 there have been 10 presidential elections, 8 legislative elections, 4 for the Assembly of Experts, 3 local councils, 3 referendums and 1 constitutional assembly, totaling 29 electoral processes in 30 years of republican history, which means that almost every year the Iranian people have been called to express their vote.

The electoral turnout is a fundamental element in evaluating the people's acceptance of the ground rules imposed by the government, and the confidence that Iranians place in their political elite. Because of that and the restrictive conditions for participating in the electoral race, every election is considered as a referendum by the Iranian elite and international analysts. And sometimes the increase in electoral turnout, along with some surprising electoral results, as for example the victories of Khatami in 1997 or Ahmadinejad in 2005 and 2009, allow us to confirm that Iranian electoral history is more relevant than many observers have considered, despite the low reliability of the official data that generated much controversy during the 29 electoral processes.

As shown in Figure 13.3, the highest participation rate was in the referendum for the acceptance of the Islamic Republic in 1979, with a turnout of 98 per cent, according the Interior Ministry. The second was the re-election of Mahmoud Ahmadinejad in 2009, with 84 per cent, and the third was the seventh presidential election in 1997, which brought Mohamed Khatami to presidency with 79 per cent. In contrast, the lowest participation was the second Assembly of Experts in 1990 with only 38 per cent. However, we have to remember that the absence of any prior voting register or electoral census complicates the determination of participation percentages, which is calculated using the total potential voting population, according to information from the population census produced by the Iranian Centre of

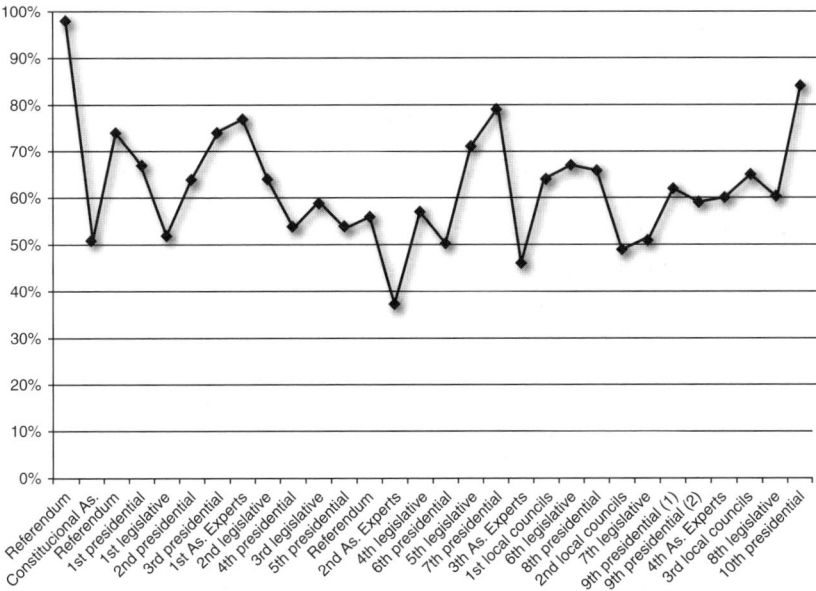

Figure 13.3 Turnout in the Iranian elections, 1979–2009.

Statistics. This complication is emphasized at provincial and municipal levels. If we analyse the official information of all the presidential elections published on the Ministry website we can find that in at least three different instances before 2009 there were cities and provinces showing a turnout of more than 100 per cent. In the second presidential election held on 24 January 1981, the provinces of Elam, Lorestan and Markazi showed 107.06, 116.54 and 100.49 per cent respectively, with the seventh one on 23 May 1997 indicating a 106.45 per cent voter turnout at Lorestan. Finally, in the ninth presidential elections of 2005, there were seven municipalities in the first round and five in the second that showed more than 100 per cent.[3]

The official turnout data was strongly contested in several provinces during the presidential elections of 12 June 2009. In this case significantly higher participation was evident on election day, especially in Tehran province, where more than 7.5 million people voted, compared with the presidential election in 2005, when around 5 million people voted. The polling stations in the capital city were crowded with people from early morning and throughout the day. It is important to note in this context that the minimum voting age had been 16 until the 2005 presidential elections, whereas it was raised to 18 for the most recent one. According to the subsequent complaints presented by the defeated candidates, in 150 cities more than 100 per cent of the potential electors voted, and in many more cases, participation was between 90 and 95 per cent, which would be, at least statistically, rather suspicious. The Guardian Council only accepted such a figure in 50 cities, adding that this was not enough to prove the existence of fraud. The official explanation – with voters allowed to choose whichever Iranian constituency and city they wished – did not convince the opposition.

The presidential elections of 1997–2005

The most significant electoral processes in Iranian republican history were the presidential ones, and in particular, the last four, of 1997, 2001, 2005 and 2009, when Khatami and Ahmadinejad gained their victories.

The seventh presidential election was the first with an unexpected result for international analysts, as well as for many Iranians. It was also the first time that opinion polls were published in the Iranian media. Some polls conducted by several newspapers and political associations had anticipated the victory of Mohamed Khatami. A survey organized by Executives of Construction, Rafsanjani's party, and published in the newspaper *Akhbar* only two days before the elections, suggested a clear majority of 59 per cent for Mohamed Khatami, followed by the official candidate, the former Parliament Speaker Ali Akbar Nateq-Nouri, with 30 per cent.[4] However, other previous polls showed quite different voting intentions by the Iranians. In early April, a survey conducted by the Center for Public Opinion Studies, belonging to the Ministry of Culture and Islamic Guidance, showed that Nateq-Nouri was in the lead with 40 per cent, followed by Khatami with 38 per cent.[5] Despite the introduction of this new element during the electoral process, the lack of method and statistical criteria and the obvious political intentions of the polls gave very low reliability to all the pre-electoral surveys. However, it is possible to say that the victory of Khatami was not as unexpected as Western observers thought.

Mohamed Khatami was elected on 23 May 1997 by 20 million votes, in a landslide victory, with 70 per cent of the votes cast. Nateq-Nouri obtained only 24 per cent, with 7.2 million votes. A more detailed analysis of the electoral data offered by the Interior Ministry showed the same confusing figures as in previous elections, as already mentioned. Khatami's second term was achieved after another landslide victory on 8 June 2001, with more than 21.6 million votes – 76.9 per cent of the votes cast. The second candidate, Ahmad Tavakkoli, obtained only 15 per cent. In comparing both elections it is clear that the absolute number of Khatami's voters had increased, but their relative support decreased notwithstanding. Bearing in mind that in 2001 there were 5.5 million more voters than in 1997 – namely those who reached 16 years of age in between – and that the turnout fell from 80 to 66 per cent because of the disillusion of many reformists supporters, Khatami actually failed to attract almost 4 million votes, including new and old voters.[6]

In 2005, Mahmoud Ahmadinejad obtained another unexpected victory in a two-round presidential election. His victory was a surprise for everybody outside Iran and for most Iranians too. All the polls and previous analyses spoke of the possibilities of victory for Rafsanjani and Moin, and in the second line Karroubi and Qalibaf, but no one mentioned the mayor of Tehran. In a very early survey of voter intention carried out by the official news agency IRNA in March 2004, 13.9 per cent of respondents chose Rafsanjani. Ahmadinejad was in 11th position with only 1.2 per cent of voter intention.[7] In another survey, also published by IRNA just one week before the elections, Rafsanjani was still first with 27.1 per cent followed by Moin (18.9 per cent), Qalibaf (16.5 per cent) and Karroubi (10.8 percent). Ahmadinejad trailed in fifth place with 7.7 per cent.[8]

In spite of such predictions, Ahmadinejad obtained 5.7 million votes – 19.4 per cent – in the first round, in second position after Rafsanjani with 6.1 million – 21 per cent. There was a very high suspicion of fraud, which benefited Ahmadinejad and was to the detriment of Karroubi, who come third in the first round with 5 million votes – 17.3 per cent. In fact, Karroubi himself sent a letter of protest to the Leader Khamenei and resigned his position in the Expediency Council. For the first and only time a second round to decide a president was necessary, since none of the candidates had reached the required 51 per cent in the first round.

The first-round votes were territorially divided and decentralized between the seven candidates. Karroubi won in the eleven western and south-western provinces, Ahmadinejad in the central nine (including Tehran), Rafsanjani in three (Gilan, Zanjan and Kerman), Mehralizadeh in three (Ardabil, East and West Azerbaijan), Qalibaf in two (North and Razavi Khorasan), and Moin and Lariyani in one province each (Mazandaran and Sistan-o-Baluchistan).

If we compare only the votes obtained by Ahmadinejad and Rafsanjani in the first round, we can see that Rafsanjani gained more votes on the periphery while Ahmadinejad did better in the centre of Iran. The support given to Ahmadinejad in those provinces provided him with the necessary votes to reach the ballotage.

In the second round, Ahmadinejad's victory was absolute: more than 17 million voted for him, compared with 10 million for Rafsanjani, who won only in Sistan-o-Baluchistan province. Ahmadinejad won more than 50 per cent in 9 provinces, more than 60 per cent in 13, and more than 70 per cent in six. However, with 61 per cent of voter turnout he was the president elected with the lowest ever popular support.

In analysing the detailed information on votes cast in every Iranian city it is possible to observe a very profound change in the orientation of votes between the first and second rounds. The 10.5 million votes obtained by the reformist candidates – Mehdi Karroubi, Mustafa Moin and Mohsen Mehralizadeh – in the first round, shifted mostly towards an ultra-conservative candidate, Ahmadinejad, instead of a pragmatist, Rafsanjani. On the other hand, Ahmadinejad was able to attract the majority of those who voted for conservative candidates – Baqer Qalibab and Ali Larijani – plus at least 5 million reformist voters. Although these figures seemed suspicious and almost impossible for any scholar specializing in electoral behaviour, we have to remember that Rafsanjani, one of the most powerful figures in the Iranian political system, was also one of the least popular, who for many Iranians represented the continuity of the corrupt system ruled by the clerics. So, it is possible to affirm that at that political moment, the choice of Ahmadinejad's represented change in the minds of millions of Iranian voters, as for Khatami in 1997. When the Iranian population had the opportunity to vote between several presidential candidates, they chose the candidate least connected to the establishment.

The electoral process was controversial because of the unexpected first-round result and the struggle between the Interior Ministry, controlled by Khatami, and the Guardian Council, regarding the publication of the final data. Particularly irregular was the slowness of the release of the Tehran results in the first round. With the 1.5 million votes obtained in this province Ahmadinejad reached the second position, allowing him to participate in the second round. Improvements in integrity and guarantees over the whole electoral process were minimal, and of the almost 300 complaints presented to the Guardian Council all were rejected. But the transparency in the final publication of all the votes cast detailed at provincial and municipal level was an important step towards the standardization of electoral procedures. This transparency was important for detecting many inconsistencies in the vote count system and the procedures established to solve problems, as for example, the scarcely explicable differences registered in thousands of ballot stations where the numbered ballots used did not correlate with the ballots actually placed in the ballot boxes.

June 2009 presidential elections campaign

The tenth presidential electoral process started officially on 25 April 2009, with the candidates' online registration via a website provided by the Interior Ministry. After two weeks, on 5 May, candidates had 4 days to personally register at the ministry's headquarters. On 20 May, the final list of candidates accepted by the Guardian Council was released, with the campaign lasting until 11 June, 24 hours before the election. However, the presidential hopefuls had begun to speak about their intention to stand and to try to gain political support more than one year beforehand. Many political figures from the reformist tendency were aiming to be the consensus candidate, such as Mohamed Khatami, Abdallah Nouri, Mehdi Karroubi and Mir Hussein Mousavi. Exactly the same happened in the conservative camp of Ali Larijani, Baqer Qalibaf, Mohsen Rezai and of course Mahmoud Ahmadinejad. In the end, some figures from the reformist camp – namely Khatami, Masumeh Ebtekar, Nouri – withdrew their candidacy to favour the reformist options, with some conservative politicians, such as Larijani and Qalibaf, also deciding not to stand.

On 20 May, the Interior Ministry released the final list of presidential candidates. Only the four pre-candidates who had been expected to pass the strict filter of the Guardian Council did so. There were no surprises in this respect, and the contenders were the president, Mahmoud Ahmadinejad, the former Prime Minister, Mir Hossein Mousavi, the former Parliamentary Speaker, Mehdi Karroubi, and the former head of the Revolutionary Guards, Mohsen Rezai. However, a total of 475 people, including 42 women, aged between 19 and 86, had appeared personally in the offices of the Interior Ministry to ratify their electronic pre-registration in the first week of May. There were notably fewer pre-candidates than the 1014 that ran in 2005. For some days, there was speculation that for the first time a woman would be accepted as a candidate, but all the female hopefuls were vetoed once again. Surprisingly, there were no complaints from rejected candidates, nor did any well-known personalities stand, in contrast to the legislative elections of 2004 and 2008.

On 21 May, the presidential electoral campaign officially began with a series of innovations intended to improve electoral participation and competition between the candidates, an effort that the political elite was making in order to overcome a crisis of unity between conservative and reformist political sectors and reinforce the legitimacy of the elective institutions of the system. More than at any other time, it was possible to read and hear criticism exchanged between different factions and between civil servants and high-level clerics regarding the performance of governmental agencies. For the first time in the history of Iranian elections, television debates between the candidates took place, with equal screen time assigned to each of the four candidates by IRIB, the Iranian state-run television. The debates took place on channel three in six 90-minute face-to-face meetings between the four candidates. In this case, television surpassed the written press as a vehicle for electoral debate and attracted a huge popular following. However, the Committee for the Protection of Votes, made up of supporters of Karroubi and Mousavi, accused Iranian radio and television of taking sides and giving much more time to Ahmadinejad in news bulletins and special programmes that presented the achievements of his presidency. The 20-minute right to rebuttal granted *in extremis* to Ahmadinejad on the last day of the campaign fed this accusation.

A record audience watched the debates whose content, because of the accusatory and critical tone – unthinkable a month earlier – left no Iranian indifferent. The direct accusations between the candidates for the presidency and the questioning aimed at key figures in the political elite surprised everyone, and revealed the cracks existing in the heart of the political elite. Ahmadinejad even criticized Hashemi Rafsanjani, the second most powerful man in Iran and political rival of Khamenei. Accusations of corruption, lies and nepotism were repeated in the debates, but political and economic programmes were conspicuously absent. However, enormous expectation was generated about the course of the vote count and the final result, encouraging mass participation in the election, even higher than during the time of Mohammed Khatami.

Campaign events were well attended in general and especially during the last week of the campaign, when Mousavi and Ahmadinejad confronted each other in the capital. The political rallies brought the city to a standstill, with scenes of festivity never seen in earlier elections.

Other procedural measures were also announced, such as the computerization of voter registration and an electronic vote count, two advances that had not been approved for earlier elections despite having been technically implemented. There were also plans for the four candidates to assign observers to the polling stations, in order to guarantee that the election would be clean throughout the entire country – although this was very difficult to implement, according the opposition complaints to the Guardian Council. In short, a series of measures were planned to bring the Iranian election closer to the parameters of integrity, transparency and fairness enjoyed by other electoral systems established around the world. Paradoxically, the presence of international observers' presence was totally neglected by the government, who also strongly criticized the creation of the Election Protection Committee by reformists candidates, as well as the establishment of a General

Inspection Organization, headed by the former Interior Ministry Mostafa Pour-Mohammadi on behalf of former Judiciary Chief, Hashemi Shahroudi, with the task of supervising the electoral process.[9]

Opinion polls were quite common during the campaign, although their reliability was still very low. Several news agencies and newspapers published many surveys with the same low scientific credibility and politically tendentious predictions as in previous elections. However, by comparing all of them, it was possible to elaborate an average, shown in Table 13.1, which gave Ahmadinejad an advantage of only 5 per cent over Mir Hussein Mousavi – 42.6 and 37.5 per cent respectively.

The contested results

According to the Interior Ministry, the final results of the tenth presidential election of 12 June 2009 were a landslide victory for Ahmadinejad, with 24.5 million votes, or 62.63 per cent of valid votes cast. Mousavi obtained only 33.75 per cent, with 13.2 million votes. The other two contenders, Rezai and Karroubi, received only around 1 million votes between them. Almost 40 million people expressed their vote, according to official information. But the transparency of the election process was strongly questioned by the losing candidates, who contested the results before the Guardian Council, and for the first time, demanded a re-run of the elections. Also for the first time, a partial recount of 10 per cent of the votes was made, without the presence of any representatives of the opposition due to their refusal to legitimize the recount, in the middle of a wave of street demonstrations rejecting the final results. More than 600 formal complaints were made to the electoral body, which rejected them after a week of negotiations and discussions between the members of the political elite and after the sermon delivered by Khamenei on 19 June which ratified the results, openly endorsing the re-elected president.

As mentioned earlier, a lack of transparency has been common in Iranian elections and the previously announced guarantees were not applied. The haste in publishing the results seemed very suspicious, since less than 15 hours after the polling stations had closed, the final results were announced, declaring an overwhelming victory for Ahmadinejad.

An analysis detailing the data broken down by province reflects many differences from historical voting trends. Mousavi won in only two provinces, while in the other 28 provinces, Ahmadinejad was declared the winner. When the results are compared with earlier elections, it is possible to verify that the ethnic vote in the peripheral areas of Azerbaijan, Kurdistan, Khuzestan, Khorasan and Baluchestan have generally chosen reformist candidates or candidates with ethnic ties to these provinces, which was not the case in this election. If this historical trend and the unreliable pre-election opinion polls had been corroborated, Mousavi, Rezai and Karroubi should have won large numbers of votes in these areas, in contrast to what took place on 12 June.

The differences in favour of Ahmadinejad in some provinces were enormous, even in Mehdi Karroubi's province and Mir Hussein Mousavi's own city, where both reformist candidates lost.

Table 13.1 Opinion polls in the presidential elections, 2009

Poll	Date	Description	Ahmadinejad	Mousavi	Karrubi	Rezai
Ayandeh News	bef. 26 May	10 cities	34	38	-	-
IRIB	bef. 26 May	Tehran	43	47	-	-
Alef News Agency	17–18 May	15,000	54.5	22	3.2	2
Entekhab News	17–18 May	2,564	23.9	27.8	22.8	25.5
Teribon Isfahan University Poll	14 May	2,682	21.2	58.49	9.35	1.02
Webgozar Internet Poll	14 May		19.8	69.7	3.8	2.6
Rayemelat	12 May		42	44	6	6
Etemad-e Melli	12 May		1st	3rd	2nd	4
Teribon.com Internet Poll	12 May		42	16.2	19.7	3.2
IRNA Student Poll	4 May	1,370	51.3	26.4	17.5	8.4
Rajanews	3–4 May	62 cities	59	22	-	-
Sada va Sima (IRIB)	3–4 May	23,898	58.2	21.9	3.6	1.4
Shafaf.ir	26 Apr.	7,678 (10 prov.)	54.1	12.7	15.3	0.6
Labour Union Association	10 Apr.		36	52	8	-
University Polling Association	9–10 Apr.		46.9	15.7	1.4	0.9
Hamedan Payam	21 Mar.		36.8	11.8	2.3	-
Tabnak.ir Internet Poll	17 Mar.	54,407	15.1	23.8	2.6	-
University Polling Association	Feb.–Mar.		44.5	8.2	1	-
Tehran University	26 Feb.	5,167	17.6	72.1	6.9	-
Baztab.com	26 Dec.	12,066	25.1	46.96	2.73	-
Average			**42.67%**	**37.5%**	**5%**	**4%**

The oft-mentioned rural backing given Ahmadinejad was not statistically very important, considering that only 30 per cent of the population in Iran is rural, as Eric Hooglund clarified.[10]

The source of the 24 million votes won by Ahmadinejad is difficult to explain sociologically when compared with the presidential elections of 1997, 2001 and 2005. Of the conservative candidates, Nateq-Nouri, with 7 million votes, was the most popular in 1997, followed by Ahmadinejad in the first round of 2005 with 5.7 million votes. On the other hand, the reformists have obtained higher numbers of votes since 1997. Khatami won 20 and 21 million votes in 1997 and 2001, respectively and in 2005 the three reformist candidates – Karroubi, Moin and Mehralizadeh – won 10.5 million votes in the first round, twice that of Ahmadinejad and much more than Rafsanjani, who won only 6.1 million. As was summarized by Ali Ansari, 'regional variations in participation have disappeared. There is no correlation between the increase in participation and the swing to Mahmoud Ahmadinejad.'[11]

Additionally, high participation rates favoured reformists in the 1997 and 2001 presidential elections, the municipal elections in 1999 and the parliamentary elections in 2000, while low participation rates benefited conservatives. This time, on the contrary, the record participation rate of 84 per cent overwhelmingly favoured Ahmadinejad.

The turnout of over 100 per cent in two provinces is not enough to prove the elections were rigged, as this was also a common feature in previous presidential elections. But taken together, all the data, and the complaints submitted to the Guardian Council by the Election Protection Committee, support the opposition's suspicion of possible electoral fraud. Despite the fact that the opposition has no reliable alternative data to offer, the dossier presented included a substantive amount of information and detailed analysis of results in provinces, municipalities and electoral districts that evidenced inconsistencies in the official results. Apart from confirmation that in at least 192 constituencies the turnout was up to 100 per cent with no geographical or sociological justification, the report denounced the concentration of votes, amounting to more than 99 per cent for Ahmadinejad in hundreds of ballot boxes.[12] In addition, not only was there a huge difference between the 46,000 fixed and 12,000 itinerant polling stations regarding the voting percentage obtained by Ahmadineyad, but hundreds of ballot boxes existed that included votes in multiples of hundreds – something totally impossible statistically.[13] The evidence presented by the Committee is impossible to hide, because all the results detailed by city, electoral district and polling station are available for the first time at the Interior Ministry. Nonetheless, the Guardian Council rejected the report, considering that those irregularities did not suppose an electoral fraud, in a final decision made public for the first time on the Guardian Council's website.

Concluding thoughts

Bearing in mind the controversy generated around the final outcome of the presidential elections of June 2009, and the information available from previous presidential electoral processes, we can elaborate some concluding remarks in comparing several aspects of these processes.

Considering the absolute numerical information, it is clear that Mahmoud Ahmadinejad is the individual candidate who has been the most voted for in the history of the Islamic Republic. His 24 million votes displaced Mohamed Khatami, who gained 21 million eight years before. On the other hand, Ahmadinejad obtained only 5.7 million votes in the first round of the 2005 election and for the first time it was necessary to put into action a second round of presidential elections. Paradoxically, he has been successively the least and the most popular of the Iranian presidents since 1979. Apart from the first two presidents – Bani Sadr, who was dismissed, and Ali Rajai, who was killed in a bomb attack – the remaining four were re-elected for a second term. Ali Khamenei, Hashemi Rafsanjani and Mohamed Khatami completed these two terms allowed by the Constitution, as presumably will Mahmoud Ahmadinejad. Leaving aside the controversy and the electoral complaints in 2009, this supposes a certain continuity in the electoral behaviour of Iranians, despite the fact that on at least two opportunities, namely 1997 and 2005, the majority did not vote for the official candidate.

The lack of reliability regarding the transparency and probity of the whole electoral process has been quite a familiar feature in the history of the Iranian electoral system, in addition to a very complicated mechanism of voting procedures, candidatures and vote counts. The impossibility of monitoring and the difficulty in complaining successfully in front of the electoral authorities have also been detrimental to the credibility of the final results of every election in the country, particularly the last two presidential elections of 2005 and 2009. However, the progressive implementation of several pre-electoral and electoral procedures in these two elections, such as televised debates, national opinion polls, electronic registration of voters, and the publication of whole national results broken down as far as polling station level, are very important achievements in contributing to legitimizing the elective institutions in the Islamic Republic.

Notes

1 The voting age was 16 until it was raised to 18 after the legislative elections of 2008.
2 In the first round of the presidential election of 2005, the turnout officially published by the Interior Ministry at Shemiranat, in Tehran province, was 797.22 per cent and in the second round climbed to 839.32 per cent!
3 Ministry of Interior, Iran, www.moi.ir (accessed 17 May 2011).
4 Quoted at http://web.payk.net/mailingLists/iran-news/html/1997/msg00257.html (accessed 17 May 2011).
5 Quoted at http://www.iran.org/news/970519.htm (accessed 17 May 2011).
6 In 1997 there were 36,466,487 potential voters and Khatami obtained 20.078.178 votes or 55.06 per cent, while in 2001 there were 42,170,230 with 21,656,476 votes for him (51.35 per cent), www.moi.ir (accessed 17 May 2011).
7 IRNA, 11 March 2004.
8 Ibid., 11 June 2005.
9 Press TV 31 May 2009.
10 Hooglund, Eric: 'Iran's Rural Vote and Election Fraud', Agence Global, 17 June 2009, available at: http://www.agenceglobal.com/Article.asp?Id=2034 (accessed 17 May 2011).

11 Ansari, Ali: 'Preliminary Analysis of the Voting Figures in Iran's 2009 Presidential Election', Chatham House, 21 June 2009, available at www.chathamhouse.org.uk/files/14234_iranelection0609.pdf (accessed 17 May 2011). A very detailed explanation of the hypothetical sources of Ahmadinejad's votes can be found here.
12 Report of complaints presented by the Election Protection Committee of Mir Hussein Mousavi to Guardian Council, Spanish translation from Persian by Manuel Llinás Aguilera, Madrid, 15 August 2009, available at http://norooznews.net/photo/jadavel. pdf consulted in 2009 (accessed 17 May 2011).
13 The ballot papers are distributed to the polling stations in batches of a hundred.

14 Concluding thoughts

Nadir Gohari

This volume has attempted to provide new insight into Iran with regard to the international system. It has also exhibited esoteric properties of the country that are often elusive from mainstream media attention. At times, little known or promoted features can contradict the irrational image of the country that is commonly portrayed to some members of the international community. Regardless of such depictions, however, Iran is indeed an enigma and will remain such for some time. Given the numerous caveats and complexities of the state, there is constant societal movement and structuring taking place, which contributes to increasing difficulty in comprehending the country. Nevertheless, one aim of this book has been to create a more balanced understanding of Iran and offer readers a perspective that cultivates such a view. Of course, establishing common ground and an element of understanding can contribute to proliferating productive engagements between Iran and other members of the international system, including those that have had strained relations with the country in the past.

Currently, Iran is a regional power in the Middle East and seeks to further solidify its global position through recognition from the international community. However, it is difficult to gain overwhelming acknowledgement in the wake of the current domestic political tensions in the country. The most recent presidential elections in Iran proved costly to the reputation of the Islamic Republic in that the country was not able to achieve a peaceful transition of power. While the regime would not be inclined to using 'democratic' terminology to describe some aspects of its political system, the fact of the matter is that there were presidential elections in which the population participated in order to determine the succeeding president. The outcome of the election astonished a portion of the population and the demonstrations that followed challenged the ruling government, gained international attention and were an unpredicted event whose reverberations were felt among the global community, with particular curiosities generated from other Middle Eastern nations. Indeed, the subsequent protests served to cast doubt on the ruling government, something which had not been so outwardly been done before. Needless to say, the move had the potential to affect multiple spheres of influence in the region including the balance of power and the energy sectors.

However, despite the internal tensions and intrastate affairs, it was noted earlier that many Iranians view their society as principled and can credit the perceived essence of morality to the religious themes that exist within the social order. Some would even argue that because religious principles have the ability to create a sense of morality and conscience in society, they should be relevant and ever-present, especially in the circles of the political structure. The reasoning underlying this claim is that religious principles are the best and therefore the correct standards to implement in order to have a flourishing society. However, such conclusions rest on several assumptions. For instance, there is a supposition that the texts provided to society are infallible and additionally carry a flawless interpretation, for lack of perfection might entail an absence of influence. Also, there is a conjecture that individuals in society will be open enough to accepting ideas to an extent that they become principled. In spite of such assumptions, the perceived set of values gives many Iranians the sense that because they are an ethical society and emphasize human virtues, they are therefore a responsible member of the international system. Consequently, they should be treated on amicable terms and be entitled to recognition from other constituents of the international system. After all, it is a fact that Iran has never attacked another country from aggression but has, rather, fought on the defensive in conflicts, notably the Iran–Iraq War and the incidents of terrorism across the country. The history of non-aggression demonstrated by Iran is enviable for many other states and even a desirable status for others. Although rhetoric from the state has occasionally been sharp, particularly in recent years, there is a noticeable lack of militaristic force employed by the country.

However, the spiritual elements in Iranian society can sometimes be extreme. Consequently, religious fervour can intimidate members of the international system and arouse suspicion as to the motivations of the country, particularly since Iran has the potential to produce a global impact with respect to hydrocarbon exports via the Straits of Hormuz in the Persian Gulf. Hence, a proposed solution to alleviate tensions within the worldwide community would be to establish and confirm that Iran has the ability to become partner to international peace-building. Opportunities for transnational cooperation can be found on a number of levels, particularly those that capitalize on Iranian influence and geographical positioning. For instance, partnering to hamper narcotics trade routes from Afghanistan to the Persian Gulf would prove beneficial to the entire international community, even to the producing country of illicit substances since such an action would make it difficult for narcotics operations to thrive. An additional example would be collaboration in an attempt to rein in human trafficking within, through, and in countries neighbouring Iran. Certainly, all forms of forced labour have been recognized as abhorrent practices that deserve international attention as well as cooperation. Partnership in this area could also exhibit and embolden certain strands in Iran that are concerned with human rights since the trade is concerned with the abuse of civil liberties. Therefore, the international community, inclusive of Iran, should work for the restoration of human dignity in this respect since it is a universal trait. In turn, Iran may even benefit further from such a joint venture in that domestic policies with respect to human rights may be reformed or encouraged to progress to new standards. Essentially, the purpose of international partnership would be to establish a mutual relationship between Iran and the international system that would assist in creating avenues for Iran to visibly cultivate an open sense of justice that would be seen by the rest of the world. In order to further craft an alleviated political atmosphere, it would be beneficial to demonstrate that models of peace and justice have been created on the foundations of Iranian teachings. Of course, the current regime may attempt to convey that the country has developed such models on the basis of Iranian interpretations of theocratic materials; however, it is highly unlikely that this would serve to convince the international system of state responsibility or genuineness of motive. Hence, it would be better for Iran to encapsulate all fields and perspectives of teachings in the formulation of theoretical models instead of limiting them to religious works. To encompass other fields would be to demonstrate that Iran is willing to extend its relations to the greater international community since it is opening potential areas for dynamic communication and interaction.

The geographical positioning of Iran ensures that it is a country that cannot be easily ignored or isolated from the international system, since it carries significant regional weight. It is after all situated at the crossroads of the Middle East and Central Asia as well as having access to the Caspian Sea and Persian Gulf. Hence, an alternative option over direct conflict or engagement in these areas can instead be to faciliate regional peace through diplomatic accord using Iranian influence; this policy would be particularly valuable when engaging the Middle East, an area where many states already regard each other with suspicion. While productive engagement in this sense can already occur, it is more likely to proliferate and progress with the mending of relations between Iran and the international system. A positive direction in which this can occur would be with the dispelling of the myths and distrust that currently serve as root causes for unnecessary tensions. One example of this is the vilification of the US as the symbol of evil and as a neo-imperialistic force that is bent on world domination. Another is labelling Iran as a terrorist or rogue state. The element of mistrust is a damaging element and impedes overall reconciliation. Indeed, the lack of success in the relationship between states can certainly be attributed to widespread malicious anecdotes. To ensure that such destructive practices are at least lessened, it would be beneficial to address them on domestic levels so that the populations of each state can come to the realization that the distances between each state are not immeasurable.

There is also the notion of the Iranian sense of victimization. Since the overthrow of the Shah, there have been events contributing to a sentiment of unfair treatment, such as the imposition of crushing economic sanctions and some members of the international system contributing to Iraqi forces during the Iran–Iraq War. Consequently, Iran has felt targeted by the international system at times and has moved to a position that the current layout and UN power structure is unsuitable for dealing with future, let alone current, affairs. Moreover, an argument deriving from this stance is that the configuration at present cannot remain the same forever; rather, that the world is steering towards a multipolar system composed of regional powers. However, realistically the calls for reformation will linger only as rhetoric since any significant reformation or change is far from happening soon, even with respect to regional powers, since countries such as the US still maintain a significant global presence. But the dissatisfaction should be noted and taken into consideration when attempting to reconcile relations in that it can be a platform for dialogue with the international system. Various methods and means can be implemented to build confidence with Iran and alleviate the severity of hostility as well as the argumentative status sometimes adopted by the country.

Energy security in the Middle East has also remained in the foreground of international relationships since the Persian Gulf possesses vast reserves of coveted hydrocarbons that are in global demand. Given that Iran is now a regional power in the area, it has the potential ability to influence energy exports from the Straits of Hormuz. Needless to say, apart from the immense oilfields located in the Arab states Iran also maintains its share of oil and gas reserves. Major conflict in this region has already proved to be undesirable as far as the economics of energy extractions and exportations are concerned since prices will adversely fluctuate, affecting many consuming members of the international community. Therefore, alleviating currently existing tensions and facilitating the creation of a more stabilized atmosphere in the Persian Gulf could prove to be valuable in that a steadier volume of oil and gas from the region could be supplied while prices in tandem could be kept within an acceptable spectrum for global consumption. Engagement and cooperation with Iran is crucial to developing such an amicable environment since the country has an extensive maritime presence in the Persian Gulf. Moreover, collaboration can provide an opportunity for Iranian hydrocarbon reserves to be accessed on a larger scale since they have not been utilized to potential. The circumvention or exclusion of Iran with regard to energy security in the region, however, keeps up an unnecessary and overbearing pressure. Since it is in the interest of all members of the international community to ensure that hydrocarbon extraction is not subject to extreme controversy or politicization, costs are not susceptible to unreasonable marginalization, and that future explorations for new oil and gas fields can continue without apprehension, a venture between members of the international system along with Iran could prove to be a productive endeavour.

Yet the potential influence that Iran holds over the Persian Gulf and its resources at the moment may be undermined by the fact that a portion of the domestic population within Iran is dissatisfied with the current regime. Prior to the elections, Iran had endured several interstate and intrastate conflicts dealing with aggressive neighbours and terrorism. Indeed, at one point Iran was about to engage the Taliban in Afghanistan when a diplomat was executed, being branded a heretic on the basis of following Shi'ism. After the invasions of Afghanistan and Iraq by the US, Iran initially found itself in a sensitive position, feeling pressured by a pincer grip forming along its borders. Steps were taken to modernize the military, and while these advancements could not match the superiority of US equipment, there was notable improvement. It seemed that the Islamic Republic was experiencing a resurgence. All that was needed was the reconfirmation of Ahmadinejad as President and for the power to remain peaceable. To the shock of the international community, demonstrations and riots gained momentum when it became clear that the outcome was strongly controversial. While the movements were temporarily managed, there was no peaceful maintenance of power, which also meant that there was a long shadow of doubt cast on the legitimacy of the Islamic Republic, since it was unable to successfully hold full and fair elections. The outcome of the elections was a clear illustration that all states must eventually answer to their public, no matter how powerful they appear. It can certainly be stated that an additional result of the Iranian elections was that neither the Middle East nor Iran will ever be the same again, with an increasing population calling for democratic reform and transparency.

In spite of these recent occurrences though, the Islamic Republic has managed to sustain itself for the time being; therefore, the question remains as to how best to resolve current issues. Obviously, major steps towards meaningful engagement would be to create confidence-building mechanisms that would assist in mending the rifts of mistrust that have developed between Iran and other members of the international system. It would be unreasonable and inconceivable to try to find an ultimate solution that will be bilaterally beneficial to Iran as well as other members of the international system, a solution that would completely end all negative sentiments. But the point is to facilitate better communication, which can be obtained realistically. Iran can prove to be a beneficial member of the international community with the potential to influence it on a global scale, although major changes and developments are necessary within the country itself in order for it to be recognized as a responsible state. To achieve such status would undoubtedly result in positive progress and direction. Many undertakings and obstacles need to be overcome, however, with efforts from all participants in the international system in order for the enigmatic state to be demystified.

Select bibliography

Abazari, Yousef and Neda Milani. (2005). 'Representation of the West in Student Periodicals', *Nameh Olum Ejtemaei*, No. 26, winter, 97–122.

Adib-Moghaddam, Arshin. (2005). 'Islamic Utopian Romanticism and the Foreign Policy Culture of Iran', *Critical Middle Eastern Studies* 14(3): 265–292.

Ahearne, Jeremy. (1995). *Michel De Certeau: Interpretation and its Other*, Cambridge, Polity Press.

Alikhah, Fardin. (2008). 'Political Consequences of Consumerism', *Iranian Cultural Studies Quarterly*, No. 1, spring, 231–256.

Amin, S. (1989). *Eurocentrism*, translated by Moore, R., Zed Book.

Appadurai, A. (1996). *Modernity at Large: Cultural Dimensions of Globalisation, Public World*, Vol. 1. Minneapolis, University of Minnesota Press.

Appadurai, A. (2000). 'Grassroots Globalization and the Research Imagination', *Public Culture* Vol. 12, no. 1, winter, pp. 1–19.

Arabi, Muhiaddin ibn, *Alfotouhat al-Makkiyah*, Beirut, Dar Sader, Bita.

Azad, Armaki. (2007). *Everyday Life in Iran: Power and Culture*, Tehran, Jihad University Institute.

Azad Armaki, Taqi and Vahid Shalchi. (2005). 'Two Iranian Worlds: Mosque and Coffee Shop', *Iranian Society of Cultural and Communication Studies Quarterly*, 1st year, No. 4, fall and winter.

Beitz, Charles R. (2000), 'Rawls's Law of Peoples', *Ethics*, No. 110, July.

Bennett, Andy. (2007). *Culture and Everyday Life*, translated by Leila Joafshani and Hassan Chavoshian, Tehran, Akhtaran Press.

Biggart, N.W. (1989). *Charismatic Capitalism: Direct Selling Organisations in America*, Chicago University Press.

Bromley, Simon. (1994). *Rethinking Middle East Politics: State Formation and Development*, Cambridge, Polity Press.

Buchanan, Allen. (2000). 'Rawls's Law of Peoples: Rules for a Vanished Westphalian World', *Ethics*, No. 110, July.

Bull, Hedley. (1977). *The Anarchical Society: A Study of Order in World Politics*, London, Macmillan.

Bull, Hedley. (1988). 'The Revolt Against the West', in Hedley Bull and Adam Watson (eds.), *The Expansion of International Society*, Oxford, Clarendon Press.

Butler, Brian E. (2001), 'There are Peoples and There are Peoples: A Critique of Rawls's The Law of Peoples', *Florida Philosophical Review*, Vol. 1, No. 2.

Castells, M. (1997). *The Power of Identity*, Oxford, Blackwell.

Castells, M. (2010). 'The Rise of the Network Society', the first volume of the *The Information Age: Economy, Culture, and Society*, Oxford, Wiley-Blackwell.

Castes, S. and Miller, M.J. (1993). *The Age of Migration, International Population Movements in the Modern World*, Houndmills, Basingstoke and London, Macmillan.

Chaney, D. (1994). *The Cultural Turn: Scene-setting Essays on Contemporary Cultural History*, London and New York, Routledge.

Chon, Gina 'China Reaches $3 Billion Deal to Develop Oil Field in Iraq', *Wall Street Journal*, 29 August 2008.

Cvetkovich A. and Kellner D. (1997). *Articulating the Global and the Local*, USA, West View Press.

Daftari, Farhad. (ed.). (2000). *Rational Traditions in Islam*, London, I.B. Tauris.

Daniels, R. (1990). *Coming to America: A History of Immigration and Ethnicity in American Life*, New York, HarperCollins.

Dawisha, Adeed. (1983). *Islam in Foreign Policy*, Cambridge, Cambridge University Press.

Dehghani F., Seyed Jalal. (2005). 'Societal Sources of Iranian Foreign Policy', *Discourse: An Iranian Quarterly* 6(3–4): 33–58.

Dehghani F., Seyed Jalal. [1384] (2005). *Tahvol Goftmani dar Syasat khareji Jomhoore eslami Iran* [Discursive Evolution in the Islamic Republic of Iran's Foreign Policy], Tehran, Entesharat Rooznameh Iran.

Dehghani, F., Seyed Jalal. [1386] (2007). 'Hoviat va mnfaat dar syasat kharejie Jomhoori eslami Iran' [Identity and Interest in Islamic Republic of Iran's Foreign Policy], in Davood Kiany, ed., *Manafe Mellie Jomhoorie eslamie Iran* [National Interests of Islamic Republic of Iran], Tehran, Pajooheshkadeh motale'at rahbordi.

Dehghani F., Seyed Jalal. (2008). 'Emancipating Foreign Policy: Critical Theory and Islamic Republic of Iran's Foreign Policy', *The Iranian Journal of International Affairs* xx(3): 1–26.

Dehghani F., Seyed Jalal. [1387] (2008). 'Syasat Khareje Dolat Nohom' [Ninth Administration's Foreign Policy], *Rahyafthaye Syasi va Binolmelali*, 13(1).

Denison, D. (1990). *Corporate Culture and Organisational Effectiveness*, New York, Wiley.

De Certeau, Michel. (1988). *The Practice of Everyday Life*, translated by Steven Rendall, Los Angeles, University of California Press.

Al-Dinvari, Abi Hanifeh Ahmad ibn Davoud. (1960). *al-Akhbar al-Tawal*, research: Abdul Muneim Amer, Cairo, Dar al-Ihya al-Kutub al-Arabiya.

Doyle, Michael W. (1983). 'Kant, Liberal Legacies, and Foreign Affairs', *Philosophy and Public Affairs* 12(3).

Doyle, Michael W. (1986). 'Kant Liberalism and World Politics', *American Political Science Review* 80(4): 1151–1690.

Ehteshami, A. and Zweiri, M. (2007). *Iran and Rise of its Neoconservatives: The Politics of Tehran's Silent Revolution*, London, I.B. Tauris.

Faist, T. (1998). 'Transnational social spaces out of international migration: evolution, significance, and future prospects', *Archives Europeennes de Sociologie* 39(2): 213–247.

Faist, T. (2000). *The Volume and Dynamics of International Migration and Transnational Social Spaces*, Oxford, Oxford University Press.

Farabi, Abu Nasr Mohammad. (2003). *Fosoul Montaze'ah*, translated by Hassan Malekshahi, Tehran, Soroush.

Fazeli, Mohammad. (2008). 'An Image of the Cultural Lifestyle of an Academic Community', *Iranian Cultural Studies Quarterly*, No. 1, spring, 175–198.

Fazeli, Ne'matollah. (2008). 'Modernity and Housing: An Anthropological Approach to the Concept of Home, Rural Lifestyle, and its Modern Developments', *Iranian Cultural Studies Quarterly* No. 1, spring, 25–63.

Featherstone, M. (ed.). (1990). *Global Culture: Nationalism, Globalisation and Modernity*, London, Sage.

Ferguson, J. (2002). 'Development', in Barnard, A. and Spencer, J. (eds.), *Encyclopaedia of Social and Cultural Anthropology*, London and New York, Routledge.

Fiske, John, (1992). 'Cultural Studies and Culture of Everyday Life', in Grossberg, L. (ed.), *Cultural Studies*, London and New York, Routledge.

Fokouhi, Nasser. (2008). 'Minority Subcultures and Lifestyle: Trends and Outlooks', *Iranian Cultural Studies Quarterly*, No. 1, spring, 143–174.

Galtung, Johan. (1964). 'Editorial', *Journal of Peace Research* 1(1).

Galtung, Johan. (1969). 'Violence, Peace and Peace Research', *Journal of Peace Research*, 3: 167–192.

Geertz, C. (1973). *The Interpretation of Cultures: Selected Essays*, New York, Basic Books.

Glick Schiller, N. (1997). 'The Situation of Transnational Studies', *Identities*, 4(2): 155–166.

Hajiani, Ebrahim. (2007). *Lifestyle Models in Iran*, Tehran, Strategic Studies Research Institute.

Halliday, Fred. (1995). *Islam and the Myth of Confrontation*, London, I.B. Tauris.

Halliday, Fred. (1999). *Revolution and World Politics*, London, Macmillan.

Hamidi, Nafiseh and Mehdi Faraji, (2008), 'Women's Lifestyle and Cover in Tehran', *Iranian Cultural Studies Quarterly*, No. 1, spring, 65–92.

Hannerz, U. (1996). *Transnational Connections: Culture, People, Places*, London and New York, Routledge.

Harper, D. (1987). *Working Knowledge: Skill and Community in a Small Shop*, Chicago, University of Chicago Press.

Hassani, Ali Akbar. (1994). *Analytical and Political History of Islam*, Tehran, Islamic Asceticism Promotion Office.

Hay, Colin. (2002). *A Critical Introduction to Political Analysis*, London, Palgrave Press.

Held, D. (1995). *Democracy and the Global Order*, Cambridge and Palo Alto, Polity Press and Stanford University Press.

Highton, Ben. (2002). *Everyday Life and Cultural theory: An Introduction*, London and New York, Routledge.

Holsti, Kalevi. (1988). *International Politics: A Framework for Analysis*, 5th edn, Englewood Cliffs, New Jersey, Prentice Hall.

Hor Ameli, Sheikh Mohammad ibn Hassan, *Wasael ush-Shia*, research: Abdolrahim Rabbani Shirazi, Tehran, Maktabat-ul-Islamiyah, 1403 AH

Hosseini Beheshti, Seyed Alireza. (2003). 'Dialogue among Cultures and Political Theory', *International Journal of Humanity of the Islamic Republic of Iran*, 12(3).

Hosseini Beheshti, Seyed Alireza. (2007). 'The Expanse of Rawls' The Law of Peoples', *Political Sciences Research Magazine*, No. 7, summer.

Hulme, D. and Turner, M. (1985). *Sociology of Development*, Manchester, Manchester University Press.

Huntington, S.P. (1996). *The Clash of Civilizations*, Simon & Schuster.

Ian, Kribe. (1999). *Modern Social Theory: From Parsons to Habermas*, translated by Abbas Mokhber. Tehran, Agah Press.

Jafari, Mohammad Taqi. (1991). *A Study of Two Universal Human Rights Systems of Islam and the West*, Tehran, Office for Propagation of International Legal Services Press.

Javadi Amoli, Abdollah. (1996). *Philosophy of Human Rights*. Qom, Asra Press.

Jones, M. (1976). *The Old World Ties of American Ethnic Groups*, London, Macmillan.

Al-Jozi, Sebt ibn, *Tazkirat-ul-Khawas*, Tehran, Maktaba Neinavi al-Hadisah, Bita.

Kant, Immanuel. (1983). *Perpetual Peace and Other Essays*, translated by Ted Humphrey, Hackett publishing company.

Kazemi, Abbas and Mohammad Rezaei. (2008). 'Dialectics of Differentiation and Removing Differentiations: Sauntering and Lifestyle of Lower Urban Classes in Tehran Shopping Malls', *Iranian Cultural Studies Quarterly*, No. 1, spring, 1–24.

Kelsen, H. (1966). *Principles of International Law*, New York, Rinehart and Winston.

Keohane, Robert O. and Lisa L. Martin. (1995). 'The Promise of Institutionalist Theory', *International Security*, 20(1).

Keohane, Robert O. and Joseph S. Ney. (1989). *Power and Interdependence*, 2nd edn, New York, Harper-Collins.

Khadduri, Majid. (1984). *The Islamic Conception of Justice*, The John Hopkins University Press.

King, A.D. (ed.). (1991). *Culture, Globalisation and the World System: Contemporary Conditions for the Representation of Identity*, Binghamton, State University of New York Art Department.

Kivisto, P. (1984). *Immigrant Socialists in the United States: The Case of Finns and the Left*, Rutherford, New Jersey, Fairleigh Dickinson University Press

Kivisto, P. (2001). 'Theorizing Transnational Immigration: A Critical Review of Current Efforts', *Ethnic and Racial Studies*, 24(4) July, 549–577

Al-Koleini, Abi Ja'far Muhammad ibn Yaghoub. (1983). *Forou'il Kafi*, Tehran, Darul Kutubil Islamiyah.

Lambton, A.K.S. (1987). *Qajar Persia*, London, I.B. Tauris.

Lasch, H. (1997). *The Radical Will: Selected Writing of Randolph Bourne*, New York, Urizen Books.

Long, E. (1997). *From Sociology to Cultural Studies: New Perspectives*, Oxford, Blackwell.

Malley, R. (1996). *The Call from Algeria: Third Worldism, Revolution, and the Turn to Islam*, Berkely, University of California Press.

Al-Massoudi, Abulhassan Ali ibn Hassan. (1991). *Moruj al-Zahab*, Abolqasem Payandeh, Tehran, Scientific and Cultural Press Company.

Meyer, J.W. and Scott, W.R. (1992). *Organisational Environments: Ritual and Rationality*. Beverly Hills, CA, Sage.

Mills, C.W. (1959). *Sociological Imagination*, Oxford, Oxford University Press.

Al-Minqari, Nasr ibn Muzahim. (1991). *War of Seffin*, Parviz Atabaki, Tehran, Scientific and Cultural Press Company.

Misbah Yazdi, Mohammad Taqi. (2001). *Legal Theory of Islam*, Qom, Imam Khomeini Educational and Research Institute.

Mohaqqeq Damad, Seyed Mostafa. (2004). *International Humanitarian Law*. Tehran, Center for Propagation of Islamic Sciences.

Mojtahedzadeh, P. [1383] (2004). 'Rouhieh edalatkhahi va Jaygah an dar Hoviat Melli Iranian' [The Spirit of Justice–seeking Spirit and Its Position in Iranian National Identity], in Davood Mirmohammadi (ed.), *Hoviat melli dar Iran* [National Identity in Iran], Tehran, Motale'at melli, 231–244.

Moran, Joe. (2005). *Reading the Everyday*, London and New York, Routledge.

Morgenthau, Hans G. (1993). *Politics among Nations*. New York, McGraw-Hill.

Moshirzadeh, H. (2007). 'Discursive Foundations of Iran's Nuclear Policy', *Security Dialogue*, 38(4): 521–543.

Motaki, M. [1385] (2006). *Syasat khareji dolat Nohom* [Foreign policy of the Ninth Administration], Tehran, Markaz Tahghighat steratejik Khavaremianeh.

Motaki, M. [1386] (2007). *Rooznameh Iran*, 1386/05/30 [Iranian Newpaper].

Muhaqqiq Helli, *Sharayeh al-Islam*, Najaf, Matba'at al-Adab fil Najaf al-Ashraf, 1389 AH,

Al-Najafi, Sheikh Mohammad Hassan. (1981). *Jawahir al-Kalam fi Sharh Sharaye al-Islam*, vol. 21, Beirut, Dar ul-Ehya al-Toras al-Arabi.

Nasr, S.H. (2003). *Islam: Religion, History, and Civilisation*, Harper Collins.

Nateghpour, M.J. (2006). 'The cultural dimensions of Anglo-Iranian relations.' Working Paper. Durham: University of Durham, Centre for Middle Eastern and Islamic Studies.

Naviri, Shahab-ud-Din Ahmad. (1985). *Nahayat al-Irb*, translated by Mahmoud Mahdavi Damghani, Tehran, Amir Kabir Press.

Neuchterlein, D. (1979). 'The Concept of National Interest: A Time for New Approaches,' *Orbis*, 23(1).

Nobahar, Rahim. (2005). 'Religion and Human Dignity', *Theoretical Fundaments of Human Rights*, Qom, Mufid University.

Pangle, Thomas and Peter J. Ahrensdorf. (1999). *Justice among Nations: On the Moral Basis of Power and Peace*, The University Press of Kansas.

Parsons, T. (1951). *The Social System*, New York, Free Press.

Philpott, D. (2002). 'The Challenge of September 11 to Secularism in International Relations', *World Politics*, Vol. 55, October, 66–95.

Polanyi, K. (1957). *The Great Transformation: The Political and Economic Origins of Our Time*, Boston, MA, Beacon Press.

Portes, A. (1995). 'Children of Immigrants: Segmented Assimilation', in Alejandro Portes (ed.), *The Economic Sociology of Immigration*, New York, Russell Sage Foundation, 248–280.

Al-Qartabi, Ahmad al-Ansari. (1966). *Al-Jami' Lil Ahkam al-Quran*, Beirut, Dar ul-Ehya al-Toras al-Arabi.

Qomi, Sheikh Abbas. *Safinat ul-Bihar*, Beirut, Dar -ul-Mortez, Bita.

Al-Qoshairi, Abdulkarim bin Hawzan. (1995). *Al-Risalat al-Qishriyah*, research: Abdulhalim Mahmoud and Mahmoud bin Sharif, Qom, Bidar Press.

Randolph, B. (1916). 'Trans-National America', in Peter B. Levy (ed.), *100 Key Documents in American Democracy*, Westport, CT: Greenwood (1994), 303–309.

Rawls, John. (1971). *A Theory of Justice*, Cambridge, MA, Harvard University Press.

Rawls, John. (1993). *Political Liberalism*, New York, Columbia University Press.

Rawls, John. (1999). *The Law of Peoples*, Cambridge, MA, Harvard University Press.

Reiters, George. (1997). *Theory of Sociology in Contemporary Times*, translated by Mohsen Salasi, Tehran, Scientific Press.

Robertson, R. (1996). *Globalization: Social Theory and Global Culture*, London, Sage Publications.

Rousseau, Jean-Jaques. (1968). *Social Contract*, Penguin Books.

Sadurski, Wojciech. (2003). 'The Last Thing He Wanted: Realism and Utopia in the Law of Peoples by John Rawls', EUI Working Paper Law, No. 2003/16.

Said, E.W. (1994). *Culture and Imperialism*, USA, Vintage Books.

Schmid, H. (1968). 'Politics and Peace Research', *Journal of Peace Research*, 3: 217–232.

Shahabi, Mahmoud. (2003) 'Subcultures of Youth in Iran: Readings and Consequences', *Iranian Sociological Letter*, No. 4.

Shahabi, Mahmoud. (2006). 'Youth Subculture in Post-revolution Iran: an Alternative Reading', in Nilan, Pam and Carlos Feixa (eds), *Global Youth? Hybrid Identities, Plural Worlds*, London and New York, Routledge.

Shahidi, Seyed Jafar. (2007). *Nahj-ul-Balagha*, Tehran, Islamic Revolution Publications and Education, 1992.

Shalchi, Vahid. (2008). 'Coffee Shop Youth Lifestyle', *Iranian Cultural Studies Quarterly*, No. 1, spring, 93–115.

Al-Sheibani, Muhammad ibn al-Hassan. (1958). *Kitab al-Seir al-Kabir*, Cairo, Mohammad ibn Ahmad al-Sorkhi.

Al-Sheikh al-Mufid, Muhammad bin Muhammad bin Nu'man. (1988). *The Battle of Jamal*, translated by Mahmoud Mahdavi Damghani. Tehran, Nei Press.

Al-Sheikh al-Mufid, Muhammad bin Muhammad bin Nu'man. (2001). *Al-Irshad*, translated by Seyed Rasoul Mahallati, Tehran, Office for Propagation of Islamic Culture.

Sklair, L. (2001). *The Transnational Capitalist Class*, Oxford, Blackwell.

Skelton T. and Allen T. (2000). Culture and Global Change. London and New York: Routledge.

Sohrabzadeh, Mehran. (2008). 'A Comparison Between Generational and Intergenerational Mentality in Academic Generations after the Islamic Revolution', *Institute for Cultural and Social Studies*, Ministry of Science, Research and Technology.

Stevens, Rob. (2000). *Great Sociologists*, translated by Mehrdad Mirdamadi. Tehran, Markaz Press.

Sullivan, Roger. (1997). *An Introduction to Kant's Ethics*, Cambridge, Cambridge University Press.

Al-Tabari, Mohammad ibn Jarir. (1979). *Tarikh al-Tabari*, Beirut, Al-A'lami Lilmatbuat Institute.

Al-Tabari, Mohammad ibn Jarir, *Tarikh Tabari*, translated by Abolqasem Payandeh, Tehran, Asatir Press, Bita.

Tabatabaei, Seyed Mohammad Hossein. (1393 AH) *Al-Mizan fi Tafsir al-Quran*, Beirut, Al-A'lami Lilmatbuat Institute.

Tabatabaei, Seyed Mohammad Hossein. (1996). *Tafsir Al-Mizan*, Seyed Mohammad Baqer Mousavi Hamedani, Tehran, Tabatabaei Scientific and Theoretical Foundation.

Tasioulas, John. (2002). 'From Utopia to Kasanistan: John Rawls and The Laws of Peoples', *Oxford Journal of Legal Studies*, 22(2).

Tibi, B. (2000). 'Post-Bipolar Order in Crisis: The Challenge of Politicized Islam', *Millennium, Journal of International Studies*, 29(3): 843–859.

Tomlinson, J. (1999). *Globalization and Culture*, Cambridge, Polity Press.

Tousi, Sheikh. (1985). *Tahzib-ul-Ahkam*, Tehran, Dar-ul-Kutub al-Islamiyah.

Van Dyke, V. (1966). *International Politics*, New York, Appleton-Century Crofts.

Vatikiotis, P.J. (1987). *Islam and the State*, London and New York, Routledge.

Vertovec, S. (1999). 'Conceiving and Researching Transnationalism', *Ethnic and Racial Studies*, 22(2): 447–462.

Williams, R. (1976). *Keywords: A Vocabulary of Culture and Society*, London, Fontana.

Wilson, R. and Wimal, D. (1996). *Global/Local: Cultural Production and the Transnational Imaginary*, Durham, NC, Duke University Press.

Wimmer, A. and Glick Schiller, N. (2002). 'Methodological Nationalism and Beyond: Nation-State Building, Migrations and the Social Sciences', *Global Network*, 2(4): 301–334.

Zokaei, Mohammad Saeed. (2007). 'Youth, Globalization and International Immigration: A Study on Young Elites', *Iranian Journal of Sociology*, 7(2).

Zokaei, Mohammad Saeed. (2008). 'Youth, Body and Fitness', *Iranian Cultural Studies Quarterly*, No. 1, spring, 117–141.

Zokaei, Mohammad Saeed and Mirzaei, Seyed Ayatollah. (2006). *Young Boys and Manliness Values*, 5(3).

Zubaida, S. (1989). *Islam, the People and the State*, London and New York, Routledge.

Zyaee-Bigdeli, M. [1368] (1988). *Eslam va Hoghooghe Bainolmelal* [Islam and International Law], Tehran, Scherkat Sahami Enteshar.

Index